Human Resource Management

Human Resource Management

Volume - I
Development of Personnel and Employment

Dr. Chakshu Pathak

KALPAZ

First Published, 2020

Published by

Kalpaz Publications
C-30, Satyawati Nagar,
Delhi – 110052
Ph.: 011-47034999, 9811692060
www.kalpazpublications.com
E-mail: kalpaz@hotmail.com

Printed at: Gyan Press, Delhi

Cataloging in Publication Data—DK
Courtesy: D.K. Agencies (P) Ltd. <docinfo@dkagencies.com>

Pathak, Chakshu, author.
Human resource management / Dr. Chakshu Pathak.
volumes cm
Includes index.
Contents: volume 1. Development of personnel and employment — volume 2. Management relation.
ISBN 9789353243098 (set : HB)
ISBN 9789353243357 (vol. 1 : HB)

1. Personnel management—India. 2. Industrial relations—India. I. Title.

LCC HF5549.P38 2020 | DDC 658.3 23

To

N.K. Pathak Ji

Contents

Perface

I have pleasure to bring out this new edition books on "Human Resource Management". This book contains a comprehensive discussion of the element that goes to make up the "Management of Human Resource". Human beings are a resource to an organisation. Like any other materials on economic resource, they represent an investment whose development and utilisation require managing (i.e. planning, organisation, leadership and evaluation). There is a fundamental truth in the clinch that "People are an organisation's most important assets". Therefore, human resource needs to be understood in their proper prospective and utilised effectively to achieve the goals of an organisation.

This edition is being produced in the twenty first century. During the last four decades, a vast change has been taken place in the economic condition of India. The government has brought in new policies with liberalisation of economy. It has also done with the bureaucratic restrictive practices, control on industry and business. The New Economic Policies has ushered in an areas of foreign collaborations, acquisition, and merger. The foreign investors have brought in new concepts, ideas of managing business and industry have been passed on to new generations managers, entrepreneur, and young dynamic managers have changed the industrial and business scenario.

In this changing environment, new concepts of management are being introduced. This book has, while retaining its old flavour, substance been revised to incorporate the new approach. I hope the readers will find this edition very useful and meet their needs.

Human resource management is increasingly getting integrated with the strategic management at corporate levels. At corporate sector Human Resource Management and Development has assumed great importance. Human Resource Management has become a driving force in success of an enterprise. The reading of this edition will be refreshing and encouraging for the scholars.

Human Resource Management and Development is now a subject of study in almost all universities besides Management Studies Institute. This will be useful to all such at postgraduates courses.

Acknowledgements

A large numbers of motivations have contributed in creating this book, "Human Resource Management". I am thankful to all of them for their help and encouragement. Like most text-books, this book has also drawn from work of a large number of researchers and authors in the field of Human Resource Management. My writing in this book has also been influenced by a numbers of standard and popular text in this field. As far as possible, they have been fully acknowledged at the appropriate places. I express my gratitude to all of them. I have tried to give credit to all sources from where I have drawn materials for this book. Still there may have remained some unintended errors. I shall fell obliged if they are brought to my notice.

I express my gratitude to all of them for making suggestion for the improvement of the book, or for extending their support and encouragement. I have mentioned the names who have been source of motivation to me.

Dr. Girish Kumar Srivastava

Dr. Vikas Kumar

Dr. Jyoti Kumar

Dr. Kamini Kumar

Dr. P. K. Verma

Dr. Vijay Raj Singh

Yugal Kishore Parsad

CMA, Neha Pathak.

I would very much thankful and sincerely acknowledge suggestion given by them. I shall be happy to acknowledge the support of the adopter of the book.

The book is dedicated to N.K. Pathak ji who has always appreciated me and been a constant source of incessant motivation and encouragement to me. Finally, my regard to My Grandparents, Shri Jaswant Rai Pathak and Sheela Devi Pathak, My parents Anil Kumar Pathak and Shubha Pathak and Almighty for bestowing upon me the courage to face the complexities of life and in completing this book.

Dr. Chakshu Pathak
Ranchi
(Jharkhand)

Chapter - 1

Personnel Management — An overview

Work Organisation

As one author has rightly said 1 + 1 makes an organisation, i.e., where there are two or more persons there is in effect an organisation. Some individuals prefer to work independently in isolated circumstances. But the vast majority of all work in today's environment takes place within the context of a structured organisation — a grouping of individuals into a unified and common effort. The structuring may be a loosely knit one in which inter-relationships are scarcely discernible (for they relate to any natural self-grouping of individuals according to their needs) or the organisation pattern may be a highly formalised one in which authority relationships (between the President/or Board of Directors and the operative workers) are clearly defined in detail and prescribed worker behaviour is expected. The former type of structure is known as the "informal" and the latter as the "formal" organisation. An organisation without some structure could be compared to an airport that has no ground or air control over the airplanes using the facilities. It would create chaos and disturb the entire working of the airport.

An organisation may be a manufacturing firm, a business concern, an insurance company, a governmental agency, social organisations, hospital, a university, a public school system, or a religious trust, cause-oriented groups and even families. It may be small or large, simple or complex. An organisation is a human grouping in which work is done for the accomplishment of some specific goals, or missions. For example, the goal of a manufacturing concern might be to produce and supply the goods and services to satisfy the demands of a market. A hospital may provide preventive and curative health services to the people of the area; or the business's goal might be not only to earn profit but also to survive in the competitive market for long. However, the goals of the organisations will not all be the same but an organisation has its own objectives, which may remain relatively constant, but they are likely to be modified over a period of time, as per the changing needs and circumstances. Organisational objectives are most likely to be modified over a period of time, as per the changing needs and circumstances. Organisational objectives are most likely to be multiple, as the organisation try to achieve several goals and to serve a number of different categories of people. In order to achieve the goal, a well-run organisation works out a set of rules sometimes called policies, programmes, rules and regulations, procedures or guidelines and sanctions. These are designed not to restrict creativity but to assist its members in accomplishment of the organisational goals.

People Who Manage

To look after the various functions set for the organisation adequate resources in men and materials have to be arranged by individuals who serve as managers or supervisors within organisations. Such people have to make things happen to aid in the achievement of the organisational objectives, to co-ordinate the resources of the organisation — 4 important Ms.viz. money, material (raw or semi-manufactured), machinery (or fixed assets and plants), and men (or human resources). It is an effective combination and dovetailing of these factors on which the success or failure of the organisation depends. The resources by themselves will not help the organisation to accomplish the objective, unless there is an effective co-ordination and utilisation of these human and non-human resources.

While the human resources available to management in an organisation are only one part of resources which must be co-ordinated, it is through the combined efforts of the people that monetary and material resources are utilised for organisational objectives. Without human efforts, organisations cannot accomplish their objectives. Rensis Likert rightly observes, "All the activities of any enterprise are initiated and determined by the persons who make up that institution, plants, offices, computers, automated equipment, and all else that make a modern firm uses are unproductive except for human effort and direction of all the tasks of management, managing the human component is the central and most important task, because all else depends on how well it is done."

Consequently, the managers have a central responsibility not only for the behaviour and performance of other people but also of their own behaviour. Managers are appointed at various levels to organise and co-ordinate the activities of the team members or fellow work associates.

This constitutes a hierarchy of management, where individuals perform different roles: some are at the top level management, others are at the intermediate and lower levels of the management group. Those at the lower levels are responsible to persons at a higher organisational level. The greater the commitment of the members to organisational objectives, the greater is the degree of effectiveness with which the organisation works.

People at Work

The principal component of an organisation is its 'human resources' or 'people at work'. Human resources have been defined as "from the national point of view, the knowledge skills, creative abilities, talents and aptitudes obtained in the population; whereas from the viewpoint of the individual enterprise, they represent the total of the inherent abilities, acquired knowledge and skills as exemplified in the talents and aptitudes of its employees." Jucius calls these resources, 'human factors,' which refer to "a whole consisting of inter-related, inter-dependent and inter-acting physiological, psychological, sociological and ethical components."

It is the human resource which is of paramount importance in the success of any organisation, because most of the problems in organisational settings are human and social rather than physical, technical or economic. Failure to reorganise this fact causes immense loss to the nation, enterprise and the individual. In the words of Oliver Sheldon, "No industry can be rendered efficient so long as the basic fact remains unrecognised that it is principally human. It is not a mass of machines and technical processes, but a body of men. It is not a complex of matter, but a complex of humanity. It fulfils its function not by virtue of some impersonal force, but a human energy. Its body is not an intricate maze of mechanical devices but a magnified nervous system."

'People at Work' comprise a large number of individuals of different sex, age, socio-religious group and different educational or literacy standards. These individuals in the work place exhibit not only similar behaviour patterns and characteristics to a certain degree, but they also show many dissimilarities. Each individual who works has his own set of needs, drives, goals, and experiences. Each has his own physical and psychological traits. Each human being is not only a product of his biological inheritance but also a result of interactions with his environment. Family relationships, religious influences, racial or caste backgrounds, educational accomplishment, the application of technological innovations, and many other environmental-experimental influences affect the individual as he works. Among the environmental factors that influence work behaviour are various organisational elements (authority relationships; organisational goals, procedures, rules and policies: informal group relationship, the type and manner of supervision received by the employee, etc.). People come to work with certain specific motives to earn money, to get employment, to have better prospect in future, to be treated as a human being while at the place of work. They sell their labour for reasonable wage/salary and other benefits. It is these people who provide the knowledge and much of the energy through which organisational objectives are accomplished.

The management must, therefore, be aware not only of the organisational but also employee needs. None of these can be ignored. The achievements for the organisations, the 'people at work,' 'the people who manage them' (i.e., managers themselves), and other groups of the public (such as the consumers, shareholders, the entrepreneurs, the governments, the suppliers, etc.) are possible through a concerted effort. The employee develops four dimensional relationships: (i) those between management and workers; (ii) those among the workers themselves; (iii) those among the managerial personnel; and (iv) those among different members of the organisation and the community. In other words, he develops "Human Relations" the purpose of which is not to enable him to discover clever techniques for winning friends and influencing people through personality development; nor to enable him to manipulate people as though they are puppets, but to assist him in working more effectively with other people in organisation."

Management of Men is a Challenging Job

"The Management of Man" is a very important and challenging job; important because it is a job, not of managing 'men,' but of administering a social system. The management of men is a challenging task because of the dynamic nature of the people. No two persons are similar in mental abilities, traditions, sentiments, and behaviour; they differ widely also as groups, and are subject to many and varied influences. People are responsive; they feel, think, and act; therefore, they cannot be operated like a machine or shifted and altered like a template in a room layout. They, therefore, need a tactful handling by management personnel. If manpower is properly utilised, it may prove a dynamic motive force for running an enterprise at its optimum results and also work as an elixir for maximum individual' and group satisfaction in relation to the work performed.

Manpower management is a most crucial job because "Managing people is the heart and essence of being a Manager." It is concerned with any activity relating to human elements or relations in organisation. Material elements, however, are beyond its domain. This view has been rightly summed up by J. M. Dietz (of Chicago). He observes: "A business or an industry can be thought of as an inter-weaving of human elements and material elements, with the human elements as the warp; while inter-locking and inter - weaving with this element are the material elements — the wool of the fabric. The warp of the fabric is the human element appearing and reappearing, the strength giving element holding the entire fabric together, and giving it life and a character of continuity." A business cannot succeed if this human element is neglected.

Aldrich has expressed the importance of personnel management thus: "The nearest - analogy is in the human body. Personnel management is not the brain, the controller, not only just a limb, a member: not yet the bloodstream, the energising force; it is the nervous system. It is a line channel, not just a duct, and in some respects has automative force. It is used in enemy action; if it atrophies, partial paralysis results, if it gets out of balance, there issues instability, chaotic action, disequilibrium which can be found in all stages of advancement, in close parallel with neurosis. But, above all, it is inherent in the whole body and intimately connected with its every movement. The nervous system can never be thought of as an adjunct of the body, no more can personnel management be an extraneous or superimposed element on the structure of an organisation. The personnel function lies embedded in the structure, is inherent in the dynamism of that structure, and is an integral part of the process of management itself."

Importance of Human Resource Management

The importance of human resource management can be discussed, after Yodder Heneman and others, from three standpoints, viz., social, professional and individual enterprise.

(a) Social Signicance: Proper management of personnel, enhances their dignity by satisfying their social needs. This it does by: (i) maintaining a balance between the jobs available and the jobseekers, according to the qualifications and needs; (ii) providing suitable and most productive employment, which might bring them psychological satisfaction; (iii) making maximum utilisation of the resource in an effective manner and paying the employee a reasonable compensation in proportion to the contribution made by him; (iv) eliminating waste or improper use of human resource, through conservation of their normal energy and health;

and (v) by helping people make their own decisions, that are in their interests.

(b) Professional Significance: By providing a healthy working environment it promotes team work in the employees. This it does by: (i) maintaining the dignity of the employee as a 'human-being'; (ii) providing maximum opportunities for personal development; (iii) providing healthy relationship between different work groups so that work is effectively performed; (iv) improving the employees' working skill and capacity; (v) correcting the errors of wrong postings and proper reallocation work.

(c) Significance for Individual Enterprise: It can help the organisation in accomplishing its goals by: (i) creating right attitude among the employees through effective motivation; (ii) utilising effectively the available human resources; and (iii) securing willing co-operation of the employees for achieving goals of the enterprise and fulfilling their own social and other psychological needs of recognition, love, affection, belongingness, esteem and self-actualisation.

Dynamic and growth-oriented organisation do require effective management of people in a fast-changing environment. Organisations flourish only through the efforts and competencies of their human resources. Employee capabilities must continuously be acquired, sharpened, and used. Any organisation will have proper human resource management: (i) to improve the capabilities of an individual; (ii) to develop team spirit of an individual and the department; and (iii) to obtain necessary co-operation from the employees to promote organisational effectiveness.

Definition of Personnel Management

We produce below a few standard definitions given by experts of personnel management, which will give an idea of what it means.

"It is that phase of management which deals with the effective control and use of manpower as distinguished from other sources of power".

"The management of human resources is viewed as a system in which participants seek to attain both individual and group goals".

"Its objective is to understand what has happened and is happening and to be prepared for what will happen in the area of working relationships between the managers and the managed".

If an analysis is made of these definitions it will be seen that personnel (or manpower) management involves procedures and practices through which human resources are managed (i.e., organised and directed) towards the attainment of the individual, social and organisational goals. By controlling and effectively using manpower resources, management tries to produce goods and services for the society.

Prof. Jucius has defined personnel administration as, "The field of management which has to do with planning, organising, directing and controlling various operative functions of procuring, developing, maintaining and utilising a labour force, such that the: (a) objectives, for which the company is established are attained economically and effectively; (b) objectives of all levels of personnel are served to the highest possible degree; and (c) objectives of the community are duly considered and served."

According to this definition, personnel administration is concerned with the managerial (planning, organising, directing and controlling) and operative (procurement, development, maintenance and utilisation) functions, with a view to attaining the organisational goals economically and effectively and meeting the individual and social goals.

Prof. Thomas G. Spates offers the following definition, "Personnel administration is a code of the ways of organising and treating individuals at work so that they will each get the greatest possible realisation of their intrinsic abilities, thus attaining maximum efficiency for themselves and their group, and thereby giving to the enterprise of which they are a part its determining competitive advantage and its optimum results".

In this definition, personnel administration has been regarded as a code which deals with the ways of organising the human resources in such a way that their potentialities are best utilised bringing them satisfaction and efficiency in their work and helping the organisation in attaining its objectives, with minimum of cost, in a competitive market.

Edward Flippo states, "Personnel Management is the planning, organising, directing and controlling of the procurement, development, compensation, integration, maintenance and separation of human resources to the end that individual, organisational and social objectives are accomplished."

This definition is a comprehensive one and covers both the management functions and the operative functions. The purpose of all these functions is to assist in the accomplishment of basic objectives.

According to French, "Personnel Management is the recruitment, selection, development, utilisation of and accommodation to human resources by organisations. The human resources of an organisation consist of all individuals regardless of their role, who are engaged in any of the organisation's activities".

This definition states that personnel management is planning, co-ordinating, and controlling of a network of sub-processes and facilitating systems pertaining to the recruitment, selection, utilisation, development of and accommodation of human resources. The sub-processes comprise the most vital aspects of personnel management — leadership, justice, determination, task specialisation, staffing, performance appraisal, training and development, compensation, collective bargaining and organisation development. According to French, "Personnel management is a major component of the broader managerial function and has roots and branches extending throughout and beyond each organisation. It is a major sub-systems of all organisations."

Personnel management, or personnel administration has been defined by Scott and others thus:

> "It is that branch of management which is responsible, on a staff basis for concentrating on those aspects of operations which are primarily concerned with the relationship of management to employees and employees to employees and with the development of the individual and group. The objective is to attain maximum individual development, desirable working relationship between employers and employees and employees and employees, and effective moulding of human resources as contrasted with physical resources".

This definition puts emphasis on the staff group personnel activities and on assisting the operational personnel in performing the personnel duties (i.e., maintenance of personnel records; selection, transfer and promotion of employees; and the responsibility for seeing that the company's policies relating to personnel practices and procedures are carried out).

In the opinion of Dunn and Stephens, "The personnel management is the process of attracting, holding and motivating people involving all managers — line and staff."

An analysis of this definition will show that personnel management is principally concerned with three activities, viz., attracting people, by offering suitable monetary and non-monetary rewards, retaining them in the organisation by improving work environment, etc. and motivating them by following progressive practices and human policies conducive to bring about personal satisfaction to the employees.

The Institute of Personnel Management, London, formulated an official definition of personnel management after the Second World War and modified it in 1965 to incorporate progressive trends and professional developments in the UK. The two definitions are reproduced/below:

> "Personnel Management is that part of the management function which is primarily concerned with the human relationships within an organisation. Its objective is the maintenance of those relationships on a basis which, by consideration of the well-being of the individual, enables all those engaged in the undertaking to make their maximum personal contribution to the effective working of that undertaking" (1945).
>
> "Personnel Management is that part of management concerned with people at work and with their relationship within an organisation. Its aim is to bring together and develop into an effective organisation the men and women who make up an enterprise and having regard for the well-being of the individual and of working groups, to enable them to make their best contribution to its success."(1965)

The essence of the definitions is that Personnel Management is concerned with man at work; and with their group relationship, with a view to achieve the objectives of the organisation through their maximum personal contribution towards the work-goal achievement. The new definition places emphasis on the 'group aspect.' In this definition three objectives are explicit: (a) to maintain good relationships within an organisation, (b) to enable each person to make his maximum personal contribution to the organisation as a member of the working group, and (c) to achieve these things through respect for human personality and the well-being of the individual.

The Indian Institute of Personnel Management (now National Institute of Personnel Management) observes that:

> "Personnel Management, Labour Management or Staff Management means quite simply the task of dealing with human relationships within an organisation. Academically the three aspects of Personnel Management are: (i) the welfare aspect concerned with working conditions and amenities such as canteens, crèches, housing, personal problems of workers, schools, and recreation; (ii) the labour or personnel aspect concerned with recruitment, placement of employees, remuneration, promotion, incentives, productivity etc. (iii) the industrial relations aspects concerned with trade union negotiation, settlement of industrial disputes, joint consultation and collective bargaining.

All these aspects are concerned with human element in industry as distinct from the mechanical."

Lawrence Appley, former President of the American Management Association, has perhaps given the best possible definition of Personnel Management. According to him, "It is a function of guiding human resources into a dynamic organisation that attains its objectives with a high degree of morale and to the satisfaction of those concerned. It is concerned with getting results through people." According to him, "all management is personnel management as it deals with human beings, its development can best be discussed in terms of human development, philosophical, psychological, spiritual and physical". The development and utilisation of human resources is not by any means an ancillary activity but a central element in the operation of a business.

Concept of Personnel Management

On the basis of the various definitions given above, a few basic facts and characteristics may be noted about Personnel Management.

- Some other definitions may also be noted such as:

  "It is method of developing potentialities of employees so that they get maximum satisfaction out of their work and give their best efforts to the organisation" Pigors, Paul and Myres, Charles A, *Personnel Administration: A Point of View and Method*, McGraw Hill Book Co., Kagakusha Ltd., Tokyo, 1961, second edition 1961, p. 11.

  "Personnel Management is an extension of general management, that of prompting and stimulating every employee to make his fullest contribution to the purpose of a business" Northcott, C.H., *Personnel Management: Principles and Practice*, Sir Issac Pitman & Sons, London, 1958, p. 12.

  "It is a function concerned with developing and utilising the manpower resources of the business to the optimum extent in achieving the objectives of that business." — Dirks, Howard M., "Personnel Administration", in Maynard, HB. (Ed.) *Handbook of Business Administration*, New York, 1967, Section 11, p. 11.

  "Personnel Administration is concerned basically with manpower of 'people', organisational resource of output". Sikula, Andrew F., *Personnel Administration and Human Resource Management*, John Wiley and Sons., Inc., New York, 1976, p. 5.

"Personnel Management involves the task of handling the human problems of an organisation, and is devoted to acquiring, developing, utilising and maintaining an efficient work force." Richard Calhoon, Harper and Row Calhoon, New York, 1964, p. 4 and satisfaction, bringing them an equitable, just and human treatment and adequate security of employment. Personnel Management seeks to provide to terms and conditions of employment and satisfying work for those employed.

First, Personnel Management is concerned with managing people to "rank and file employees" at work. Such people or personnel do not simply refer to "rank and file employees" or "unionised labour" but also include "higher personnel" and "non-unionised labour." In other words, it covers all levels of personnel, including blue-collared employees (craftsmen, foremen, operatives and labourers), and white-collared employees (professional, technical and kindred workers, managers, officials and proprietors, clerical workers and sales workers). The shape and form that personnel administrative activity takes, however, may differ greatly from company to company; and, to be effective, it must be tailored to the individual needs of each organisation.

Second, it is concerned with employees, both as individuals as well as a group, the aim being to get better results with their collaboration and active involvement in the organisation's activities, i.e., it is a function or process or activity aiding and directing individuals in maximizing their personal contribution.

Third, personnel management is concerned with helping the employees to develop their potentialities and capacities to the maximum possible extent, so that they may derive great satisfaction from their job. This task takes into consideration four basic elements, namely, the capacities, interests, opportunities and personality of the employees:

Capacities - referring to those abilities or attainments, inherited or acquired, that a worker has, is capable of and must to a certain degree at lease exercise in his work.

Interests - not only an individual's desires and ambitions, but also his instinctive impulsive tendencies, vague yearnings, and ill-defined cravings that may or may not stir him to his fullest action in performing his duties.

Opportunities - not only opportunities for advancement, but opportunities to exercise his capacities and satisfy his interests.

Personality - the sum total of a workers' reaction to his experiences and environment, personality is manifest by an individuals' reception by others. The workers' personality has great influence upon his opportunities.

Since the employee is both a social and economic entity, possessing different characteristics in various work situations; there can be a perfect adjustment of the worker in his work unit if the worker possesses the exact capacities required for the work. The work similarly affords the opportunity for exercising these capacities, and the worker's interests are generally satisfied in the performance of his job. However, a happy combination of the four elements are seldom achieved in actual practice; and a lack of balance forms one of the major causes of waste in production. The best or ideal personnel management, therefore, recognises the individual differences involving these elements and tries to eliminate or reduce them.

Fourth, since recruitment, selection development and utilisation of, and accommodation to people are an integral part of any organised effort, Personnel Management is inherent in all organisations. It is not confined to industry alone; it is equally useful and effective in government departments, military organisations, and non-profit institutions. It is a major part of the general management function and has roots and branches extending throughout and beyond each organisation. Therefore, it is rightly the central pervasive system of all organisations. This point has been summarised by Pigors and Myers in these words: "Personnel administration permeates all types of functional management, such as production management, financial management, sales management and research management. It applies in non-industrial organisations, government, non-profit institutions, and armed services. Unless these managers themselves expect to perform all the duties for which they are responsible, they have to secure the co-operation of other people within their part of the total organisation. In short, every member of the management group, from top to bottom, must be an effective 'personnel administrator' because he depends on the co-operative efforts of his subordinates."

As Bakke says: "Human relations, industrial relations and personnel relations are just new names for an aspect of the general managerial function as old as management itself". It is more than the management of people by supervisors; and it is also more than the responsibilities assigned to the personnel department. As a field of discipline, personnel management is faced with many challenging problems centering around social responsibility, work design, staffing, style of leadership and supervision, compensation and appraisal, collective bargaining, organisational development and organisational climate.

Fifth, personnel management is of a continuous nature. In the words of George R. Terry: "It cannot be turned on and off like water from a faucet; it cannot be practised only one hour each day or one day a week. Personnel management requires a constant alertness and awareness of human relations and their importance in everyday operations".

Finally, personnel management attempts at getting the willing co-operation of the people for the attainment of the desired goals, for work cannot be effectively performed in isolation without the promotion and development of an esprit de corps.

Taking the above characteristics into consideration, it may be observed that personnel management is an approach; a point of view; a new technique of thinking and a philosophy of management, which is concerned not only with managing people, but also with solving the human problems of an organisation intelligently and equitably, and in a manner which ensures that employees' potential is properly developed, that maximum satisfaction is derived by them from their work, that the objectives of the organisation are achieved and that good human relations are maintained within the organisation.

Personnel management can be of full value to an organisation only when it is consistently thought out and applied at all levels and to all management functions; in corporate policies, in the systems, procedures and in employment practices, etc. This integrative aspect of personnel management is, therefore, of vital importance.

Terminology: The Name of the Game

Different terms, such as 'Personnel or Staff Management,' 'Personnel Administration,' 'Labour Management,' 'Manpower Management,' 'Employee Relations,' 'Industrial Relations,' etc., have been used interchangeably. The phrase 'staff executive' in-charge of 'personnel management', 'personnel administration,' has been variously designated, reflecting changes in status and functions. Richard Calhoon points out: "From the earliest term 'employment manager' evolved the more general term of 'Personnel Manager' in the 20s and 30s. During the late 30s and 40s, the terms 'Industrial Relations,' and 'Labour Relations' became more popular concurring with the rise of collective bargaining and the expansion of other functions (the executive being known as 'Industrial Relations Officer' or 'Labour Relations Director' or 'Manager' or 'Labour Welfare Officer' or simply 'Labour Officer'). Then, in the late 40s and 50s, a limited number of organisations and industries espoused the designation

'Human Relations' (the executive being known as 'Director' or 'Manager') as more in keeping with the over-all organisational behavioural responsibilities. As of 60s, however, the key word is 'personnel' to describe the general functions in the vast majority of cases.

This chronological growth variation in terminology indicates that Personnel Management as a branch of knowledge is still in a formative stage, and an exact connotation cannot be given to it. However, during the late 60s and 70s, a growing feeling of social responsibility in personnel administration has further warranted the use of even a broader term, including "Public and Community Relations." To Prof. Yoder goes the credit of using the term "Industrial Relations," which is the most inclusive of these terms and which describes the more all-inclusive functions of "Manpower Management."

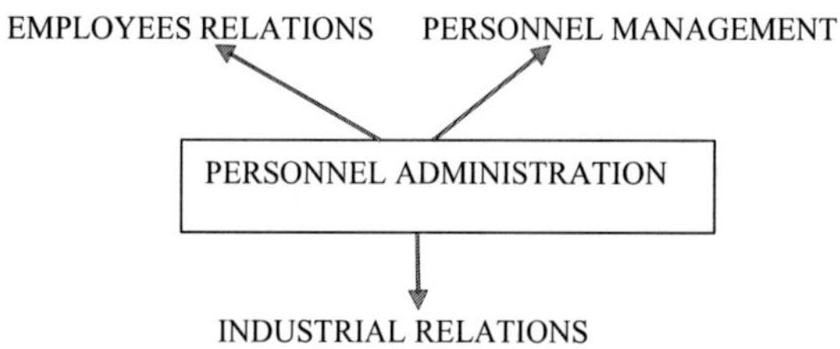

Fig. 1.1: Personnel Management Terminology.

Manpower management relates to procedures through which human resources are organised and directed towards the attainment of organisational, social and individual goals. Yoder further subdivides it into "Personnel Management/Personnel Administration" and "Labour Relations." He uses the first two terms interchangeably to refer to the management of manpower. They represent the employers' relationships with individual employees (in different activities); and "Labour Relations" represent the relationship between the management and organised unions, and indicating the negotiation and administration of collective agreements or labour contracts. I have preferred the use of "Personnel Management", "the Management of Human Resources," because it is highly inclusive and embraces all the above concepts. Even otherwise, at present, the terms "Personnel Management" and "Industrial Relations" for purpose of accuracy are widely used and the executives are designated as Personnel Officer, Personnel Director, Personnel Man, Personnel Executive, Staff and Personnel Manager, Employment Manager, Labour Welfare Officer, Labour Liaison Officer, or Labour Officer or Chief Industrial Relations Officer, in India he is called 'Labour Officer', 'Labour Welfare Officer,' 'Personnel

Officer,' 'Personnel Manager,' 'Employee Relations Officer,' 'Industrial Relations Officer', and so on.

Characteristics and Qualities of a Personnel Manager

Personnel Management is a delicate subject, and often it matters more to know 'who' says something than to know 'what' he says. Unless the personnel manager has the active support of the top management, he will be like a ship without a rudder. On the other hand, if he does not win the confidence of the employees and their union, he will not be respected by the management. Moreover, he has to earn the esteem of his colleagues especially those in the line who are more interested in immediate rather than long-term results. He walks on a tight rope. Tact and imagination are his only guides.

To be successful in his job, a Personnel Manager must be a specialist in organisation theory and as such be an effective adviser to top management in organisational matters as well as being able to organise his own Department/ Division in such a manner as to minimize frictions, promote goodwill, and release the latent energies of his own people and associates to be expended on their primary assignments.

He should have real expertise in personnel administration — knowledge of relevant laws, procedures, techniques and of developments in theory and practice in comparable economies, behavioural sciences' contribution to personnel management, a bent for research in man-management, and should have an adequate knowledge of behavioural sciences which study the reactions of individuals and the groups to particular sets of conditions and environments in an organisation or a factory.

Prof. Jucius has emphasised that personnel managers should possess the following types of general knowledge, besides their specialisation in the field of personnel areas?

(1) Philosophy, which seeks for the underlying explanations of human nature and conduct.

(2) Ethics, which is concerned with moral and value judgments.

(3) Logic, which is concerned with the rules and principles of reasoning.

(4) Mathematics, which treats of exact relations between quantities, magnitudes and systems.

(5) Sociology, which deals with the forms and functions of human groups.

(6) Anthropology, which is concerned with physical and environmental relations to people's social and cultural patterns.

(7) Medicine, which in all its branches is concerned with the well-being of the people.

(8) History, which seeks to record and explain past events.

(9) Economics, whose interests are in optimizing choices among competing uses of limited resources.

(10) Management which is concerned with a skilful leadership of organisational groups.

(11) Political Science, which, in the best sense, is concerned with how people are governed and how they govern themselves.

He must have a keen sense of social justice and be fully appreciative of the rights and interest of the men and women at work, as well as of the economic necessities of management. His philosophy of social justice should include two fundamental concepts:

(i) industry is a partnership between management, men and owners whose objective is to earn profits through service;

(ii) industry can profit greatly by developing and co-ordinating the capacities, the interests, and the opportunities of each worker and of each of management. He must be able to couple this sense of social justice with a warm personal interest in people. This is turn, must be controlled by a wealth of common sense, which will protect him from sentimentality on the one hand and from coldness on the other.

The other important qualities that a personnel manager should possess are:

(i) a mind with a capacity for creative thinking, for analyzing situations and reasoning objectively;

(ii) he should know problem-solving techniques and have an ability to inspire, motivate and direct employees;

(iii) a devoted sense of vocation and faith in humanity;

(iv) capacity for leadership, a sense of social responsibility and a standard of social justice;

(v) personal integrity so that employees may repose confidence in him;

(vi) capacity for persuasion, coupled with patience and tolerance;

(vii) a friendly, approachable nature, which is tactful and sympathetic, and a pleasing personality, a well-groomed appearance, sophisticated taste and habits, and capable of working with and through other people;

(viii) initiative and decision-making ability;

(ix) mobility of facial expression (which encourages confidence, conveys interest, registers sympathy and allays distrust);

(x) an ability to generate trust among his colleagues and develop acceptability, recognition for himself and his ideas of communication with readiness and fluency;

(xi) a readiness to co-operate the subordinates in times of difficulty and never to interfere or thrust his advice on them; and finally,

(xii) a promptitude in giving them the feedbacks in their handling of personnel matters whenever necessary in the interest of functioning of the organisation and established personnel policies of the company.

Regarding the qualities of a personnel manager, Northcott has rightly observed: "The personnel requirements are admittedly high, but a profession which deals with so large a part of industrial life will always be held in honour and calls for men and women of sterling qualities."

In sum, a personnel man must be a person who has the human relations skill, a sensitivity to behavioural issues, and a conceptual skill to see the broad picture and predict situations rather than react to problems as they occur.

The Role of Personnel Man

Looking back at the historical manifestation of the role of a Personnel Manager in industry, it may be said that by and large it reflected the top management's own concept of the personnel function and the methods of managerial control they believed in. The personnel manager has been playing a variety of roles at different stages in the past, like that of a police agency, a legal defender of rights and a negotiator, a catering man meeting the welfare needs of the employees. But the theme has always been set by the thinking at the top level management".

It is difficult precisely to relate the present day functions of personnel to his role as conceptualised earlier. If the personnel management is what personnel managers do, the picture that emerges is indeed confusing, for what personnel managers do can be compared to a Sunday morning jumble sale — a collection of incidental chores, fire-fighting tasks, welfare functions, and a watch-dog function.

As Professor Chatterjee puts it: "The personnel man first appeared as a low powered functionary who was no better than a files clerk or record keeper concerned with the payment of the dues of the workers. Out of this arose a kind of role as a liaison man or channel of communication between the boss and the man. To start with he was essentially an odd-job-man. Then came the next stage when he administered the welfare schemes which were being gradually provided for in the statutes. As the workers were organising themselves into strong unions and industrial conflicts were multiplying the employer used the Personnel Man as a kind of trouble shooter or fire-fighting — either to advise him on how to find loopholes in the labour laws or other statutes so that the union demands could be resisted with a measure of legitimacy or to come to a settlement where concessions were inescapable. There was a tendency at this stage to make him responsible for handling all kinds of labour trouble. Gradually his work was realised as more of the nature of staff function rather than line function; and that he was an expert rather than a controller or manager of men".

In the modern era, the personnel manager typically performs a variety of roles, such as the roles of conscience, of a counsellor, a mediator, a company spokesman, a problem-solver and a change agent. He performs many miscellaneous roles in accordance with the needs of a situation, such as.

(i) The conscience role is that of a humanitarian who reminds the management of its moral and ethical obligations to its employees.

(ii) The personnel manager plays the role of a counselor to whom the employees frequently go for consultation and with whom they discuss their marital, health, mental, physical and career problems.

(iii) As a mediator, he plays the role of a peace-maker, offering to settle the disputes that may arise among individuals or groups. He acts as a liaison and communicating link between an individual and a group and between labour and management.

(iv) The personnel manager has always been a frequent spokesman for or representative of the company because he has a better overall picture of his company's operations, since he deals intimately with many key organisational activities and functions.

(v) The personnel manager also acts as a problem-solver with respect to the issues that involve human resources management and overall long range organisational planning.

(vi) He works as a change agent within the organisation because he is best suited to introduce and implement major institutional changes. He takes initiative for installing organisational development programmes and convinces the top management of their need. It is he who alerts the top management regarding managerial obsolescence in his organisation.

(vii) He helps line managers learn to detect and solve their problems.

(viii) The personnel manager plays many other roles as well. Any matter which needs someone's attention and which nobody wants to deal with is often handled by the personnel department. Such activities may be peripheral but important and crucial to the efficient and effective operation of an organisation.

It has been now fully recognised that the basic role of the Personnel Manager is "the management of manpower resources". Such management is concerned with both in group and individual relationship, and labour-management relations. It effectively describes the process of planning, and directing the application, development and utilisation is now considered as one of the four main functions, viz., finance, production, marketing and human relations.

The functions of the personnel manager are very comprehensive' and varied and are determined and influenced by such factors as the size, nature and organisation, business or industry, its short and long-term objectives, nature of industry and product, market conditions, degree of competitiveness among rivals economic, cultural, political and legal environment the structure of the executive and administrative officers, the mental make-up of the personnel managers, and the over-all organisational philosophy of business.

The personnel manager undertakes all those functions which are concerned with "human elements" or "relations in organisation as well as in material elements." Whatever items are listed therein (as the functions), the main objective is to see that human resources are purposefully utilised for the optimum good of the organisation and there should be meaningful co-operation for achieving the objectives of management. Expertise is brought together in a scientific manner and attitude so created that motivate the group to achieve the organisational goals economically, effectively and speedily, and also fulfil and satisfy its physiological, psychological, economic and social needs and realise its potential abilities.

Chart 1.1: The role of a personnel manager

Personnel role	*Welfare role*	*Administrative role*	*Fire-fighting legal role*
a. Advisory – advising management on effective use of human resource. b. Manpower planning, recruitment and selection, etc. c. Training and development of line man. d. Measurement and assessment of individual and group behaviour.	a. Research in personnel and organisational problems b. Managing service canteen, grains shops transport co – opertaive crèches, etc. c. Group dynamics groups counseling, motivation, leadership, communication, etc.	a. Time –keeping . b. Salary &wages administrative incentives. c. Maintenance or records d. Human engineering man –machine relationship.	a. Grievance handlings b. Settlements of disputes c. Handling disciplinary action. d. Collective bargaining e. Joint consultation,

The role of personnel manager is ever expanding and is strengthened by greater interest shown in human relations problems by specialists such as behavioural scientists, industrial engineers, social psychologists, labour and legal advisers, industrial and computer technologists — all of whose researches have enriched the field of personnel management, its functions and changed their nature making them wide and humanitarian.

The ideal personnel manager is not a "decision-maker" but a counsellor not "a collector of responsibilities" but "an advisor" to help the management make more reliable personnel decisions. In any enterprise it is these "line men" who determine the "personnel climate" for the entire organisation. If the personnel man can meet the challenge of "staff role" he would make the most effective contribution to industry.

Objectives of Personnel Management

One of the principles of management is that all the work performed in an organisation should, in some way, directly or indirectly, contribute to the objectives of that organisation. This means that the determination of objectives, purposes or goals is of prime importance and is a prerequisite to the solution of most management problems. Objectives are pre-determined ends or goals at which individual or group activity in an organisation is aimed.

The formulation of the objectives of an organisation is necessary for the following reasons:

(i) Human beings are goal-directed. People must have a purpose to do some work. Announced organisational goals invest work with meaning.

(ii) Objectives serve as standards against which performance is measured.

(iii) The setting of goals and their acceptance by employees promotes voluntary co-operation and co-ordination; self- regulated behaviour is achieved.

(iv) The objectives stand out as guidelines for organisational performance. They help in setting the pace for action by participants. They also help in establishing the "character" of an organisation. Ralph C. Davis has divided the objectives of an organisation into two categories: (a) Primary objectives, and (b) Secondary objectives:

(a) Primary objectives, in the first instance, relate to the creation and distribution of some goods or services. The personnel department assists those who are engaged in production, in sales, in distribution and in finance. The goal of personnel function is the creation of a work force with the ability and motivation to accomplish the basic organisational goals. Secondly, they relate to the satisfaction of the personal objectives of the members of an organisation through monetary and non-monetary devices. Monetary objectives include profits for owners; salaries and other compensation for executives; wages and other compensation for employees; rent for the landowners and interest for share/stock-holders. Non-monetary objectives include prestige, recognition, security, status, or some other psychic income. Thirdly, they relate to the satisfaction of community and social objectives, such as serving the customers honestly, promoting a higher standard of living in the community, bringing comfort and happiness to society, protecting women and children, and providing for aged personnel.

(b) The secondary objectives aim at achieving the primary objectives economically, efficiently and effectively. The fulfillment of the primary objectives is contingent upon:

(i) The economic need for, or usefulness of, the goods and services required by the community/society.

(ii) Conditions of employment for all the members of an organisation which provide for satisfaction in relation to their needs, so that they may be motivated to work for the success of the enterprise.

(iii) The effective utilisation of people and materials in productive work.

(iv) The continuity of the enterprise.

The methods adopted by business organisations in fulfiling the primary purposes must be consistent with the ethical and moral values of society and with the policies and regulations established by legislative action.

On the personnel men lies the responsibility for ensuring a satisfactory accomplishment of the objectives of an organisation and of its employees, for if they are not reasonably achieved, the basic objectives of the organisation will suffer. It is for this reason that, while framing company personnel objectives care is taken to consider the interests and needs of the employees and of employee goals. This is done by integrating the employee interests and the management interests with a view to achieving the objectives of the entire organisation. The concept of integration of employee-management interests, and the relationship between objectives and programmes, have been illustrated in the following chart:

Chart 1.2: Integration of Interests of Employees and Management

Employee's Interests	*Managements interest*
1. Recognition as an individuals	1. Lowest unit personnel
2. Opportunity for expression or development	2. Maximum productivity of employee
3. Economic security	3. Availability and stability of employees
4. Interest in work	4. Loyalty of employee
5. Safety, healthy working conditions	5. Co-operation of employee
6. Acceptable hours of work and adequate wages	6. High organisational morale
7. Fair and efficient leadership	7. Intelligent initiative of employee

Executive Leadership

According to the professional personnel executives, who met in a conference at Armstrong Manor, Lancaster, Pa, the objectives of personnel administration are:

(a) To utilise human resources effectively;

(b) To establish and maintain a productive and self-respecting relationship among all the members of an organisation; and

(c) To bring about maximum individual development of the members of an organisation.

In the opinion of Scott, Clothier and Spriegel, "The objectives of personnel management, personnel administration or industrial relations in an organisation are to obtain maximum individual development, desirable working relationships between employers and employees, and employees and employees, and to effect the moulding of human resources as contrasted with physical resources."

Dirks states that "the objectives of personnel administration include the utilisation of human resources effectively, establishment and maintenance of productive and self-respecting working relationships among the participants and attainment of maximum individual development of the members in the organisation.

Pigors and Myers observed, "Managing is organisational leadership, and one of its central tasks is effective co-ordination and utilisation of available human and non-human resources to achieve the objectives of the organisation. These objectives may be, for example, to maximise profit or increase the firm's share of the market in business enterprises; to improve efficiency or expand the scope of services provided by a governmental department; to get more members or to bargain more effectively for members in a labour union; or to improve the quality of instruction, expand facilities for training and undertake research".

The American Management Association has very succinctly summarised the objectives of personnel administration. It says: "The purpose of a business enterprise is the profitable production of goods and services to fulfil economic needs in such a way as to provide satisfactory returns to both economic and social suppliers, owners and members of the organisation, under conditions which provide for the maximum conservation of human and material resources over a continuing period".

Following this statement, the objectives of personnel administration may be laid down as follows:

(i) To achieve an effective utilisation of human resources (besides resources) in the achievement of organisational goals (which may be the production and distribution of goods and services needed by society).

(ii) To establish and maintain an adequate organisational structure and a desirable working relationship among all the members of an organisation by dividing of organisation tasks into functions, positions, jobs, and by defining clearly the responsibility, accountability, authority for each job and its relation with other jobs/personnel in the organisation.

(iii) To secure the integration of the individuals and groups with an organisation, by reconciling individual/group with those of an organisation in such a manner that the employees feel a sense of involvement, commitment and loyalty towards it. In the absence of such an integration, friction may develop in an organisation which may lead to its total failure. Friction produces inefficiency. Friction may result from political aspirations, from difficulties in communication, and from faults inherent in a particular organisational structure. The behaviour of individuals and groups in any organisation also involves frictions – personal jealousies and rivalries, prejudices and idiosyncracies, personality conflicts cliques and factions, favouritism and nepotism."

(iv) To generate maximum individual/group development within an organisation by offering opportunities for advancement to employees through training and job education, or by effecting transfers or by offering retraining facilities.

(v) To recognize and satisfy individual needs and group goals by offering an adequate and equitable remuneration, economic and social security in the form of monetary compensation, and protection against such hazards of life as illness, old age, disability, death, unemployment, etc., so that the employees may work willingly and co-operate to achieve an organisation's goals.

(vi) To maintain a high morale and better human relations inside an organisation by sustaining and improving the conditions which have been established so that employees may stick to their jobs for a longer period.

Personnel management tries to improve morale by giving adequate training to workers and by achieving for itself a knowledge of human nature which is "the totality of motives that cause human actions; it is a mosaic of relexes and instincts, of inherited and acquired habits, of individual and group traditions."

The American Management Association observes: "These basic objectives remain the same whether or not certain groups among the members of the organisation belong to a labour union. Further, the objectives are not in opposition to those objectives of organised labour which are consistent with the private enterprise system.... The objectives are in the best interests of all those to whom management is responsible; owners of enterprises, the community, the consumers of its goods and services, and members of the organisation itself, including groups who may belong to unions".

Pre-requisites for the Achievements of the Objectives

In brief, the objectives of an organisation may be: the fullest contribution of human resources for the achievement of the organisation goal, of long and short-term plans, and of the operations of the organisation in an environment of high morale and vitality consistent with profitability and social milieu, with the ethical values of society and with the policies and regulations established by the country's legislature.

To achieve these objectives, the following pre-requisites must be satisfied:

(a) Capable people should be picked up on the basis of the qualifications fixed.

(b) Individual and group efforts/potentialities must be effectively utilised by providing suitable work opportunities, tools and raw materials, by showing an appreciation of work well done, and by offering better chances for future advancement and training.

(c) Willing co-operation of the people to achieve the objective must be available by creating such feelings as "people work with us" rather than saying that "people work for us."

(d) The tasks of an organisation should be properly divided in accordance with a sound plan into functions and positions, each indicating clear-cut authority, responsibility and duties, as also the relationship of one position with another.

(e) The goals to be achieved should be specially made known to all concerned in the language best understood by them. Specificity and clarity are both important in defining the objectives. The objectives should also be comprehensive.

(f) Since objectives have to be shared by many senior persons in an organisation, a wide-scale enquiry and consultation should be undertaken before their formulation and efforts should subsequently be made to develop a common understanding of the objectives among managers at various levels.

(g) The objectives should be clearly defined, failing which a great deal of confusion may arise. Without clear-cut objectives, the management of organisational records cannot be kept in balance, and the management of one section may interfere with that of another. Moreover, without clear-cut objectives, the management of organisational records cannot be kept in balance, and the management of one section may interfere with that of another. Moreover, without clear-cut objectives, there can be no standards by which to evaluate the performance of an individual or that of the whole organisation. Again, an absence of objectives often leads to organisational disaster. On the other hand, the refining or revising of objectives is the most fundamental task of all managers at all levels.

(h) Suitable monetary and non-monetary incentives, in the form of adequate and reasonable pay-packets, service benefits and security against hazards of life and of employment and against the arbitrary actions of supervisors should be available to employees. A properly prepared grievance handling procedure and disciplinary plan should also be available.

A determination of objectives is the responsibility of the top management, particularly of the President or Chairman and the Board of Directors.

Impact of Environment on Organisational Objectives

Various aspects of the national environment have a decided impact upon the objectives. These are:

(i) National or commercial attitudes, such as a growing social consciousness on the part of the management to fulfil its responsibilities of providing employment to special category of people (the women, the handicapped, the scheduled tribes or scheduled castes people), meeting employee needs, etc.

(ii) State or Central legislation, which may prohibit the production of alcoholic beverages during the period of prohibition, or curtail the production of harmful drugs or food articles.

(iii) The needs of national defence on an emergency situation, or shortage of critical materials, may force certain organisations to change their objectives from earning high profits to a proper distribution of goods and services in the community.

(iv) Innovations in technology and service such as television, refrigerators, new vaccines have had a great impact on the objectives of an organisation, by making them more useful.

(v) Union-management relations and the need for the payment of higher wages may force some marginal producers to go out of the market or may force organisations to instal new equipment or systems in order to compete successfully in the market. Trade union checks on management may have the effect of forcing the executive to define or revise objectives.

(vi) The marginal skills and attitudes, the imagination and capability of managers may affect the proper realisation of objectives which in turn, would determine whether those objectives are continued, dropped or supplemented.

(vii) The personal likes and dislikes of owners or directors of an organisation also have an effect on objectives. Some directors may refer rapid growth, others may want only a moderate growth at all. Some owners or directors may not be interested in certain products or services, even though may be economically feasible to enter into competition with those particular goods or services.

(viii) The relationship of power among the various categories of employees and their bosses also affects organisational objectives. This is specially so when a new organisation is set up, in which the willingness of various entrepreneurs to manage certain aspects of certain goods are important factors in determining organisational goals.

(ix) The labour market also has an important effect on organisational objectives.

Tools, Techniques and Methods Needed to Achieve Objectives

To achieve the objectives of an organisation, in the first place, it is necessary to develop an appropriate organisation and an administrative system. This requires that systematic data should be collected both from within the organisation and from external sources (such as the universities and other enterprises). In the second place, there must be a periodic review of administrative practices in the organisation and of the changes made, whenever necessary. In the third place, the personnel manager should assume the responsibility of attaining the requirements of his enterprise and those imposed upon it by environmental changes.

Process-Systems Approach to Personnel Management

Just as it is useful for the architect to build miniature models of a proposed building, so it has been found useful to have some type or model for personnel management, which may be based upon "a symbolic representation of a perceptual phenomenon." This type of model is given the name of "Process-Systems Approach to Personnel Management." Such an approach provides for:

(i) a description of personnel management as a dynamic sub-aspect of the total management process and as integral part of all subdivisions of an organisation;

(ii) an analysis of the inter-dependence between various aspects of personnel management and between personnel management and other managerial processes; and

(iii) an analysis of the Ecology of personnel management (i.e., relationship between the various personnel processes and their environments).

Before we proceed to discuss this Approach, it would be fruitful to know what 'process' and 'systems' mean.

A process is "an identifiable flow of inter-related events moving toward some goal, purpose, or end." Wendell has analysed this definition thus: "flow, implies movement through time and in the direction of a result. Inter-related, implies, interaction within the process and between events. Events, are activities, happenings, or change. Goal, and purpose suggest a human objective. End implies some conclusion or consequence that may not necessarily be sought or planned by man." A process may, or may not, have consequences intended by man.

System, on the other hand, has been defined as "a particular linking of inter-related and inter-dependent components having a facilitating effect, on the carrying out of one or more processes." In this definition, "particular may be different in some respect from other systems; components may be devices, raw materials, techniques, procedures, plans, policies, rules and/ or people; inter-related and inter-dependent signify inter-dependency among components; facilitating effects suggest that systems are ordinarily designed as means of carrying out of regularising processes." The system has a goal-sequence or end-oriented.

Coming to the personnel management, for instance, employment process is facilitated by a unique linkage of people, policies, devices and procedures for hiring employees such as application blank, a battery of tests, and a series of interviews. The employment systems of various companies might differ in some aspects, and even people involved may also differ. However, some aspects, and even people involved may also differ.

However, some aspects of the system, such as the types of tests used, might be similar. This example of employment system is a sub-system relative to the broader personnel management system of organisation. And the total organisation itself or any of its departments/units can be systems.

Every system in operation (in process) includes a flow of inputs (materials, energy or information), a processor or transforming mechanism (a machine or the human being doing the work), and a flow outcomes or outputs (the product or services and waste). A system may also have a mechanism of feedback.

In the process systems terminology, "personnel management" is the planning, co-ordinating, and controlling of a network of organisation wide sub-processes and facilitating sub-systems pertaining to recruitment, selection, utilisation, development of, and accommodation to human resources. The sub-processes comprise the most vital aspects of personnel management; leadership, justice determination, task specialisation (job and organisation design), staffing, performance appraisal, training and development, compensation and reward, collective bargaining, and organisation development. These processes are found, in more or less degree, in most, if not all kinds of organisations.

The leadership process involves in influencing the individual and group behaviour towards achievement of organisation goals. It is concerned with traits, philosophy, and behaviour of the leader, the characteristics of subordinates, and the superiors.

The justice determination process is concerned with the giving of awards and penalties to the employees in proportion to their relative contribution to the output. This provides for "equal treatment to all and a fair compensation for the work."

The task- specialisation process consists of division of the total task into individual jobs. In other words, it consists of setting of organisational objectives; job designing; communication of the job design to employees through job descriptions and performance standards and training; job specification and the work rules.

Personnel Management

<table>
<tr><td rowspan="9">PLANNING
COORDINATION
CONTROL</td><td>1. Lerdership</td></tr>
<tr><td>2. Justice determination</td></tr>
<tr><td>3. Task specialisation</td></tr>
<tr><td>4. Staffing</td></tr>
<tr><td>5. Performance appraisal</td></tr>
<tr><td>6. Training and development</td></tr>
<tr><td>7. Compensation and rewards</td></tr>
<tr><td>8. Collective bargaing</td></tr>
<tr><td>9. Organisational development</td></tr>
</table>

Fig. 1.2: Major Personnel Management Process in Organisation.

The staffing process is the more complex and important process, involving manpower planning, authorisation for staffing, developing sources for recruitment; evaluation of applicants, employment decisions; offers, induction and orientation, transfers, promotions, demotions, and separations, etc.

The performance appraisal process is concerned with continuous evaluation of the employees work so that when necessary, promotion, pay raises, transfers, training etc. may be given.

The training and development process is a combination of many subprocesses which aim at correcting the quality of work of the individual, through provision of training and development programmes, employee counselling, offering suggestions, etc.

The compensation and reward process determines the mechanism and form for giving ûnancial and non-financial rewards, fringe-benefits, etc. to the employees with a view to motivate them for work.

The collective bargaining process is a process that determines the relationship between the union and the employer in regard to wages, benefits, hours and working conditions, etc.

From the above, it is obvious that personnel management is a major component of the broad managerial function and has roots and branches extending throughout and beyond each organisation. It is a major sub-system of all organisations which are inter-related and inter-dependent. Every personnel manager's responsibilities include planning for people; organising people; staffing with people; directing people; gaining the commitment, interest and effect of people; and applying controls to people.

Chapter - 2

Functions of Personnel Management

Introduction

As the term implies, personnel management is the management of human resources in an organisation and is concerned with the creation of harmonious working relationship among its participants and bringing about their utmost individual development. Such management is concerned with leadership in both groups and 'individual relationship' and 'labour relations' and 'personnel management.' It effectively describes the process of planning and directing, development and utilisation of human resources in employment. In fact, personnel management undertakes all those activities which are concerned with human elements or relations as well as with material elements in an organisation. Whatever functions are listed therein, the main objective of these functions is to bring together expertise in a scientific way and to create attitudes that motivate a group to achieve its goals economically, effectively and speedily.

Classification of Functions

Broadly speaking, experts have generally classified the functions into two major categories, viz., managerial functions and operative functions. Others have classied functions as general and specific functions, and yet others as 'Personnel Admininstration Functions' and 'Industrial Relations Functions.' Functions have also been classified on the basis of the capacities; or on the basis of authority. This type of classification of functions has been discussed as below:

(a) **The General and Specific Functions:** Under 'General' type of functions, the personnel management is required: (i) to conduct personnel research, (ii) to assist in the programmes of personnel administration, (iii) to develop appraisal plans, (iv) to launch education and training programmes, (v) to develop a competent work force, and (vi) to establish and administer varied personnel services delegated to personnel department. Under specific functions, the personnel management may involve itself in areas of employment, safety, wage and salary, benefit schemes, community relations and advice and counselling the employees.

(b) Personnel Administration and Industrial Relations Functions: Personnel administration functions relate to the function of managing people from the lower to the upper level of the organisation and embraces policy determination as implementation of policies by the personnel at the lower levels. Accordingly, "Personnel administration" refers to "creating, developing and utilising a 'work group' and involves all types of inter-personnel relationships between superiors and subordinates."

The 'Industrial Relations' functions, on the other, are "not directly related to the function of 'managing people', but refer to interactions between the management and the representatives of the unions." Such functions involve all activities of employer-employee relationship, such as organisation of the union members, negotiation of contracts, collective bargaining, grievance handling, disciplinary action, arbitration, etc. — the purpose of all these being to prevent conflict between the two participants. The above two functions are inter-related and inter-dependent and, hence, the most common term used is "Personnel Management/ Administration and Industrial Relations."

(c) Functions Classified on the Basis of Capacities: This classification has been adopted by Saltonstall. According to him, "Although Personnel managements' function is the 'staff function,' it also performs three roles," viz;

(i) He performs a line function not only because he directs the work in his own department but also in some service functions such as recruitment, administration of benefits, the plant canteen and allied activities.

(ii) He functions as a co-ordinator of personnel activities, in so far as he controls the functions of other departments. This he does through regular reporting on labour turnover, absenteeism, accidents and grievances to different levels of management. He also assists/advises the top management in accomplishing personnel objectives, policies and procedures.

(iii) He performs a typical staff function in the form of assisting and advising the line personnel to solve their problems.

Saltonstall suggests two approaches for the development of line officials, viz., (a) "the reductive" or "threat approach"; and (b) the "augmentive" or "source of help" approach. The latter approach is more close to "behavioural approach to management".

Thus, according to him:

The typical staff functions are indirectly related to action and characterised by development, consultation, planning, interpretation, evaluation, diagnosis, research, investigation and recommendation; and the typical line functions are related to command action and characterised by direction, control, decisions, enforcement, application, performance and instruction.

(d) Functions According to the Degree of Authority: Dale Henning and French made an interesting observation that "The personnel man is described in the textbooks and journals is like 'Abominable Snowman' much talked about but seldom seen." They have classified his functions into three categories thus:

(a) Area of maximum authority, e.g., direction of payroll calculations, orientation procedure, transfer rules, etc.

(b) Area of combined use of authority and persuasion, e.g., establishment of disciplinary procedure, inter-departmental data gathering, determining the number of participants in a training programmes, etc.; and

(c) Area of maximum persuasion, e.g., salary changes under the rules of the plant, employment of individuals recommended by the personnel department in other departments, initiating disciplinary action, etc.

We now discuss below the functions of personnel management under two broad heads, viz., (1) Managerial functions, and (2) Operative functions.

Inputs	*Planning*	*Organising*	*Direction*	*Controlling*	*Outputs*
Human (management of men) and economic (materials, machinery and money) resources interacting with environment changes	Determination to shorts long range plans to accomplish organisation objectives	Developments of the organisation structure according to predetermined plans	Stimulations and motivation of organisation personnel according to predertermined plans	Assurance that directed action is taking place according to predertemined plans	Goods and services needed by the organisation's customers

Feedback of significant deviation from planned performance

Fig 2.1 Function of Managements

Managerial Functions

"Management is a multi-purpose organ which has three jobs, two of which are directly related to personnel managing a business: 'managing managers' and 'managing workers' and the work." Lawrence Appley says that "Management is the accomplishment of the results through the efforts of other people." In the opinion of Harold Koontz, "It is the of getting things done through people and with informally organised groups".

In our view, management may be thought of as the process of allocating an organisation's inputs (human and economic resources) by planning, organising, directing and controlling for the purpose of producing outputs (goods and services) desired by its customers so that organisation objectives are accomplished. In the process, work is performed -with and through organisation personnel in every changing business environment.

Management is, thus, personnel administration, It is the development of the people and not the direction of things. Managing people is the heart and essence of being a manager. Thus, a Personnel Manager is a manager and as such he must perform the basic functions of management. He exercises authority and leadership over other personnel. His function involve (what Luther Gullick calls) POSD CORB, i.e., planning, organising staffing, directing co-ordinating, reporting and budgeting the work of those who are entrusted with the performance of operative functions. In other words, managers procure, process and peddle, find and employ resources, develop services, and find markets for their output.

(a) Planning: "Is a pre-determined course of action." According to Allen, "it is a trap laid to capture the future". Terry is of the view that "planning is the foundation of most successful actions of any enterprise." Planning is the determination of the plans, strategies, programmes, policies, procedures, and standard needs to accomplish the desired organisation objectives. In fact, "planning today avoids crisis tomorrow." Planning is a hard job for it involves the ability to think, to predict, to analyse, and to come to decisions, to control the actions of its personnel and to cope with a complex, dynamic fluid environment. They bridge the gap between where "they are and where they want to go." For this purpose they determine personnel programmes well in advance. The two most important features of planning are research and forecasting. These two are inter-related, for forecast is possible only as a result of research. Personnel administration should be able to predict trends in wages, in labour market, in union demands, in other benefits and in personnel policies and programmes. The task of forecasting personnel needs in relation to changes in production or seasonal variations and the levelling out of differences in production is extremely important, both for employees and for management. Therefore, planning or decision-making has to be undertaken much in advance of an action so that unforeseen or anticipated problems and events may be properly handled. This is also stressed by the saying: "Good managers make things happen".

(b) Organising: After a course of action has been determined, an organisation should be established to carry it out. According to J.C. Massie, "An organisation is a structure, a framework and a process by which a cooperative group of human beings allocates its tasks among its members, identifies relationships and integrates its activities towards common objectives". This is done by designing the structure of relationships among jobs, personnel and physical factors. An organisation is the wedding of authority and responsibility because, in its essentials, it consists of the assignment of specific functions to designated person or departments with authority to have them carried out, and their accountability to management for the results obtained. It seeks to achieve the maximum return with minimum effort by decentralisation, whereby the power of decisions is brought down as near as possible to the individual concerned. How far this can be done will depend upon the top management's philosophy and appreciation of the benefits of delegation and decentralisation. In the words of Drucker: "The right organisational structure is the necessary foundation; without it, the best performance in all other areas of management will be ineffectual and frustrated.

(c) Directing (Motivating, Actuating or Commanding): Directing the subordinates at any level is a basic function of the managerial personnel. According to McGregor, "many managers would agree that the effectiveness of their organisation would be at least doubled if they could discover how to tap the unrealised potential present in their human resources." Directing is involved with getting persons together and asking them (either through command or motivation) to work willingly and effectively for the achievement of designated goals. Directing deals not only with the dissemination of orders within an organisation units and departments, but also with the acceptance and execution of these orders by the employees.

The decisions are taken by the top management, but only after consultation with the personnel department. A review or checking of the safety instalments, wage rate ranges, disciplinary action and general wage changes are all the responsibility of the personnel department. Final action is taken only when the green signal has been obtained from it. However, securing acceptance and execution generally requires a certain amount of motivation of individuals and groups. Otherwise, the actual performance level may be well below that which is desired.

(d) **Co-ordinating and Controlling:** Coordinating refers to balancing timing and integrating activities in an organisation, so that a unity of action in pursuit of a common purpose is achieved. In the words of Terry, "Co-ordination deals with the task of blending efforts in order to ensure a successful attainment of an objective." Co-ordination in the management of personnel takes place at all levels, from the top management through to the supervisor and those for whom he is responsible. The personnel department has to co-ordinate the tasks of developing, interpreting and reviewing personnel policies, practices and programmes, such as safety programmes, employee benefits, job evaluation, training or development, and communication." These activities are generally put into operation by and through the line people; but it is the personnel department which follows them through, unifies them, and checks to see how they work.

"Controlling is the act of checking, regulating and verifying whether everything occurs in conformity with the plan that has been adopted, the instructions issued and the principles established." It is greatly concerned with actions and remedial actions. "It is not just score-keeping. It is not just plotting the course and getting location reports; but rather it is steering the ship." "It is through control that actions and operations are adjusted to pre-determined standards; and its basis is information in the hands of the managers." "By check, analysis, and review, the personnel department assists in realising the personnel objectives. Auditing training programmes, analysing labour turn-over records, directing morale surveys, conducting separation interviews, interviewing new employees at stipulated intervals, comparing various features of the programme with other organisation programmes in the area, industry and nation — these are some of the means for controlling the management of personnel."

This monitoring process provides management with actual performance information for comparison with pre-determined performance standards.

If there are unavoidable deviations from the planned performance, corrective action can be taken immediately.

This last function of control closses the system loop by providing feedback of significant deviations from the planned performance. The feedback of pertinent information can affect the inputs or any of the management functions.

Though all the above functions are performed at all levels of management, the amount of time devoted to each function varies for each management level the top management performs planning functions more than does the supervisory management. On the other hand, supervisors at the third rung of the management pyramid devote more of their time to directing and controlling production.

Operative Functions

The operative functions of personnel management are concerned with the activities specifically dealing with procuring, developing, compensating, and maintaining an efficient work force. These functions are also known as service functions.

(1) The procurement function is concerned with the obtaining of a proper kind and number of personnel necessary to accomplish an organisation's goals. It deals with specifically with such subjects as the determination of manpower requirements, their recruitment, 'selection and place' (comprising activities to screen and hire personnel, including application forms, psychological tests, interviews, medical check-up reference calling), induction, follow-up, transfers, lay-offs, discharge and separation, etc.

(2) The development function is concerned with the personnel development of employees by increasing their skill through training so that job performance is properly achieved. Drafting and directing training programmes for all levels of employees. Arranging for their on-the-job, office and vestibule training, holding seminars and conferences, providing for educational and vocational counselling and appraising employee potential and performance are undertaken under this function.

(3) The compensating function is concerned with securing adequate and equitable remuneration to personnel for their contribution to the attainment of organisational objectives. Functions related to wage surveys, establishment of job classifications, job descriptions and job analyses, merit ratings, the establishment of wage rates

and wage structure, wage plans and policies, wage systems, incentives and profit-sharing plans, etc., fall under this category.

(4) The integration function: after the employee has been procured, his skill and ability developed and monetary compensation determined, the most important, yet difficult of the personnel management is to bring about an "integration" of human resources with organisation, and to cope with inevitable conflicts that ensue. "Integration" is concerned with the attempt to effect a reasonable reconciliation of individual, societal, and organisation interests. It rests upon the premise that significant over lappings of interests do exist in the organisation in such programmes as job enlargement, job evaluation, variable compensation plans. The greater the overlap, the more productivity would coincide with employees that they would prefer to avoid, e.g., assignment to narrow and repetitive tasks, meeting high output standards, acceptance of managerial decisions. For this reason, organisations have disciplinary action programmes as well as some freedom to do away with the services of particular employees. On the other hand, there are certain things that employees desire which the organisation is reluctant to provide, e.g., increased wages, totally safe working conditions, time off with pay, shorter hours of work, premium pay for overtime work, etc. To get these benefits, outside pressure might be brought upon the employers.

Managerial activities that bring about a reasonable integration of human resources and the organisation objects, are termed as "human relations." The goal is to lead to productive and creative collaboration toward mutual objectives. 'Human relations' programme tend to decrease accidents, absenteeism, turnover and operating errors, while simultaneously raising morale, quality and productivity such programmes also prevent undesirable behaviour such as sabotage, insubordination, strikes, etc. All these problems are handled under grievance procedure, disciplinary action and labour union programmes.

(5) The maintenance function deals with sustaining and improving the conditions that have been established. Specific problems of maintaining the physical conditions of employees (health and safety measures) and employee service programmes are the responsibility of the personnel department.

Flippo rightly says: "The purpose of all of these activities is to assist in the accomplishment of the organisation's basic objectives. Consequently, the starting point of personnel management as of all management, must be a specification of those objectives and a determination of the sub-objectives of the personnel function. The expenditure of all funds in the personnel department can be justified only in so far as there is a net contribution toward company objectives.

It may be noted that the personnel management cannot afford to lay greater emphasis on one and neglect the other two major functions. In this connection the observations of John F. Mee merit mention: "It is essential to grasp the significance of this dual division of personnel functions if the mistake of becoming pre-occupied with the demand of detailed problems to the neglect of managerial duties is to be avoided. It is easy, as many executives have learned to their regret, to become so busy with such tasks as hiring, transferring, counselling, and training that they fail to foresee the shifting condition which call for the changes in operating function they fail to recognised the work of subordinates satisfactorily and the fail to keep a good check up on the work of the subordinates."

Functions of Employee Welfare and Personnel Administration

A. Employee Welfare

I. Conditions of Work Environment

(1) Working Conditions: (a) Temperature; (b) Ventilation; (c) Lighting; (d) Dust, smoke, fumes and gases; (e) Noise; (f) Humidity; (g) Posture — simple, and (h) hazard and safety complex devices.

(2) Factory Sanitation and Cleanliness: (a) Provision of urinals in factories (b) Provision of spittoons; (c) Provision for the disposal of waste and rubbish; (d) Provision for water disposal (drainage); (e) Provision of proper bathing and washing faculties; (f) Cleanliness, white-washing and repair of buildings and workshops; and (g) Care and maintenance of open spaces, gardens, roads, etc.

(3) Welfare Amenities: (a) Provision and care of drinking water; (b) Canteen services; c) Lunch; (d) Rest room; (e) Crèches: (f) Cloak rooms; and (g) Other amenities.

II. Employees' Health Services

(1) Factory Health Services: (a) Medical examination of employees; (b) Factory dispensary and clinic treatment; (c) First aid and ambulance room; (d) Treatment of accidents; and (e) Health education and research.

(2) Recreation: (a) Playgrounds for physical recreation (athletics, games, gymnastics, etc.) and (b) Social and cultural recreation (music, singing, dancing, drama. etc.).

(3) Workers Education: (a) Education to improve skills and earning capacity; in Literacy; (c) Library, audio visual education, lecture programmes; and (d) Workers' educational scheme and its working.

(4) Economic Services: (a) Employees' co-operative societies; (b) Grain shops and fair price shops and (c) Housing co-operatives.

(5) Housing for Employees and Community Services.

(6) Study of the Working of Welfare Acts: (a) Factories Act; (b) Employees State insurance Act; and (c) Minimum Wages Act.

(7) Social Work in Industrial Setting: (a) Family Planning; and (b) Employee counselling.

B. Personnel Administration

I. Recruitment

(1) Recruitment: (a) Recruitment of personnel; (b) Knowledge of sources of employee apply; (c) Receiving application interviews; (d) Investigation of references; and (e) Physical 'tests, trade tests and aptitude tests.

(2) Job Descriptions, Job Specifications, Job Analysis.

II. Manpower Administration

(1) Placement: (a) Job Assignment; (b) Job enlargement; and (c) Personnel development.

(2) Introduction: (a) Introduction to supervisor; (b) Introduction to job and work place; (c) Introduction to colleagues; (d) Introduction to welfare activities and other facilities; (e) Authorities and procedures; (f) Service conditions; and (g) Sponsor system follow-up interviews).

(3) Wage and Salary Administration (Job Evaluation): (a) Wage scales, increments and E.B. (Efficiency Bar), (b) Salary and wage standardisation; (c) Incentives payments and allowances; (d) Working hours and over-time; (e) Profit sharing, bonus; (f) Holidays, leave; (g) Executive compensation plans; and (h) Fringe benefits and perquisites.

(4) Discipline: (a) Instances of indiscipline and misconduct; (b) Causes of indiscipline; How to deal with indiscipline; domestic enquiry; (d) Handicaps of management in the maintenance of discipline and enforcement of certain rules; and (e) Shop floor supervision and its responsibilities.

(5) Transfer and Promotion: (a) The procedure to be adopted; (b) Causes of transfer and promotion; (c) Personnel for transfer and promotion and (d) Records of transfer and promotion.

(6) Merit Rating and Evaluation of Employees: (a) Assessment techniques, and (b) Counselling.

(7) Time, Motion and Work Study.

(8) Prevention of Losses: (a) Material loss; (b) Work loss; and (c) Time loss.

(9) Administration in Relation to: (a) Absenteeism; (b) Late coming; (c) Loitering; and (d) Employee turnover, its causes, incidence, effects, remedies, and statistical analysis.

(10) Personnel Training and Development Programmes for:

(a) Apprentices;

(b) Workers;

(c) Foremen and Supervisors;

(d) Junior Executives;

(e) Management Staff.

(11) Personnel Records and Statistics: (a) Accident records; (b) Employee turnover studies; (c) Absenteeism; (d) Wage levels and cost of living; and (e) Research into industrial relations and personnel management relations and personnel management problems.

III. Retirement

(1) Provident Fund and Pension Plans,

(2) Gratuity Provisions,

(3) Exit Interviews,

(4) Long Service Awards, and

(5) Retirement Plans, Housing, Medical Aid, etc.

IV. Study of the Working of

(1) Apprentice Act,

(2) Employment Exchanges. (Compulsory Notification of Vacancies) Act,

(3) Payment of Wages Act and Payment of Bonus Act;

(4) Shops and Establishments Act; and

(5) Employees Provident Fund Act. Employees State Insurance Scheme.

It should be noted that the listing made by different authors is by no means comprehensive or necessarily representative of the work of personnel administration; it is only indicative of the nature of activities which are usually included in functional areas of a modern company of large dimensions.

Functional Areas of Personnel Management

On the basis of the various functions which the personnel management undertakes, the functional areas of personnel management may be set forth as below:

(i) Organisational Planning, Development and Task Specialisation;

(ii) Staffing and Employment;

(iii) Training and Development;

(iv) Compensation, Wage and Salary Administration;

(v) Motivation and Incentives;

(vi) Employee Services and Benefits;

(vii) Employee Records;

(viii) Labour or Industrial Relations; and

(ix) Personnel Research and Personnel Audit.

I. Organisational Planning and Development

"Organisational planning" is concerned with the division of all the tasks to be performed into manageable and efficient units (departments, divisions or positions) and with providing for their integration. Both differentiation and integration are vital for the achievement of pre-determined goals.

(1) A determination of the needs of an organisation in terms of a company's short and long-term objectives, utilisation of technology (industrial engineering, industrial psychology, and mechanical engineering) of production, deciding about the nature of product to be manufactured, keeping in view the external environment and public policy.

(2) The planning, development and designing of an organisational structure through the fixing of the responsibility and authority of the employees, so that organisational goals may be effectively achieved.

(3) Developing inter-personal relationship through a division of positions, jobs and tasks; the creation of a healthy and fruitful interpersonal relationship; and the formation of a homogeneous, cohesive and effectively interacting informal group.

II. Staffing and Employment

The staffing process is a flow of events which results in a continuous manning of organisational positions at all levels from the top management to the operative level. This process includes manpower planning, authorisation for planning, developing sources of applicants, evaluation of applicants, employment decisions (selection), offers (placement), induction and orientation, transfers, demotions, promotions and separations (retirement, lay-off, discharge, resignation, disability, and death).

(1) Manpower planning is a process of analysing the present and future vacancies that may occur as a result of retirements, discharges, transfers, promotions, sick leave, leave of absence, or other reasons, and an analysis of present and future expansion or curtailment in the various departments. Plans are then formulated for internal shifts or cut-backs in manpower, for the training and development of present employees, for advertising openings, or for recruiting and hiring new personnel with appropriate qualifications.

(2) Recruitment is concerned with the process of attracting qualified and competent personnel for different jobs. This includes the identification of existing sources of the labour market, the development of new sources, and the need for attracting large number of potential applicants so that a good selection may be possible.

(3) Selection process is concerned with the development of selection policies and procedures and the evaluation of potential employees in terms of job specifications. This process includes the development of application blanks, valid and reliable tests, interview techniques, employee referral systems, evaluation and selection of personnel in terms of job specifications, the making up of final recommendations to the line management and the sending of offers and rejection letters.

(4) Placement is concerned with the task of placing an employee in a job for which he is best fitted, keeping in view the job requirements, his qualifications and personality needs.

(5) By induction and orientation is meant the introduction of an employee to the organisation and the job by giving him all the possible information about the organisations history, objectives, philosophy, policies, future development opportunities, products, goodwill in the market and in the community, and by introducing him to other employees with whom and under whom he has to work.

(6) Transfer process is concerned with the placement of an employee in a position in which his ability can be best utilised. This is done by developing transfer policies and procedures, counselling employees and line management on transfers and evaluating transfer policies and procedures.

(7) Promotion is concerned with rewarding capable employees by putting them in higher positions with more responsibility and higher pay. For this purpose, a fair, just and equitable promotion policy and procedure have to be developed; line managers and employees have to be advised on these policies, which have to be evaluated to find out whether they have been successful.

(8) Separation process is concerned with the severing of relationship with an employee on grounds of resignation, lay-off, death, disability, discharge or retirement. Exit interviews of employees are arranged, causes of labour turnover are to be analysed and advice is given to the line management on the causes of, and reduction in, labour turnover.

A number of devices and sub-systems are used in the systems designs to manage the staffing process. These are: (a) Planning tables and charts; (b) Application blanks; (c) Interviews; (d) Psychological tests; (e) Reference checks; (f) Physical examination; (g) Performance reviews; and (h) Exit interviews.

III. Training and Development

It is a complex process and is concerned with increasing the capabilities of individuals and groups so that they may contribute effectively to the attainment of organisational goals. This process includes:

(1) The determination of training needs of personnel at all levels, skill training, employee counselling, and programmes for managerial, professional and employee development; and

(2) Self-initiated developmental activities (formal education), during off-hours (including attendance at school/college/professional institutes); reading and participation in the activities of the community.

Under this area, the training needs of the company are identified, suitable programmes are developed, operatives and executives are identified for training, motivation is provided for joining training programmes, the line management is advised in matters conducting training programmes, and the services of specialists are enlisted. The training programmes has to be evaluated by arranging follow-up studies.

IV. Compensation, Wage and Salary Administration

It is concerned with the process of compensation directed towards employees for services rendered and motivating them to attain the desired levels of performance. The components of this process are:

(1) Job evaluation through which the relative worth of a person is determined. This is done by selecting suitable job evaluation techniques, classifying jobs of various-categories and then determining their relative value in various categories.

(2) Wage and salary programme consists of developing and operating a suitable wage and salary programme, taking into consideration certain facts such as the ability of the organisation to pay, the cost of living, the supply and demand conditions in labour market, and the wage and salary levels in other firms. For developing a wage and salary programme, wage and salary surveys have to be conducted, wage and salary rates have to be determined and implemented, and their effectiveness evaluated.

(3) The incentive compensation plan includes non-monetary incentives which have to be developed, administered and reviewed from time to time with a view to encouraging the efficiency of the employee.

(4) The performance appraisal is concerned with evaluating employee performance at work in terms of pre-determined norms/standards with a view to developing a sound system of rewards and punishment and identifying employees eligible for promotions. For this purpose, performance appraisal plans, techniques and programmes are chalked out, their implementation evaluated, and reports submitted to the concerned authorities.

(5) Motivation is concerned with motivating employees by creating conditions in which they may get social and psychological satisfaction. For this purpose, a plan for non-financial incentives (such as recognition, privileges, symbols of status) is formulated; a communication system is developed, morale and attitude surveys are undertaken, the health of human organisation diagnosed and efforts are made to improve human relations in the organisation. The line management has to be advised on the implementation of the plan and on the need, areas and ways and means of improving the morale of employees.

V. Employee Services and Benefits

These are concerned with the process of sustaining and maintaining the work force in an organisation. They include:

(1) Safety provision inside the workshop. For this purpose, policies, techniques, and procedures for the safety and health of the employees are developed; the line management is advised on the implementation and operation of safety programmes; training has to be given to first line supervisors and workers in safety practices; the causes of accidents have to be investigated and data collected on accidents; and the effectiveness of the safety programmes evaluated periodically.

(2) Employee counselling is the process through which employees are given counsel in solving their work problems and their personal problems. The line management has to be advised on the general nature of the problems which the employees may face from time to time.

(3) The medical services include the provision of curative and preventive medical and health improvement facilities for employees, free or otherwise. A periodical medical check-up of employees, training in hygienic and preventive measures are undertaken.

(4) The recreational and other welfare facilities include entertainment services like film shows, sports and games; and housing, educational, transport and canteen facilities, free or at subsidised rates. Suitable policies and programmes are framed and efforts are made to administer these services satisfactorily. The effectiveness of such programmes has also to be evaluated.

(5) Fringe benefits and supplementary items are made available to employees in the form of: (a) Old age survivor's and disability

benefits, unemployment and workmen's compensation; (b) Pensions, gratuities and such other payments as are agreed upon - death benefits, sickness, accident and medical care, insurance, expenses of hospitalisation, voluntary retirement benefits; (c) Paid rest periods, lunch periods, wash-up time, travel time, get-ready time; (d) Payments for the time during which no work is done – paid vacation or bonus in lieu of vacation, payment for holidays, paid sick and maternity leave; and (e) Profit-sharing benefits, stock options contribution to employees' provident fund, employees educational expenditure and special wage payments ordered by the courts.

These benefits are usually given to employees in order to tempt them to remain in the organisation, to provide them social security, and to reduce absenteeism and labour turnover. Policies and programmes for implementing these have to be properly developed.

VI. Employee Records

In employee records complete and up-to-date information is maintained about employees, so that these (that is the records) may be utilised, if need be, at the time of making transfers/promotions, giving merit pay, or sanctioning leave and at the time of termination of service.

Such records include information relating to personal qualifications, special interests, aptitudes, results of tests and interviews, job performance, leave promotions, rewards and punishments.

VII. Labour Relations

By labour relations is meant the maintenance of healthy and peaceful labour - management relations so that production/work may go on undisturbed.

Under this area:

(1) Grievance handling policy and procedures are developed, after finding out the nature and causes of grievances, and locating the most delicate areas of dissatisfaction.

(2) Rules and regulations are framed for the maintenance of discipline in the organisation, and a proper system of reward and punishment is developed.

(3) Effort are made to acquire a knowledge of, and to observe and comply with, the labour laws of the country and acquaint the line management with the provisions which are directly concerned with

organisation. Collective bargaining has to be developed so that all the disputes may be settled by mutual discussions without recourse to the law court. Such bargaining, negotiating and administering agreements relating to wages, leave, working conditions and employee-employer relationship falls in this area.

VIII. Personnel Research and Personnel Audit

This area is concerned with:

(1) A systematic inquiry into any aspect of the broad question of how to make effective an organisation's personnel programmes - recruitment, selection, utilisation of, and accommodation to human resources;

(2) Procedures and policies and findings submitted to the top executive;

(3) Data relating to quality, wages, productivity, grievances, absenteeism, turnover, strikes, lock-outs, accidents etc., which are collected and supplied to the management so that it may review, alter or improve existing personnel policies programmes and procedures;

(4) Morale and attitude surveys.

In large organisations, some of these functions are performed by persons other than personnel men; but in smaller organisations, all these functions are discharged by the personnel administrator.

In most companies, staffing, appraisal, training and development, compensation. collective bargaining and health and safety are included in the purview of the personnel department. Only a few firms have departments which specialise in some of these functions and which are separate from personnel department. The practice of separating "personnel" from "labour/ industrial relations" has declined in recent years. Today, in the vast majority of companies, the personnel department is expected to be concerned about all major "people aspect" of the enterprise.

The principal categories of functions performed by personnel department may include many sub-functions. For example, the administration of employee benefit programme may include representing the company's interest in unemployment compensation and workmen's compensation. Occasionally the personnel department may be involved in such matters as parking lots, preparing the annual report to shareholders etc. McFarland calls this tendency to assign such miscellaneous functions to the personnel department the "trashchen hypothesis." He believes that indiscriminate assignment of functions to the personnel department weakens the potential impact of the personnel programme and diverts the energies and attentions of the departments members from those functions which should be their central concern. Furthermore, the chief executives believe there should be little restriction on what is assigned to the personnel department, while personnel director resents the tendency to make the department a dumping ground" of miscellaneous functions. Thus, conflict and frustration result from neglecting to clearly define the role of personnel department.

The organisation of the personnel department will reflect not only the functions assigned to it, but also the size of the enterprise. When a company is small, the personnel department may consist of one man and his secretary. In a large company, the Personnel Director may have several subordinate managers reporting to him, including a safety director, a medical director, a wage and salary administrator, a training director, and a labour relations director. Many firms may group two or more of these sub-functions under subordinate administrators.

Wendell French suggests that in a complex enterprise, the chief executive should take the following questions into consideration while assigning the function to the personnel department:

1. Does the particular function require a total — enterprise philosophy about the utilisation of human resources?
2. Do any activities related to the selection, utilisation, and development of human resources necessitate centralised attention?
3. Does the administration of human resources demand specialised skills which would be impracticable for sub-divisions of the enterprise to recruit or develop?

Changing Scope of Personnel Administration

The scope of personnel administration has changed somewhat over the last few decades. However, this change has been relatively slow in comparison to the changes in other areas of business, management and administration. Sikula observes: "Changes definitely are taking place in personnel administration. Some personnel sub-functions seem to be breaking away from personnel, others seem to be new sub-areas while still either seem to be changing only in terms of their relative emphasis and degree of importance. Many of these changes depend on the size of an organisation in which personnel function occurs, the managerial personnel philosophies, the growing importance of the functions, the changing organisational demands, employee needs and societal concerns." Managerial and organisational development, manpower planning, organisational planning are incoming areas, i.e., they are now going to receive substantially more attention; they did not have any prominence in the past. Training and managerial development and personnel research have become increasingly important today; while the importance of personnel appraisal, wage and salary administration, has somewhat declined in terms of relative emphasis. Employee benefit and services, and worker's health and safety have always been important personnel concerns. Labour relations, public relations and plant security are "outgoing" personnel sub-areas which have been taken away from the personnel department because of their increased organisational importance.

Emerging Role of Personnel Management

It has been rightly apprehended that there are dangers of the personnel manager giving way to the new specialists who are coming up — the experts in information technology, in the management of research and development, and in manpower and planning, unless the personnel manager tries and acquires advance knowledge of and prepares for the change. He should, therefore, concern himself with the following major areas of change which are emerging:

(a) changing composition of work force, with the white-collar gradually becoming a dominant group;
(b) growing unionisation among the work force is greatly increasing their strength to demand increasing participation in the decision-making activities influencing their interests;
(c) increasing role of government in enacting protective legislation to bring about a balance in the interests and rights of the participants in the organisation;
(d) revolution in information technology and other technological innovations, which might adversely affect the interests of the work force and their occupational mobility;
(e) rapidly changing jobs and skills requiring long-range man-power planning; and
(f) increasing concern of many firms for accepting greater social responsibility.

In all these areas of change, personnel management people would be needing larger amount of training, re-training, mid-career re-training. Furthermore, they must also be familiar with the findings of the Behavioural Sciences so that they could rely more on management by integration of professional goals with the goals of the organisation and by self-control rather than on management by centralised direction and control. They also cannot afford to neglect the "bread and butter" problems of day-to-day personnel administration.

Richardson considers that "Personnel" is "industrial counterpart of the Behavioural Sciences in the same way Engineering is of the Physical Sciences." But he observes that "This function seems to have lost any direct connection with business results it once may have had." According to him, "the personnel people live in a world untouched by business realities. But in future they will have to make an 'integrative approach' to systems analysis with a view to understanding the link between their activities and business outcome. For example, productivity might be one such link. Negotiations with a trade union for a wage increase might be another link which will have their effect on the probability of achieving desired future business results.

People at work and their interpersonal relations are in a state of transition. Although personnel management and personnel departments have witnessed an almost universal recognition and acceptance by top executives of the important role that personnel management can perform in planning and administering systems of human resources, the coming decade presents major new challenges in various fields, as described below.

The individual is and will be the basic unit of activity. Individual human beings supply the knowledge, skills, and much of energy utilised in organisations. It would not be incorrect to presume that each individual human being will continue to have needs, drives, and expectations; but no two people would be identical in their goals, ambitions, strengths and weaknesses. Such people may expect even more from their employment relationship. For example, Bennis has suggested that the increased level of education and mobility will change the values people have towards work. "People will be more intellectually committed to their jobs and will probably require more involvement, participation and autonomy in their work".

The educational level of the work force is expected to continue to rise. The work force will become more diverse in backgrounds, age concentrations, and ideological philosophies. Groups previously considered to be minorities of the work force (such as the women, the handicapped persons, the members of the scheduled castes, etc.) will increase in number and percentages, and their demands will become more vocal. Many workers might be having more leisure time because of change in work patterns. Managers will be required to face a wide variety of demands from employees.

Changes in the institutions of the society - the family unity, religion, education, organised labour - are likely to occur. The effect of these changes will be significant upon people at work.

The over-supply of unskilled labour, the under-supply of skilled labour in some education of some workers for jobs available will result in organisational areas, and over stress.

Social applications, both formal and informal, will have a large influence on the attitudes and behaviour of people at work. Because people are normally socially oriented, the attitudes and values of organisational peer groups, family members, off-the-job friends, and others to whom they may socially relate will influence heavily their perceptions and actions. The job of managing may therefore, become more challenging and more variable than it has hitherto been.

The organisations of the future would be larger, more complex and with more inter-related structurings of the people. Accordingly, such organisations will become more impersonal and more dehumanising. Such organisations might be required to decentralise decision-making and other activities. They might also expect that the employees should recognise a common set of objectives, plans, and goals so that they can contribute collectively toward mutually beneficial goals. High level managers will need to devote more of their time to integrative decision-making to unite the efforts of all organisational members.

Technology, discoveries and innovations will result in new pressures on organisations and individuals and call for changes in objectives of organisations and methods and procedures to achieve their objectives. Skill requirements will be altered as a result of technology. In some instances, technology might cause workers and their tasks to become more interrelated, while in others there might be tendencies toward separation and even social isolation. Computer technology may result in the reshaping of a number of organisational roles and goals and will have a particularly significant impact on decision-making. These changes indicate the challenge that lies ahead for future managers.

Being human being managers are and will be subject to their own mental and physical limitations, to their own philosophical commitments, to their own biases and prejudices, and to outside pressures from many directions. However, future managers should be able to profit from the increasing body of knowledge and experiences of the present and past managers so that they are in a position to serve more effectively and more constructively the various sectors of people.

Role of the Personnel Managers of Tomorrow

The future manager will be more knowledgeable about people, organisations and the total environment, as observed by Bergey and Slover. They state:

> "The future manager will be better grounded in social sciences, world affairs, and the humanities in general. He will effectively integrate the techniques of information technology with the human resources available to him."

To meet future challenges, professionalism among the managers will be on the increase. They will be receiving more formalised educational training in managerial techniques and responsibilities. These managers will also need different types of skills, e.g., top managers will need more conceptual, analytical, and decision-making abilities; first line supervision may need technical skills and interpersonal leadership abilities, and middle-level managers may need a blend of the above skills in addition to coordinative abilities. However, all managers will be benefitted from the development and utilisation of skills and abilities in interpersonal relations.

Future managers should develop the ability to be perceptive toward themselves, their superiors, colleagues and subordinates; their organisation, its goals, resources, etc, and many additional elements. They should be sensitive and empathetic to the people, events, and objects around them. They must be perceptive in discerning changes in knowledge, attitudes, behaviour, value systems, need levels, technical requirements, etc. They must have the ability to get to the real heart of the situation.

Because the managers will have to constantly encounter changes, they must be open-minded, and receptive to new ideas and new operational techniques and innovations. They must also possess patience and tolerance so that they may not only perceive the problems, but also diagnose cause, work with other individuals, bear their views, and find out suitable solutions.

The strength of future manager would be in helping others make decisions for themselves. This means that he should know how to lead group efforts, how to counsel with individuals and how to be a good listener. The personnel manager should put more emphasis on "positive motivation"— on helping people achieve personal goals while striving toward organisational objectives. This type of environment induces employees to be more productive because they are forced to perform. At the same time, the manager should not avoid the use of "negative motivational techniques" when they may be useful.

Besides, he and his staff should be deeply involved in encouraging "participative management" or "job enrichment", either of which may have a major impact on job design. The corporate personnel staff should be increasingly concerned with organisational planning, preparation of organisation manuals, and advice to the chief executive on over-all organisational structure, and implementing plans of reorganisation.

The future personnel staff must seek opportunities to be heavily involved in manpower planning, initial selection, orientation, promotional decisions, and career planning. It should also fulfil several other functions, such as "training for change," "systems counselling", "developing new incentives", and "building collaborative problem-solving teams."

Conclusion

In conclusion, it may be said that future has many challenges for the managers of tomorrow. The most important challenge is how personnel executive and his staff can help in improving organisational effectiveness; and how best he can utilise the results of behavioural scientists for the benefit of the people at work. One part of the challenge lies in "how to create and manage the various personnel sub-systems in a way compatible with the thrust toward more participative, results oriented, adaptive, and humanistic organisation." Systems of job design, staffing, appraisal, compensation, collective bargaining, organisational justice, and training and development must all be examined and improved toward these ends."

In the words of French, "This challenge is made all the more real and urgent by two sometimes seemingly contradictory imperatives which are rapidly overtaking us —— the imperative toward more efficient production of quality goods and services, and the imperative toward a higher quality of life in organisations. Personnel management must — and will — play a major role in furthering a creative synthesis of these two imperatives'.

Chapter - 3

Personnel Policies, Procedures and Programmes

Personnel Policies

The dictionary meaning of "policy" is a "plan of action" and that "plan" is a policy. Policy-making and planning are, therefore, synonymous. "A policy," says Flippo, "is a man-made rule of pre-determined course of action that is established to guide the performance of work toward the organisation objectives. It is a type of standing plan that serves to guide subordinates in the execution of their tasks." According to Calhoon, "Personnel policies constitute guides to action. They furnish the general standards or bases on which decisions are reached. Their genesis lies in an organisation's values, philosophy, concepts and principles." "Policies are statements of the organisation's over- all purposes and its objectives in the various areas with which its operations are concerned—- personnel, finance, production, marketing and so on."

Yoder observes: "A policy is a pre-determined, selected course established as a guide towards accepted goals and objectives.... They (policies) establish the framework of guiding principles that facilitate delegation to lower levels and permit individual managers to select appropriate tactics or programmes. In contrast to these, personnel policies are those that individuals have developed to keep them on the track towards their personnel objectives. Management policies are developed by working organisations to keep them on course headed and directed toward their organisational objectives. These define the intentions of the organisation and serve as guidelines to give consistency and continuity to total operations. They provide a base for management by principle as contrasted with management by expediency." He adds: "Personnel or labour or industrial relations policy provides guidelines for a wide variety of employment relationships in the organisation. These guidelines identify the organisation's intentions in recruitment, selection, promotion, development, compensation, organisation, motivation and otherwise leading and directing people in the working organisation. Personnel policies serve as a road map for managers.

Thus, personnel policies refer to principles and rules of conduct which "formulate, redefine, break into details and decide a number of actions" that govern the relationship with employees in the attainment of the organisation objectives.

Personnel policies are:

(i) The Key-stone in the arch of management and the life-blood for the successful functioning of the personnel management because, without these policies, there cannot be any lasting improvement in labour management relations.

(ii) The statements of intention indicating an agreement to a general course of action, indicating specifically what the organisation proposes to do and, thus, suggest the values and viewpoints which dominate the organisation's actions; and

(iii) A positive declaration and a command to an organisation. They translate the goals of an organisation into selected routes and provide general guidelines that both prescribe and proscribe programmes which, in turn, dictate practices and procedures.

Aims and Objectives of Personnel Policies

A management's personnel policy should have two types of objectives, general and specific. The statement of general objectives should express the top management's basic philosophy of human resources and reflect its deep underlying convictions as to the importance of people in an organisation and of the management activity which deals with people, i.e., personnel administration. The management must formulate and develop a basic creed, which should contain a clear-cut statement of the possibility. The statement of specific objectives should refer to the various activities of personnel administration connected with staffing, training, developing, wage and salary administration, motivation, employee services and benefits, employee records, labour relations and personnel research.

The aims of personnel policies should be/are:

(i) To enable an organisation to fulfill or carry out the main objectives which have been laid down as the desirable minima of general employment policy;

(ii) To ensure that its employees are informed of these items of policy and to secure their co-operation for their attainment;

(iii) To provide such conditions of employment and procedures as will enable all the employees to develop a sincere sense of unity with the enterprise and to carry out their duties in the most willing and effective manner;

(iv) To provide an adequate, competent and trained personnel for all levels and types of management; and motivate them;

(v) To protect the common interests of all the parties and recognise the role of trade unions in the organisations;

(vi) To provide for a consultative participation by employees in the management of an organisation and the framing of conditions for this participation, which, however, shall not take place in technical, financial or trading policy;

(vii) To provide an efficient consultative service which aims at creating mutual faith among those who work in the enterprise;

(a) by developing management leadership which is bold and imaginative and guided by moral values;

(b) by effectively delegating the human relations aspects of personnel functions to line managers;

(c) by enforcing discipline on the basis of co-operative understanding and a humane application of rules and regulations; and

(d) by providing for a happy relationship at all levels;

(viii) To establish the conditions for mutual confidence and avoid confusion and misunderstanding between the management and the workers, by developing suggestion plans, joint management councils, work committees, etc. and by performance appraisal discussions;

(ix) To provide security of employment to workers so that they may not be distracted by the uncertainties of their future;

(x) To provide an opportunity for growth within the organisation to persons who are willing to learn and undergo training to improve their future prospects;

(xi) To provide for the payment of fair and adequate wages and salary to workers so that their healthy co-operation may be ensured for an efficient working of the undertaking;

(xii) To recognise the work and accomplishments of the employees, by offering non-monetary incentives rewards;

(xiii) To create a sense of responsibility, on the part of those in authority, for the claims of employees as human beings, who should be guaranteed protection of their fundamental rights and offered enough scope for developing their potential.

In brief, personnel policies should respect human dignity and personal integrity, ensure fair treatment for all, irrespective of caste, creed, or colour, and offer reasonable social and economic security to employees. They should be so designed as to ensure that work and accomplishment are properly recognised, that safe and healthy conditions of work are created, that common interests are promoted and employee participation is encouraged, that the role of trade unions is recognised and their functions and responsibilities are respected, and that the employees' satisfaction and motivation and their development as individuals are properly looked after.

Scott and others have very succinctly described the objectives of these policies thus: "Carefully defined personnel policies serve as a stabilising influence to prevent the waste of energy in following programmes not in harmony with the company objectives. They promote cooperation in the organisation as a whole and foster initiative, particularly at lower levels of supervision. Policies not only establish goals; they also form the basis of controls and procedures (so that managers are restricted from taking undesirable action or from mishandling situations). In substance, they may be thought of as the fight plan to be followed in getting from where the business is to where it wants to go. Business policies serve as a directive in the planning, organisation, and control of business enterprise."

Peter Drucker has rightly said: "The management must gear its policies and objectives in such a fashion that the employees perform their work and do their assigned tasks. It implies a consideration of human being as a resource, i.e., as something having peculiar psychological properties, abilities and limitations that require the same amount of engineering attention as the properties of any other sources, e.g., copper. It implies also a consideration of the human resources as having, unlike any other resources, personality, citizenship, control over whether they work, how much and how well, and thus requiring motivation, participation, satisfaction, incentives, and rewards, leadership, status and function. And it is management, and management alone, that can satisfy these requirements. For they must be satisfied through work and through the job within the enterprise and management is the activating organ of the enterprise."

Need for Personnel Policy

The raison d'etre for formulating personnel policy is basically two-fold:

one, to have a formal statement on corporate thinking which will serve as a guideline for action. Two, to establish consistency in the application of the policies over a period of time so that each one in the organisation gets a fair and just treatment.

Personnel policies need be specifically created because of the following reasons:

(i) The basic need and requirements of both an organisation and its employees require deep thought. The management is required to examine its basic- convictions as well as give full consideration to practices in other organisations.

(ii) Established policies ensure consistent treatment of all personnel throughout an organisation. Favouritism and discrimination are thereby minimised.

(iii) A certainty of action is assured even though the top management personnel may change. The tenure of the office of any manager is finite and limited; but the organisation continues, and along with it continue the policies; and this continuity of policies promotes stability in an organisation.

(iv) Because they specify routes towards selected goals, policies serve as standards or measuring yards for evaluating performance. The actual results can be compared with the policies to determine how well the members of an organisation have lived up to their professed intentions.

(v) Sound policies help to build employee enthusiasm and loyalty. This is specially true when they reflect established principles of fair play and justice, and when they help people to grow within an organisation.

(vi) They set patterns of behaviour and permit participants of plan with a greater degree of confidence.

(vii) Policies are "control guides for delegated decision-making." They seek to ensure consistency and uniformity in decisions on problems "that recur frequently and under similar, but not identical, circumstances."

Principles of Personnel Policies

In designing personnel policies, the management must balance the needs, goals, objectives and values of both the employers and the employees. Since these policies are rules of conduct, they are based on the following principles:

(i) Put the right man in the right place by a careful selection and placement to make sure that he is physically, mentally and temperamentally fit for the job he is expected to do and that the new employee may be reasonably expected to develop into a desirable employee, so that "there will be the minimum number of square pegs in round holes."

(ii) Train everyone for the job to be done, so that they qualify for better jobs, so that their accomplishments are limited to their ambitions and abilities, so that they do their present work very efficiently.

(iii) Make the organisation a co-ordinated team through a proper co-ordinate and administration of different departments and divisions, so that there is a minimum amount of friction and unproductive or unnecessary work. This calls for proper planning and organisation, control and direction of the entire organisation without destroying the initiate of the individual employee.

(iv) Supply the right tools and the right conditions of work, for the better the tools, facilities and working conditions, the larger the output produced with the same human effort at lower costs so that, ultimately, higher wages may be paid and more good jobs provided.

(v) Give security with opportunity, incentive, recognition. In order that he may stick to his job, each employee should have sound incentives for work, such as fair compensation, recognition for results achieved, reasonable security, and opportunity and hope for advancement in the organisation.

(vi) Look ahead, plan ahead for more and better things. Superior products should be produced and distributed, and these should be attractive and meet the demands of consumers. This calls for research and a policy of continuing product planning and development.

In brief, the principles should ensure that equity and justice are accorded to all the employees; that wages and salaries are adequate and fair; that every employee has scope for development to the limit of his capabilities; that fairness is guaranteed in maintaining discipline and that these principles are followed without discrimination against any grade of employees.

Essential Characteristics/Tests of a Sound Personnel Policy

The main features of a good personnel policy are:

(i) The statement of any policy should be definite, positive, clear and easily understood by everyone in the organisation so that what it proposes to achieve is evident.

(ii) It should be written in order to preserve it against loss, to stimulate careful consideration before its formulation and to prevent the promulgation of numerous, differing and temporary oral policies from multiple sources.

(iii) It must be reasonably stable but not rigid, i.e., it should be periodically revised, evaluated, assessed and revised and should, therefore, be in tune with the challenge of changes in the environment and should have a built-in resilience for adjustment from time to time.

(iv) It must be supplementary to the over-all policy of an organisation, for if departmental policy is made such as to come into conflict and violate the company policy, it would be tantamount to insubordination. Peter Drucker has observed: "The policies of an enterprise have to be balanced with the kind of reputation an enterprise wants to build up with special reference to the social and human needs, objectives and values."

(v) It should indicate that the management knows that workers prefer to deal with the management on an individual basis.

(vi) It should recognise the desire of many workers for recognition as groups in many of their relationships.

(vii) It should be formulated with due regard for the interests of all the concerned parties - the employers, the employees and the public community.

(viii) It should be the result of a careful analysis of all the available facts.

(ix) It must provide a two-way communication system between the management and the employees so that the latter are kept informed of the latest developments in the organisation and the employers are aware of the actions and reactions of the employees on particular issues.

(x) It should be consistent with public policy, i.e., with the spirit rather than the letter of the law, so that the intentions and settled course of an organisation are appreciated in terms of public opinion from the standpoint of national, economic and social justice for the employees and for the community at large.

(xi) It should be generally known to all interested parties.

(xii) It must have not only the support of the management but the co-operation of employees at the shop floor level and in the office.

(xiii) Before evolving such a policy, trade unions should be consulted in matters of industrial relations; and the role of trade unions should be restricted only to this area.

(xiv) It should be progressive and enlightened, and must be consistent with professional practice and philosophy.

(xv) It must make a measurable impact, which can be evaluated and qualified for the guidance of all concerned, especially in the field of the three 'R's of personnel management, viz., recruitment, retainment, and retirement.

(xvi) It should be uniform throughout the organisation, though, in the light of local conditions, slight variations may be permitted in specific policies relating to staffing, compensation, benefits and services.

(xvii) It should have a sound base in appropriate theory and should be translatable into practices, terms and peculiarities of every department of an enterprise.

(xviii) Except in rare cases, policies should not prescribe detailed procedures.

Calhoon suggests that such a policy, being a guide for management decisions, should include these features.

(a) It should affirm the long-range purposes of personnel relations. At best, such purposes are derived from well thought out principles of philosophy, sociology, and ethics. Thus, they reflect mature social principles or ideals in human relations.

(b) It commits management representatives at all levels to a reaffirmation and reinforcement of this purpose in their daily decisions and behaviour.

(c) It indicates the scope for discretion when a long-term purpose is interpreted in a variety of specific situations and over a period of time.

Origin and Sources of Personnel Policies

Policies stem from a wide variety of places and people. They are not created in a vacuum but are based on a few principal sources, which determine, the content and meaning of policies. These are:

(i) The past practice of an organisation; and future objectives, needs;

(ii) The prevailing practices among sister concerns in the neighbourhood and throughout the country in the same industry; and internationally;

(iii) The attitudes, ideals, and philosophy of the Board of Directors, top management and middle and lower management;

(iv) The knowledge and experience gained from handling day-to-day personnel problems;

(v) Employees suggestions and complaints;

(vi) Collective bargaining programmes;

(vii) State and national legislation;

(viii) Changes in the country's economy;

(ix) International forces, economic policies of the Government and the world trade practices increasing international markets;

(x) The culture of the plant and its technology, its business environment, its social and political environment;

(xi) The extent of unionism;

(xii) The attitudes and social values of labour;

(xiii) The ethical points of view or the social responsibility of the organisation toward the public;

(xiv) The goals of the organisation; and

(xv) The development in technology, science.

Types of Personnel Policies

There are various types of policies. Jucius identifies two types, viz., functional or organisational groupings of policies; and the centralised policies. The functional grouping of policies are those policies which are grouped for different categories of personnel, e.g., for the management dealing with personnel planning, organising and controlling or for management concerned with functions of procuring developing and utilising manpower. The centralised policies are framed for companies with several locations. They are formulated at the head office and apply throughout the organisation.

Policies may also be classified as major and minor. Major policies pertain to the over-all objectives, procedures and control which affect an organisation as a whole. They cover in a general way nearly every phase of an enterprise and its product and methods of financing, its organisational structure, plant location, its marketing and personnel. Such policies are formulated by the Board of Directors, and a framework is established within which major executives fit the remaining policies necessary to carry out the major objectives of an organisation. Minor policies, on the other hand, cover relationships in a segment of an organisation, with considerable emphasis on details and procedures. Such policies are the outgrowth of major policies and preserve their unity of purpose.

Coverage of the Policies

The subject matter of personnel policies is as varied as the practices of the Personnel Department; and any itemisation would serve merely as a laundry list. The norms of personnel policy vary from industry to industry and with its management structure, the economic and social conditions prevailing in it at a particular time, the attitudes and ideals of top management. They also vary with changes in public opinion, area and regional traditions, customs and practices, the country's industrial system, the labour and industrial policies of the State and the Central Governments, the influence of trade unions, national agreements between representatives of employers, managers, employees and the government. The policies and influences of business associations, employers' federations, technological development, competition and social approval, the prevailing attitude of the organised labour, government regulations, the extent of unionisation in a particular industry, the decisions of tripartite conferences, Industrial or National Tribunals or Labour Courts - these, too, determine the norms of personnel policies. In other words, they cover such a wide variety of items and are so broad based that every possible item which affects the interests of anyone in an organisation is included in them. However, it is virtually impossible for any organisation to have policies which cover every type of contingency because new issues or questions usually crop up from time to time for which no policies exist or for which an organisation is still in the process of writing a policy. In such cases, therefore, it has to work without policies until such time as it frames them.

The National Industrial Conference Board of the USA is of the view following matters should be included in a personnel policy:

(i) History of the company's growth.

(ii) Employment practices and conditions of employment — minimum hiring qualifications, preferred services for recruiting personnel, physical examination, psychological and occupational interest and aptitude test; methods of wage payment and pay period; hours of work, overtime work, shift work and shift relationship the basis of promotion and promotion channels, lay-offs, re-hiring, discharge, voluntary separations; seniority rights, guaranteed employment after attaining a certain length of service and when an employee is considered as a regular employee.

(iii) Grievance redressal procedure.

(iv) Safety rules and regulations, and responsibilities of employees while at work.

(v) General practices - employee identification, punching time cards and reporting in and out of the plan or department, checking of tools, purchase of company usually at a discount; procedure for getting pay, absence, leave of absence, change of address and solicitation on company premises.

(vi) Mutuality of interests and need for co-operation between management and men.

(vii) Employee financial aids - savings, loans, credit co-operatives, mutual benefit associations, group insurance, profit sharing, bonus plans, incentive plans, partial or full payment of tuition fees for attendance at professional institutes.

(viii) Educational opportunities - apprentice training, factory schools, vestibule schools and on-the-job training; training for promotion, provision of training facilities.

(ix) Employees news sheet and house journals.

(x) Communication media, and suggestion system, employee motivation involvement.

(xi) Health and hospitalisation programmes.

(xii) Vacation with pay.

(xiii) Sickness, death and maternity benefits or allowances.

(xiv) Freedom for the employees to discuss any item of interest with the management.

(xv) Company's policy on compensation, rewards.

(xvi) Social security and other kinds of combinational and unemployment and accident compensation, provident fund, pension, gratuity, compensation for employees injured while on duty, invalidity.

(xvii) Collective bargaining and recognising the employee's rights to join any union of his choice, recognition of a particular bargaining agency, procedure to be followed in settling grievances or the interpretation of a bargaining contract, and the right of an individual to be heard.

(xviii) Procedures for disseminating information on company policies.

(xix) Maintenance of discipline and adherence to rules; penalties available.

(xx) Garnishments.

(xxi) Public relations.

(xxii) Labour-management relations and union-management co-operation.

(xxiii) Prohibited activities - smoking, gambling, imbibing liquor and soliciting on company premises and during working hours.

It may be noted that this list is by no means exhaustive; it is only indicative of the scope of personnel policies. In India, ordinarily personnel policies cover the following:

(a) Policy on Recruitment or Hiring of Employees, i.e., in finding and selecting right calibre and number of people required to perform the operations of the organisation, these subjects are taken into account: (i) whether recruitment needed, (ii) how much manpower required and at what levels, (iii) selection procedures, (iv) age limits for employment, (v) marital status, minority status, minority groups, SC/ST, women, disabled persons, (vi) pre-employment medical check-up; and (vii) establishing order of preferences, between relations of employees, employment exchange candidates, and outsiders in matter of selection: and (viii) induction and placement, etc.

(b) Policy of Manpower Planning and Development, this covers: (i) work study, job evaluation, (ii) selection and recruitment techniques, (iii) identifying training needs and preparing training programmes, (iv) promotional avenues and (v) opportunities for self-development and advancement in organisation etc.

(c) Policy on Terms and Conditions of Employment, which covers terms such as hours of work, overtime, shift working, lay-off, termination of services, and welfare, wage policy, payment methods, pay period, job evaluation, etc.

(d) Policy on Industrial Relations, in broad terms considers: (i) whether to recognize trade unions, and conditions of recognition, (ii) collective bargaining, (ii) grievance handling procedure, (iii) workers' participation in management, etc.

(e) Policy on Communication with Employees on all levels, covers: (i) suggestions system; (ii) formal/informal meetings between top management and junior management.

In broad, personnel policy consists essentially of the following parts:

(a) The objective stated in broad general terms, indicating the top management's deep and underlying intents and convictions as to the importance of the people in the organisation.

(b) Procedures for the attainment of the objective. Procedure lay down the step that must be followed in order that the spirit of the policy is retained intact and is reflected in management's action.

(c) Rules and regulations arising from the policy and procedures are aimed at clearly defining the do's and dont's that have to be observed by the employees at all levels.

Responsibility for Policy-making

The actual formulation of personnel policies manager; but its ultimate approval, or any change or modification in it, comes from the top executives; and his decision depends upon the financial ability of a company, the obligations imposed upon it by legislation, the agreement between employers and employees, the repercussions of such decisions of the various levels of employees as well as on neighbouring industries and on the community. The executive role is one of mediating, reconciling, persuading, convincing, expressing and communicating the policy; developing tools and machinery, guiding, directing and evaluating the effectiveness with which those tools are used in the application of policy. The responsibility for personnel administration rests squarely upon the shoulders of the line management. The personnel department assists in communicating policies to those for whom they are meant and exercises control over it in order to ensure fairness and uniformity. If it is not communicated and interpreted correctly, even a sound policy may lose much of its usefulness.

Therefore, personnel policies should be made known to the employees through supervisors at each level. Superiors may be informed of the changed policies and kept informed of the accepted policies by any of the following methods:

1. Written standard practice, procedures issued to cover company policies, with supplements to cover changes.
2. Booklets or Bulletins, issued to new employees setting forth rights, privileges, and responsibilities.
3. Verbal instructions from immediate superiors.
4. Group meetings of new employees convened regularly.
5. Union contract.

6. Company paper or house organ, giving details about company policies.
7. Conference conducted as a part of executive training programme.

When the supervisory force has been familiarised with company policies, much of the purpose of informing the employees has been accomplished. However, as a matter of safety, it is always wise to take steps to inform workers directly through the medium of published booklets and through the representatives of the Personnel Department to new employees in group meetings. It is also advisable to publicise them in a company news sheet or house journal, which may also carry a copy of the company's contract with its employees.

Policy Administration

Essentially, in the administration of a personnel policy

(i) A large sum of money is involved;

(ii) An unsound decision may endanger the company's bargaining power and position.

Therefore, a thorough consideration must be given to the following issues:

(i) What purpose and objectives will it serve?

(ii) What principles, concepts, practices and philosophies of the organisation will it project?

(iii) How much would its implementation cost?

(iv) What benefits will it offer and to whom?

(v) Is it administratively feasible and fair to the employees?

(vi) What areas will it cover?

(vii) What authority will it give to personnel at different levels?

(viii) Will it be acceptable and consistent?

Mechanism of Policy Formulation

Policy generation is a complex process, calling for the help of experts. Personnel policies are so designed as to reflect the current good practices in society. The first step in the mechanics of formulating a policy is the identification of a problem area or situation in which decisions of a similar and repetitive nature are involved. To some extent, policy-making involves all levels in the working organisation. It is the personnel staff who study the existing documents, survey industry and community practices, review the prevailing conditions in the company, interview other executives in the organisation to collcct appropriate information and get their suggestions and co-operation on personnel activities. The formulation of a policy is not a job for any ivory-tower specialist. The person preparing a draft of it must be thoroughly familiar with the subject from personal experience and involvement.

After the policy draft has been prepared, the second step is to circulate its copies among all those who may be expected to operate under it. Their constructive criticism and suggestions would be very valuable. A second draft is then prepared and finalised, and the policy statements are given shape and promulgated throughout the organisation. Policies are developed after a thorough discussion so that all the managers involved in related areas of responsibility are personally committed to them. Developed in this manner, these policies will stand the test of time, and will hold even "under conditions of stress." A set of policies may be compared to the rope holding the mountain-climbers together; since they are thus together, no climber can be lost, but they must co-ordinate their activities, "or the rope will get in their way."

The third step is to undertake a periodic review, evaluation and revision of the policies. This is essential if organisational complacency and managerial stagnation are to be avoided. It is a part and parcel of the means of keeping an organisation "vibrant" and on its toes. If a policy is cancelled or withdrawn, it should be substituted by a new one, failing which mismanagement is likely to result.

In brief, the steps necessary in designing a policy are:

(i) Initiating a policy.

(ii) Uncovering of facts by the personnel department.

(iii) Recommending a policy to the top management and eliciting the views of all concerned.

(iv) Putting down a policy in writing.

(v) Explaining and discussing the proposed policy with members of the organisation.

(vi) Adopting and launching it.

(vii) Communicating it to employees at all levels.

(viii) Administering it.

(ix) Initiating follow-up action on it.

(x) Evaluating it; and

(xi) Restating or reformulating the policy.

It should be clearly understood that "the authority for implementing personnel policy must come from the top management. The responsibility implementation rests with the line management at the department head and that of administration with the line management at the level of the department head and that of administration of day-to-day matters with the lower level of management. The responsibility for assessment, review, and follow-up action should lie with the personnel department.

Personnel Policies should be in Writing

Someone has said that an idea does not exist unless it can be put in writing. A. policy, conceived as a management tool, also does not exist unless it is in writing.

There distinct advantages of written formal policies. In the first place, the writing of policies makes a commitment on the part of an organisation. When they are written, it should be apparent to management representatives, employees and union officials that the "top management does what it says." Secondly, writing ensures uniformity of application minimises favouritism and discrimination among the personnel and assures continuity of action even when the top management is changed, for a policy is not just a fad of one particular boss, to be jettisoned when he leaves the organisation. Thirdly, it comes the loyalty of and builds enthusiasm among the members of an organisation in so far as they are assured of fair play and justice. Fourthly, it limits the freedom of action on the part of the management, for a supervisor cannot go off half-cocked and come up with his personal interpretation of the organisation's intent. Fifthly, writing helps to ensure that the professed policies are "right", for an organisation tries to put its best foot forward. Finally, written policies provide something concrete on which to base an appeal if there is any disagreement about what the organisation's policy is.

All well-established concerns, should have published Policy Manuals for all its managers, supervisors, and employees. Handbooks, house bulletins and booklets may also be used for the purpose. The moment a policy is written down or published, it encourages the staff to be constantly alert so that it may be properly implemented. Francis Clarence says: If you write it (policy) down, you have got to live up to do it or dye trying. 'If you set a high standard you will fall far short of perfection. But your performance, simply because you have pledged yourself to the standard, will be better than it would be if you lacked a special goal.

Personnel Policy is, therefore, always written in words which are neither vague and unnecessarily academic, nor in any way offensive to those who read it either before or after it had been explained to them. Words, sentences be complete and precise. It should not contain irritating words or expressions which antagonise some, or cast aspersions on others. For example, the words you are forbidden should be replaced by it will be appreciated." The tone should be warm, without the use of any legalistic phraseology.

The form should be convenient and handy for management reference an application spacing encourage reading. Short sentences are always better than long sentences linked together with some such phrases as "subject to" "provided," "whereas".

Each policy item is numbered, and its paragraphs are usually sub numbered. Sometimes each subject begins with the phrase, "we believe," and then indicates what it is that the organisation does believe in. This is invariably the statement of policy, which is immediately followed by a paragraph beginning "to give effect to belief, we do the- following things," and then follows a list of procedures and practices.

Conclusion

In conclusion, it may be observed that personnel policies are an expression of intents and plans of managements' design to attain the objectives of an organisation: they are a guide for managements' decision and plans of action: and which govern the enterprise in its relationship with its employees. Such policies are established in consultation with the employees themselves; and to ensure uniformity in action and to give the security of knowing what to expect, they are generally always put into writing.

The success of personnel policies is determined largely by three areas of activity:

1. The success of the top management in determining labour policies wisely.
2. The success of the personnel manager in interpreting these personnel policies properly, in achieving their proper execution through the line executives, and in making the personnel department render as nearly perfect service as possible to the line executives.
3. The success of the line executives themselves, particularly the first line supervisors, in fulfilling their obligations to management and to the workers by interpreting policies wisely and interestedly and in promoting the effectiveness of their workers by dynamic leadership.

Chapter - 4

Growth, Philosophy and Principles

Growth of Personnel Management

Although the field of personnel administration as a discipline of study is relatively recent, the precepts upon which its current concepts are based had their origins deep in history. For example, the "minimum wage rate" and "incentive wage plans" were included in the Babylonian Code of Hammurabi around 1800 B.C. The Chinese, as early as 1650 B.C. had originated the principle of "division of labour" (specialisation) and they understood the meaning and implications of labour turnover even in 400 B.C. The "Span of Management" and the related concepts of organisation were well understood by Moses around 1200 B.C. and the Caldrons had incentive wage plans around 400 B.C. The ancients, with their stone axes, adages and other flint tools, may not have appreciated the principle of "transfer of skill from the humans to the machine", but they were nevertheless applying the principle of "transfer of skill from the humans to the machine", and this separated them from large numbers of other human beings.

In India, Kautilya has observed that there existed a sound base for systematic management of human resources as early as the fourth century B.C. The Government then took active interest in the operation of public and private sector enterprises and provided systematic procedures for regulating employer-employee relationship. Charm has described the contribution of Kautilya in the field of "staffing and personnel management" in the form of table reproduced below:-

Stage - 1	INDUSTIAL REVOLUTION ERA
Stage - 2	PATERNALISTIC ERA
Stage - 3	SCIENTIFIC MANAGEMENT ERA
Stage - 4	INDUSTRIAL ERA

Stage - 5 BEHAVIOURAL ERA
Stage - 6 HUMAN RELATION ERA
Stage - 7 PERSONNEL SPECIALISTS ERA
Stage - 8 WELFARE ERA

Fig. 4.1: Stage of the Evolution of Personnel Management

Some authorities have preferred to study the growth of personnel management on the basis of the classification given above:

This classification is rather very broad. We would like to describe the chronological growth of the science of Personnel Management somewhat on the following lines:

(i) Era of Industrial Revolution;
(ii) Era of Trade Unionism;
(ii) Era of Social Responsibility;
(iv) Scientific Management Era;
(v) Industrial Psychology Era (including Human Relations Era);
(vi) The Behavioural Science Era; and
(vii) The Personnel Specialists and Welfare Era.

Kautilya's Contributon to Staffing and Personnel Management

Modern management concepts	*Kautilya contribution*
Job description	Very elaborate job description of superintendents is laid down in term of their responsibilities
Job qualifications	(i) For the high officials qualification in terms of family backgrounds and responsibility traits are laid down very precisely (ii) For the lower officers a decreasing degree of qualifications is considered to be sufficient.
Selection procedure	(i) Reference; (ii) On the job test; (iii) Spy information; (iv) Discussion by various steps envisaged in the selection procedure for high officials
Executive development	(i) An elaborate training programme for the king is laid down. (ii) For lower officers the need of training has been emphasized.
Incentive system (carrot and stick approach)	Monetary incentives and punishment in the form of penalties for controlling the performance and conducts of employees and citizen.
Performance evaluations	Regulars supervisions and espionage are the two methods of performance and conducts evaluations.

I. Era of Industrial Revolution

Modern personnel management has evolved from a number of significant inter-related developments which date back to the beginnings of what is popularly known as the Industrial Revolution or, as some prefer to call it, Evolution. Prior to it, there were several distinct types of relationships involving employers and employees, which were variously termed as "slaver," "serfdom" and the "guild system." The initial stage of the guild system is said to be early beginnings of personnel management, for the three classes — the masters, the travelling journeymen and apprentices — were all a closely knit group; and the system involved "selecting, training, developing, rewarding and maintaining workers." Wage and salary administration and collective bargaining over wages and conditions of work were in evidence. "In the course of time, economic and social changes brought about a change in the old economic, social and political system. These changes were precipitated in manufacturing by a new economic doctrine and by invention and utilisation of new tools, processes, and machines. The economic doctrine was based upon the French concepts of laissez faire and laissez-passer, which meant that a person should be permitted to make what he wanted and to go where he pleases.

The Industrial Revolution consisted essentially in the development of machinery. The use of mechanical energy and the consequent establishment of factories employing large number of people — all resulting in tremendous increase in the productive power of man. The factory system gradually replaced the "putting out" or "cottage" system. This doctrine of the cottage system arose out of the ability of factory owners to pay a family higher wages than would be earned by it in some other manufacturing work, primarily because of the speed of machines and efficiencies gained through a further subdivision of labour. As a result of this subdivision of labour, an individual, instead of acquiring skills in a number of jobs, now specialised in one task.

The Industrial Revolution brought about a greatly expanded mass production of goods. Science and technology began to be applied to all aspects of the work of modern industrial corporations. It affected the personnel administration system in many ways. For example: (a) The place of work changed from the home to a central work area, where people worked under a common roof. (b) The method of production changed from manual to machine operations because of the transfer of skills from the workers to the machines. (c) The migration from rural areas to urban areas started with the decline of cottage industries and because there was no land to fall back upon for employment and consequent heavy concentration of industry in certain areas. (d) As a result of the separation of owners and managers, it was difficult to maintain the close relationship which owners had with their employees in the past. (e) Mechanisation made the work so simple that a large number of women and children began to be employed, and these replaced men. (f) With the introduction of machines, heavy physical labour was eliminated, work now became less arduous and easy though, at the same time, it reduced the opportunities of employment for unskilled labour. (g) Because of the complexity of the process of production and advanced technology, a new class of professional employees had developed in industry who exercise tremendous power in the affairs of the company. (h) The increased use of computer technology has made it possible to efficiently control the various aspects of industrial activity. Production control, method control, inventory control, financial control and manpower control have all become more effective because of the introduction of computerised techniques and procedures. (i) There has been a change in the nature of the job. More new jobs are of the nature best suited to the white collar and managerial groups who guide, regulate, and co-ordinate the production process. Formerly this co-ordination was either the responsibility of blue-collar production workers or artisans. (j) Specialisation has developed to an unimaginable extent; there is mechanical, electrical and civil engineering research; there are development and production engineers and such personnel specialists as labour relations managers, wage analysts, training directors and safety engineers. (k) Mass production, which calls for a continuous fkow of materials, was made possible by complex, integrated, power driven automatic and electrically controlled equipment. (l) Not only was geographical mobility facilitated, but occupational and industrial mobility also increased. Jobs were more simplified, with the result that the labour force readily adapted itself to a variety of positions instead of a single craft or trade (m) There had been a decline in the number of semi-skilled and unskilled workers but an increase in professional and skilled workers, who handled a vast quantity of records, reports, and data needed by the management "to keep its finger on the pulse of the business." (n) There has also been a increasing participation of women in the labour force for secretarial and other clerical jobs.

However, these results were achieved at a great price, because: (i) There were great concentrations of people among many machines in small, dingy, dirty factories; (ii) Working and living conditions were unsatisfactory and very unhygienic; (iii) Adults had to work from 9 to 11 hours a day and children from 14 to 15 hours as a day and they were all treated harshly by the owners of factories; (iv) Labour was looked upon as a commodity that could be bought and sold, and the government, because of the prevailing political philosophy of laissez faire, did little to protect the workers; (v) Monotony and boredom were the results of division of labour. Because their tasks were repetitive, the workers did not have much interest in their work; and because the completed products were not their own creation they felt no pride in their accomplishment; (vi) A shut down in one sector of the industry threw the entire system out of gear bringing about great economic suffering; (vii) The worker was required to follow strict discipline; there was a web of rules binding the industrial workers. They had to live by the clock or else would be fired and punished; (viii) The increased use of machinery resulted in changes in the employment situation. Since their operation called for specialised knowledge, and unskilled workers found it difficult to adjust themselves to the new equipment, a large number of them, therefore, could not find gainful employment.

In sum, "the new industrial era brought about materialism, discipline, monotony, boredom, job displacement, impersonality, work interdependence, and related behavioural phenomena. The benefits of the Industrial Revolution, however, have far outweighed the costs of increasing industrialisation. Economically, the industrial revolution brought about great increases in output and in the accumulation of goods and capital. In turn, business and commerce were greatly accelerated, owners and entrepreneurs did well, but the average citizen fared poorly. Labour was considered a commodity to be bought and sold.

II. Era of Trade Unionism

Shortly after the advent of the factory system, groups of employees began to get to other to discuss their common problems. Initially, these problems arose out of child labour, long hours of work, and poor working conditions. Later, economic problems, including the question of employee benefits and services, became the major concern. Workers joined together on the basis of their common interests to improve their lot. The basic philosophy underlying trade unionism was that through strength and collective support, the management could be forced to listen to the workers and redress their grievances. "The weapon used was that of strikes, slowdowns, walkouts, picketing, boycotts, and sabotage. Sometimes, even physical force was used. This trade unionism, however, did influence the Personnel Management in such fields of activity as "the adoption of employee grievances handling systems, the acceptance of arbitration as a means of resolving conflicts of rights, disciplinary practices, the expansion of employee benefit programmes, the liberalisation of holiday and vacation time, clear definition of job duties, job rights through seniority and the installation of rational and defensible wage structures."

Organisational units were created by the companies to deal with union relationships and representatives. In some cases, unions were sponsored by the companies as a means of controlling their activities. Where unions brought about wage increases, greater attention was paid to the study of jobs, methods improvements, connecting wages to performance, and the more careful selection of personnel.

III. Era of Social Responsibility Feeling

In the past, employers were not very sympathetic toward their workmen. It was Robert Owen (1913) who for the first time, adopted a somewhat paternalistic attitude towards his employees. He was a British businessman, reformer and humanitarian. He believed that "the principal social and economic environments influence the physical, mental and psychological development of workers." Therefore, in order to increase productivity, it was necessary to improve the conditions of employees by removing them from an adverse environment or by changing the environment with the provision of more satisfactory living and working conditions.

Owen implemented this philosophy by "organising model villages next to his cotton mills in Scotland; by introducing such unheard of facilities as shower baths and toilets into the factories which were cleaned and painted and in which windows were installed for light and ventilation; by organising day schools for the children and night schools for the workers; and by raising the minimum age for the employment of children to 11 years and shortening their work day to 10 hours. Later, he abolished child labour entirely."

He regarded the workers like children who must be cautiously guided, trained and protected. He, therefore, advised his brother manufacturers to devote as much attention to their vital machine (i.e., workers) as they did to their inanimate machines. By doing so, profit would be maximised. Adam Smith emphasised that "if each individual worked for his own economic self-interest, the society would gain." These views were supported by Charles Babbage. He observed that "the emphasis should be on mutuality of interests between employers and workers and on the division of labour, for such division of labour would reduce the waste in raw materials, achieve savings through more effective placement of workers, produce economies through a different wage scale based on skill level, save time by not switching from task to task, gain efficiencies stemming from familiarisation with special tools, and stimulate workers' inventions pertaining to tools and methods." He held the view that "hard work and high productivity were a source of good wages for the worker and higher profits for the employer." But he denounced any unionisation of workers.

IV. The Scientific Management Era

This era began in 1900, reached its peak approximately in 1930, and then dwindled relative importance, though it has remained alive somewhat even to the present times. The scientific management movement owes its origin to Frederick W. Taylor (1556-1955) who is known as the Father of Scientific Management. He started his experiments in the steel industry in the Midvale and Bethelem plants, in 1885. He developed the "four great principles of management":

(i) The development of a true science of each job;

(ii) A scientific selection of the right person for the job;

(iii) Training a person to perform his job in a scientific manner; and

(iv) Friendly co-operation between the management and the men.

Taylor believed that "planning should be the result of co-operation between the management and workers and that a provision should exist for compensating the personnel with financial incentives. He also believed that workers were "sources of untapped energy," which could be properly utilised if they are trained and fairly treated. He strongly recommended that when workers failed to respond to initial training, they should not be brutally discharge but given more time to familiarise themselves with their transfer to the job for which they were better suited. He also emphasised the value of worker ideas and anticipated the modern suggestion system by recommending case bonuses for developed suggestions." He believed that, "by a scientific measurement on work —— that is, by a time study, methods study, job classification and methods improvement functional foremanship, standardisation of tools, specifications method, a differential piece-rate system, instructional cards for workmen and a control system most of the sources of conflict between labour and management would disappear.

The scientific management movement has had a great influence on employee-employer relationships and on management in general it has elevated management by plan, system and design, and led to the decline of management by hunch and intuition. It has greatly contributed to the professionalisation of management. The use of his approach improved management methods, procedures and standards and strengthened production and supervision. Taylor's approach was accepted by labour and management because it placed a strong emphasis on the mutual benefits of productivity: the organisation produced more and thus increased its profits, while workers made more money and lived better lives. One name given to his outlook is Welfare Capitalism. Taylor's ideas led to a separate discipline called "Human Engineering." It is the study of "people at work and of work methods; it includes a study of equipment design; pacing of work, hours of work, and environment conditions of work: its purpose is to improve productivity and job-satisfaction.

But after thirty years, this approach has begun to lose its popularity, for it has been discovered that many of the management problems are the result of 'human' and not 'mechanical factors'. Taylor's approach stressed the need for techniques which ensure higher performance at the work place and eliminate unnecessary movements, and gave greater importance to 'technology' than to the 'men at work'. Fragmentation of an operation so that each man did only one little job (specialisation) encouraging a mechanistic conception of 'men at work', ultimately led to a situation where at times symptoms of alienation, frustration, conflicts, etc. leading to loss of production, were evident. This knowledge brought about a new thinking in recent years, such as those of Douglas McGregor in the USA, and Eric Trist in UK, who pointed out that "the best results were obtained in industrial occupations when human beings were treated in the totality of their physical and psychological characteristics."

Among others who modified Taylors' views were Henry Gantt and Frank and Lilian Gilbreth. Henry Gantt propounded "Task and Bonus Wage" system which removed the penalties provided under Taylor's wage system. Under Gantt's "system, the worker was paid a guaranteed hourly rate, a bonus of 20 percent if he reached the standard output, and a high piece-rate for output that was above the standard output. Further, the foreman was given a bonus for each man who was successful".

Frank Gilbreth made an extensive use of motion pictures of tasks being performed in order to analyse body movements. From these studies, he formulated the "laws of efficient motion." Lilian Gilbreth worked closely with her husband and is credited with the publication of Psychology of Management (1914), the first book relating to the application psychology to the principles of scientific management.

V. Industrial Psychological Era

During this period, psychologists were introduced to the field of industrial management to study systematically many personnel problems. The development of Industrial Psychology owes a great deal to Hugo Munsterberg's book, Psychology and Industrial Efficiency, which was published in 1913. He is regarded as the Father of Industrial Psychology. His contributions to industrial management were particularly notable in respect of his analysis of jobs in terms of their mental and emotional requirements and in terms of the development of testing devices (such as the Alpha and Beta tests). Advances were made in selection, placement, testing, training and research practices. Industrial psychology introduced the "matching of employees to jobs, for different jobs require different skills and abilities." It emphasised the use of psychology in the field of personnel testing, interviewing, attitude measurement, learning theory, training, failure and monotony study, safety, job analysis and human engineering. Of these, the major applications of the knowledge and techniques of industrial psychology have been in the field of recruitment, testing for employment, job replacement, promotion and training. The tools and practices of industrial psychology are applied through education, publication and consultation services. The human relations movement is an outcome of the reaction against the impersonality of scientific management. Top management personnel began to realise that "human resources are the most valuable assets that any organisation posseses and that, without these, other resources are useless." Experiments were conducted at the Hawthorne Works of the Western Electric Company in Chicago during the late 1920s and early 1930s by Elton Mayo (1818-1949), F. Roethlisberger and W. J. Dickson of the Harvard Graduate School of Business Administration. They concluded that "human and social factors, not physical variables, accounted for the productivity phenomenon". As a result of this experiment, employee productivity began to be analysed in such behavioural terms as 'team-work'. 'participation', 'cohesiveness', loyalty and esprit de corps, instead of in terms of engineering alternative.

The findings of the "Hawthorne Studies" put emphasis on the importance for an understanding of the needs of both management and workers of the special aspects of work performances. The message was that interpersonal relationships (between the workers and their supervisors) should be fostered for the fullest realisation of the potential of individuals and groups. The basic conclusion was the "sociological and psychological phenomena often exerted even greater influence on output than physical measurable conditions of work did". Accordingly, concepts such as the "social system, informal organisation, group control of behaviour, equilibrium and logical and non-logical behaviour entered the field of Human Relations and Personnel Management specialists." "Therefore, there was a swing from the "scientific management" with standards of performance, impersonal engineering by efficiency experts towards the new "human relations" approach. The human relations movement was mainly concerned with the informal, spontaneous behaviour of work groups and the sentiments and attitudes of employees. The scientific management movement was mainly concerned with an organisation as a technical — economic system; the human relations movement viewed it as a social system."

VI. The Behavioural Era

The behavioural science movement is outgrowth and of the human relation studies and began around 1955; and its major impact lasted some 10 to 15 years. The Behavioural Sciences include Anthropology, Economics, History, Physiology, Mathematical Biology, Medicine and Psychiatry, Sociology, Social Psychology and Psychology. The research in these disciplines has provided the subject matter for Personnel Management. Behavioural scientists are concerned with the impact of various methods of pay and individual performance with the effect of different styles of leadership and different philosophies on total organisations performance; with job design and its relationship to personality growth; with the impact of different appraisal systems, with group influences, and the effects of organisation communications on productivity and change. The method of research made use of data obtained from experiments, observations, surveys, programme-or-action research and the theory of model-building.

Abraham Maslow (1954) propounded a theory regarding an individual "hierarchy of needs" - also known as "Deficit Theory Motivation." He stated that "there is a series of needs some of which are lower in the scale or system of values, in individual or social and some are higher. Higher needs cannot be satisfied or even felt while the lower needs remain unsatisfied. A satisfied need is not a motivator." Herzberg advanced a Two Factor Theory of motivation: Some organisations used hygiene considerations: money, supervision, job, frills, and the physical aspects of work to motivate people; but these factors served only human "maintenance needs" rather than the "job itself." Another consideration, motivators provided opportunities for personal realisation (achievement, responsibility, advancement, interesting work, recognition, and a sense of controlling one's destiny).

Douglas McGregor formulated two contrasting kinds of management beliefs or views about the nature of man at work. His 'Theory X' stands for the set of traditional beliefs generally held, while, 'Theory Y' is concerned with a different philosophy or understanding of man at work. His Theory X (or Hard Approach) involves, strict supervision, coercion and threat which might breed organised worker-protest, restriction of output, etc.; and his Theory Y (or Soft or Permissive Approach) might be exploited by the subordinates; and, therefore, he suggests a via media, that of the Carrot and Stick approach to motivate work people."

Rensis Likert says that "Assumptions like these reflect themselves in two basic systems of organisations, namely, system I and system IV. System I of organisation based upon Theory X assumption, while system IV on Theory Y assumptions."

This type of approach is also known as the Human Relations Approach. It is an aid to the process of integration of employees, however partial, with their organisation. It tries to understand human behaviour at the work place and to 'utilise' or 'modify' that behaviour to achieve the objectives of organisation and fulfill the aspiration of the employees. This approach has led to the development of some sound management practices, such as the two-way communication, participation of employees in decision-making, individual goal setting (or management by objectives) and importance of social relationship of informal groups, acceptance of work place as a social system, management development, adjustment to change, etc.

VII. Personnel Specialist and Welfare Era

With the introduction of the factory system, thousands of persons began to be employed under one roof, and had to be controlled if the goals of an organ to be achieved. For work in the administrative office, clerks or manual employees : to be recruited. These were entrusted with the responsibility of hiring men to work of an organisation. Later, they were concerned with the recruitment, placement and selection of personnel. With the increase in the size of an organisation, these functions had to be allotted to a full time 'manager.' With further increase in the number of employees a separate personnel executive had to be appointed to develop systematic methods, determine wage rates, develop job discipline and descriptions and job specification. Later, his duties were enlarged to cover additional responsibility of looking after the benefits and services provided for the employees. In the course of time, arrangements had to be made to train the existing personnel; and hence a manager for training was also appointed. Ultimately safety experts, physicians, behaviour researchers, labour relations specialists and others were appointed. For administrative and organisational effectiveness, it was then found feasible to merge these different functions into a single position, viz., the Personnel Manager and Welfare Officer.

Subsequently, "organisational planning, manpower planning, manpower selection and other allied problems regarding the management of managers and high talent manpower assumed significance in the organisation. High talent personnel emerged as the key human resources, and personnel management was turned to the existing economic structure." The emphasis now is on 'management of human resources'. So that personnel management has now passed through vast changes. Beginning with 'welfare work', its responsibilities have grown wider and deeper. In the words of Yoder, "its members have now developed technical competence in manpower planning and other related jobs, besides acquiring expertise in such matters as wage and salary administration, employee benefit schemes and services, training and development and other specilised activities".

The present day personnel management has been entrusted with three main responsibilities, viz.,

First, to assist the line management in 'manning the organisation' and to maintain the work-force at optimum efficiency - through (i) recruitment, induction and placement; (ii) wage and salary administration; (iii) training for key non-management personnel; (iv) administration of benefits and allied services; and (v) development of employee communication programmes.

Second, to provide a task force to render services to the management in the field of: (i) labour relations with particular reference to Union-Management relations; (ii) management of staff development functions; (iii) training for key non-management personnel; (iv) development of grievance procedure; and (v) development of personnel policies and procedures.

Third, to control functions regarding employee services such as (i) housing and transport; (ii) promotion and recreational facilities; (iii) financial aid to employees; and (iv) educational activities.

It will thus be noted that personnel management is entrusted to undertake a multiple of "personnel jobs." In sum, it may be noted that the personnel management function has been historically intertwined and associated with the times and events of history. Social, economic, political, technological and cultural factors have influenced the nature and scope of personnel administration. Further, the historical evolution of the personnel function is evolutionary and not revolutionary, i.e., the changes that have occurred in the personnel field have been caused mostly by gradual cultural changes, and not by drastic events. Again, the periods of movement represent applied operational philosophies and progressive sequences of events.

Factors Responsible for the Development of Personnel Management

Personnel Management is not the creation of a day or a year; its growth has been a long-drawn process and is the result of various changes that have taken place during and after the Industrial Revolution. For a clear understanding of the growth of this science, it would be fruitful to study the factors that have influenced its emergence and development.

1. **Cultural and Social Changes:** These have brought about striking changes in the attitudes and actions of employees and their families; and these changes have been the result of changes in knowledge, beliefs, art, morals, laws, customs, language, values and norms of individuals as members of society. A close relationship exists between one's values and judgment and the family background. Cultural elements to determine the creative abilities of family, its position and movement up the social ladder, and affect its desire for achievement and prestige. A larger proportion of the population is now exposed to education, because it has been recognised that skills and knowledge, like machine and technology easily become obsolete. Individual members must keep abreast of the changes in the environment if an organisation is to survive. This increased knowledge has raised the productivity of employees and enhanced their earning capacity. At the same time, however, this knowledge has tended to limit the employment opportunities of the unskilled and uneducated, and generated unemployment. Increased education has led to a high mobility and, therefore, a high turnover.

   There have been changes in social stability because of the mobility of workers and of transport and communication, and new occupations. The stability of social relationships has been affected. Older ties have broken. New social values have developed; and the generation gap has become much wider than before. Younger people in employment need extensive programmes for training; and this has necessitated the formulation and implementation of training programmes on a much wider scale.

2. **Change in Government and Labour Relations:** Earlier, the government's attitude towards labour problems was rather passive. The force of circumstances has now brought about a change in its attitude; it has now become a protagonist and a guardian of the interests of employees. Frequent strikes and lockouts, public concern for sweated labour, poor working conditions and

organisations of labour have all led to the enactment of various protective laws pertaining to the conditions of labour, industrial safety, industrial disputes, payment of wages and compensation, and laws which ensure equal opportunities of employment, irrespective of creed, caste, sex and colour.

3. **Changing Role of Employees:** Formerly, the relations between the management and the employees were those of masters and servants or of the boss and his followers. But now the employees feel that they are equal partners in industry and should be treated as human beings. Employees are individuals; as groups, they demand redressal of grievances, acceptance of suggestions, sharing of power in management, and the right to organise trade unions.
4. **Management Attitude:** Till recently, labour was a factor of production, and was handled like other technical and economic resources. However, after 1900, employees began to be recognised as human beings; and therefore, recreational, insurance, social security programmes and fringe benefit plans were launched by employers. With the passage of time, labour became mature; and employees began to be accepted as join: collaborators in an organisation. Personnel problems are now tackled not only by a rule-of-thumb method but on the basis of personnel experience and by learning from the experience of others; by means of attending courses meant for the personnel management: by discussions with others and by visits to other plants; by a study of business literature and scientific methods; and by gathering, analysing and interpreting the pertinent data. Higher education in the humanities and the social sciences too, have influenced labour relations in business.

Professionalism in Personnel Management

With the passage of time, personnel management has become mature and professionalised. Professional management is that form of management where the decision-making process rests with the professional managers, where there has been a divorce between capital and control, and where the owners of business are functionless owners. Brandeis says: "The attributes of a profession are that the training for its practice be intellectual in character, that it be pursued not for one's own sake but for others, and that the amount of financial reward should not be considered a measure of success." In the opinion of Morris L. Cagan: "A profession is an avocation whose practice is founded on an understanding of the theoretical structure of some department of learning or science, and upon the abilities accompanying such understanding. These understandings and these abilities are applied to the vital practical affairs of man. The practices of profession are modified by knowledge of a general nature and by the accumulated wisdom and experience of mankind, which serve to correct the errors of specialism. The profession, serving the vital needs of man, considers its first ethical imperative to be altruistic service to the client."

A profession is an avocation which has been analysed and written about. Its theory and practice have been systematised and are passed on through written documents, textbooks, seminar papers, research experiments and formal and methodical training, recognised by society. A profession is usually directed towards meeting wider social needs. It is not primarily directed towards the fulfilment of individual needs. A profession claims to be a social service and, hence, demands a higher status and recognition from society, than is the case with crafts and skills. In return, society also expects a certain mode of behaviour that is inner controlled or prescribed by the brotherhood of those who follow the same profession.

Characteristics of a Profession and a Professional

In the opinion of Beach, a profession should have the following features:

(i) It requires advanced, specialised formal education and training;

(ii) It required a consists exercise of discretion and independent judgement;

(iii) It is based on a deep and recognised body of knowledge;

(iv) Efforts are constantly made to expand the knowledge of the profession and right have a keenly developed sense of ethics and public responsibility;

(v) The members of the profession have a sense of common identity and purpose. There is a professional organisation which seeks to advance the field and uphold profession standards; and

(vi) It demands certain recognised standards of competence in terms of education, training, experience and human performance.

We shall discuss these characteristics as under:

A professional needs formal training and educational progammes to acquire a basic knowledge of the economic, psychological and sociological concepts affecting the proper working of an organisation. Besides, he should also have specialised in some discipline of management like production, finance, marketing, personnel, etc.

A Corpus of Knowledge: Personnel management possesses a recognised body of knowledge, which is gathered from the literature dealing with the concepts, procedures and methodologies involved in attempts to co-ordinate personnel matters within an organisation. A vast research and other literature is available, which deals with the theories and techniques of personnel administration, method of handling labour problems, wage and salary issues, training, safety, health and employment problems. Throughout the career a professional believes in continuously improving his professional skill by exposing himself to new concepts and techniques in his area of expertise.

Professional Bodies: A profession is organised as a body with its own experts. These bodies are organised on voluntary basis and are zealous of their independence. The professionals have developed a number of administrative societies, associations and institutions which have a large membership of those who have qualified in personnel affairs. The National Institute of Personnel Management, the Indian Labour Economics Society, All India Management Association, the Industrial Relations Research Association, the International Personnel Management Association and the American Society of Personnel Administration are some of such bodies.

Service Motive or Social Responsibility: Professions have, for their objective, not only longevity, survival, expansion, profit earning, but also the need for catering to the requirements of the public and act on the basis of the doctrine of social responsibility. Most professionals are concerned about both the service and profit motives. In other words, a professional has a value system which is often different from the tunnel vision of typical owner-manager for profit. His it is to optimise the results through inputs and maximal outputs.

Ethical Code or a Code of Conduct: A profession claims to be ruled by its own 'moral guidelines' rather than by 'rules of the state'. Professions do possess some type of ethical codes which guide the behaviour of their members. In India, we have a Code for the members of the National Institute of Personnel Management.

On the basis of this discussion, it may be said the personnel management is now regarded as a profession. The professional manager brings into operation the elements of scientific management — planning, organisation, staffing, direction, control and co-ordination, and the dynamics of a unified programme of growth; he unites and co-ordinates the work of technologists and professional experts to achieve predetermined goals. Those in the personnel department are concerned specifically with the employment function (recruiting, screening and selecting employees), the compensation function salary administration, employee benefits administration, job analyses, job design and job evaluation), the training and development function (operative training and management development), the labour relations function (contract negotiation and administration), and the function of administration, which includes the formulation and climate and of implementation of over-all policies, the creation of an organisational motivational systems, and organisational development. The major inputs of a social organisation are employees (workers and managers).

Professional managers cope with three central manpower problems:

(i) Attracting people into an organisation;

(ii) Motivating people to perform and develop in an appropriate manner; and

(iii) Holding people within the system.

These problems they are able to tackle efficiently because they have had a long training and education, and have also a knowledge of the managerial tools and techniques of achieving the "profit-cum-growth maxim of an organisation."

Code of Ethics of Members of National Institute of Personnel Management

Recognising and accepting the responsibilities of the profession of personnel management, I as a member of the National Institute of Personnel Management, shall:

- Uphold the honour and dignity of the profession and the Institute;
- Observe and maintain integrity as the keynote of professional conduct and shall perform my professional duties with fairness, impartiality, fidelity, and dedication to the cause of the profession;
- Recognise and accept the dignity and worth of an individual as a human being, irrespective of race, religion, language, caste or creed, and strive for the development of his personality;
- Co-operate in maximising the effectiveness of the profession by exchanging freely information and experience with others and by contribution to the development of the profession to the best of may ability;
- Maintain at all times an open mind with regard to problems that I have to deal with in the course of my work and approach the problems of others with understanding;

- Not allow any interest other than professional to interfere with any official work;
- Strive unceasingly for self-development by acquiring ever increasing knowledge, skill and experience related to the profession;
- Endeavour to extend public knowledge on professional matters and try to eliminate misconceptions and misunderstandings about the profession;
- Express publicly an opinion on professional matters only when it is founded on adequate knowledge and honest conviction;
- Not damage, directly or indirectly, the professional reputation or practice of other members;
- Exercise due restraint in criticising the work of other members;
- Endeavour to give credit for professional work to those to whom it is due;
- Endeavour to provide opportunities for the development and advancement of professional men who work with me;
- Uphold the principle of appropriate remuneration for those engaged in professional work;
- Not associate in work with another member who does not conform to ethical standards and not hesitate to bring to the notice of the Institute any unethical practice adopted by any member of the Institute;
- Be faithful to my employer or client, and present clearly to him the consequences to be expected if my professional advice is not accepted;
- Advise engagement of specialists when I am convinced that such services are in the best interests of my employer or client and shall co-operative with them in their work;
- Follow professional principles and practices tactfully and courageously, keeping in mind the principles of equity in the fair distribution of work and rewards;
- Promote the concepts, methods, skills and techniques in the fields that contribute to productivity, growth, profitability and employee satisfaction;
- Not a disclose any information of a confidential nature that I may acquire in the course of professional work without obtaining the consent of those concerned; and

- Not accept or offer any improper gratification in any form or manner whatsoever in connection with, or in the course of, my professional work.

Personnel Administration as a Discipline

Personnel management is now recognised as an academic discipline, so much so that practically every university in India and elsewhere offers courses leading to a or degree in personnel management. These courses generally deal with the concept of personnel management, selection techniques and employment, training and development employees and executives, salary and wage administration, health and safety management, human relations, group dynamics, etc. Courses in personnel management either offered by departments of business administration or by specialised institutions are personnel management and relations or institutes of management or institute of public administration. The universities also conduct these courses under the department of sociology and social work.

In the last three decades, a large body of literature, research papers, textbooks, etc. has been produced by university professors and practising executives which are based on their experience and research findings. A large number of professional journals are also published for the benefit of those in personnel field.

Personnel Administration — An Art or a Science?

Personnel management has been recognised, as science as well as an art. A science exact and systematic classification of knowledge of some subject. In view of this definition, personnel management may definitely be regarded as a science, for its principles concept laws, rules and procedures, methods and techniques have been presenting a systematic way. They are not static and rigid, but existable and adaptive; they can meet the changing circumstances of an organisation.

On the other hand, "art is an application of skill or knowledge in a unique and creative manner." To identify personnel management as a career implies that as a qualities are associated with personnel practices, which are recognised as a result of unique creative management styles rather than as a result of set of personnel rules and procedures.

Personnel Management as a Career

As the discipline of personnel management is of growing importance the chances for young person's making a career in this field are bright — at least for quite some years. A person with a highly specialised knowledge of, and training in, personnel management and with a general background has many opportunities for employment in business and industry. Highly qualified persons in different branches of behavioural sciences may be absorbed in a college or a university which offers facilities for a full-time or a part-time diploma or post-graduate course in personnel management, especially in the areas of labour economics, personnel management, industrial relations, industrial psychology, industrial sociology, industrial engineering, labour laws, public personnel administration, behaviour. Or they may find jobs in industrial concerns as industrial psychologists in charge of personnel research; as legal advisors on labour issues; as accountants who deal with employee benefit and retirement programmes; as trainers who conduct training and development programmes for employees and executives at the lower and middle levels; as labour economists concerned with labour relations or wage and salary administration; as engineers who deal with safety management; as journalists undertaking the communication and publication work of an organisation; as clinical psychologists who offer counsel and appraise employees for promotions and salary hikes.

Corporate personnel directors
Divisional personnel directors or corporate personnel functional directors
Personnel managers directors or corporate personnel specialist
Personnel manager or staff specialist division personnel department
Personnel manager (small plants) or labour relations personnel department . safety
Employment supervisor or salary administrative supervisor or communication supervisor
Employment or assist. Or salary administrative assistant or communication assistant.

Fig. 4.2: Steps form New Personnel Man to Corporate Personnel Directors.

Their expertise can also be utilised by such professional and consulting organisations as accounting firms, law firms, actuarial firms, psychological consulting firms, labour relations consultants, etc.

Persons equipped with the general management knowledge may find work in an organisation, initially as job analysts, employment interviewers, wage and salary technicians, labour relations assistants, communication assistants and personnel trainers. From there, they may move upward to various specialised areas, such as training and development, wage and salary administration, etc. Some may head the personnel and industrial relations activities of various sections of an organisation. In some instances, people may shift backward and forward, from specialised to general positions in the organisation. It has been shown the career progression pattern used by a large chemical industry in the USA.

In many organisations, the chances for moving upward are very clear. Instances have not been uncommon when a person entering at the lowest level reaches positions of middle and even top level personnel director, depending upon his acumen, perseverance, hard work and experience in different jobs.

Philosophy of Personnel Management

Personnel actions in any company are guided by the philosophy which a company may profess for dealing with people. Such a policy may or may not be in writing; but it does exist, if not openly, at least in an informal or subconscious manner. Personnel philosophy may tend in many directions. First, labour may be viewed as a technical factor, which more or less passively or actively resists managerial leadership. Therefore, it is necessary to mould, control and closely supervise the people so that company goals may be achieved in a manner beneficial for individuals, groups and even the organisation itself.

Second, the modern view is that labour is not a commodity of change but a precious asset which has inherent constructive potentials. These potentials may be utilised in an efficient manner if the management has an enlightened attitude towards labour and encourages participative management. In this way, employees may be assisted to grow and advance in the same manner as the business grows and advances. The quality of human resources can be effectively increased by implementing programmes of education, training and personnel development.

Third, "management is getting work done by and through others." In other words, it is a human relations job which is handled through several major activities — planning, organising, directing and controlling. Employee performance can best be achieved by recognising and enhancing the human dignity of each employee.

To get work done, various measures have to be adopted — mutual involvement or participation can be allowed; proper incentives or motivating devices can be used; the right things at the right moment are communicated to bring home to employees an awareness of the issues involved in the functioning of an organisation; authority to command or take decisions is delegated within certain limits; and a provision is for career planning and development opportunities.

Factors Influencing Personnel Management Philosophy

(i) **Top Management Philosophy:** To some extent personnel management philosophy is preordained, based mostly on the experience, education and background of the top management. It may or may not be stated, it is usually communicated by their actions and permeate every level and department of the organisation. For example, here is a part of the personnel philosophy of Thomas J. Watson Jr. Chairman of International Business Machines Corporation

"I firmly believe that any organisation, or order to service and achieve success, must have a sound set of beliefs on which it premises all its policies and actions. Next, I believe that the most important single factor in corporate success is faithful adherence to those beliefs, finally, I believe that if an organisation is to meet the challenge of the changing world, it must be prepared to change everything about itself except those beliefs as it moves through corporate life." "IBM's philosophy is largely contained in three simple beliefs: (i) our respect for the individual. (ii) IBM means success. We want to give the best customer service of any company in the world. (iii) An organisation should pursue all tasks with the idea that they can be accomplished in a superior performance from its people in whatever they do." IBM's philosophy was greatly influenced by the values of Mr. Thomas Watson (the father of Mr. Watson Jr.): "The important values as he learned them, were to do every job well, to treat all people with dignity and respect, to appear neatly dressed, to be clear and forthright, to be eternally optimistic and above all loyal." In India, Tata Steel's personnel management philosophy is influenced by its founder Shri Jamshedji Nussarwanji Tata, whose concern for the man, his management and welfare have been prime. The philosophy of the Tata Steel has been: "(i) Realistic and generous understanding and acceptance of their needs, rights and an enlightened awareness of the social responsibility of industry; (ii) Adequate wages, good working conditions, job security, an effective machinery for speedy redressal of grievances and suitable opportunity for promotion and self development; (iii) Promoting feelings or trust and loyalty through a humane and purposeful awareness of their needs and aspirations; and (iv) creating a sense of belonging and team spirit through their closer association with management at various levels."

(ii) Changing Environment: Fundamental changes occurring in the environment also influence personnel management philosophy. Such factors are:

(a) Dissatisfaction among the workers due to their getting such employment for which they are over qualified. This not only affects the quality of work but also compel the management to learn how to motivate a better educated worker.

(b) People are getting more interested in choosing a life style and career than just a job. This needs that personnel philosophy should be so changed as to make the career development and to make the work force more consistent with the changing interests of the workers.

(c) New changes in law require that no discrimination should be made in providing equal employment opportunity on the basis of age, sex, caste, religion, etc.

(d) Basic work values are changing. Previous "work ethics" motivated workers to work hard. With the decline of the ethics, motivating employees is becoming a difficult task.

(iii) Influence of One's Assumption about People: Personnel management philosophy is also influenced by the basic assumptions one make about people, i.e., neither one believes in Theory X or Theory Y of McGregor or in Lickerts' System I or System IV. Accordingly the philosophy is framed.

(iv) The Need to Motivate People: Managers get things done through others therefore, if they cannot motive employees to get their job done, they are destined to fail as managers. So methods of motivation also influence management philosophy.

Bench-marks Principles of Personnel Management

From the philosophy are derived the guidelines or bench-marks, which are generally exible. These principles change as conditions change, including human behavioural patterns. The main principles of personnel management may be set forth as follows:

(1) People are to be Dealt with as Complete Individuals: Persons are recruited because they possess the requisite technical, professional and other qualities. But whether they co-operate with one another, with the group and with the management is largely governed by their personal feelings, cultural and social attitudes, ethical standards and family background. These and technical factors should be programmed into organisational operations. The management should be quick to understand how employees feel about contemplated work assignments, personnel policies, and decisions which affect their interests. Employees should, therefore, be treated as a whole and not piecemeal.

(2) **Employees Should be Made to Feel Worthwhile:** "Men do not live by bread alone." There is something other than money which motivates them to work toward organisational goals. Personal feeling of accomplishment, pride in one's work, harmonious relations with other co-workers and co-operation with the management - all these factors need to be taken into consideration by the management if the efficiency and productivity of the employees are to be maintained and increased.

(3) **Fairness and Justice:** These should guide a managements policies and actions. Fairness in dealing with his employees would win for the employer the confidence of his employees.

(4) **Rewards Should be Earned, not Given:** The rewards to be given should be commensurate with the efforts put in to win them. Such rewards should be given to an employee because of what he has accomplished and not merely as a gift. Gifts are not so well appreciated as rewards for work well done.

(5) **Supply Employees with Relevant Information:** An organisation should have a properly developed two-way communication channel so that the necessary have a properly develop information, instructions, orders and rules are passed on to employees and a proper response is evoked. Information must be given at the right moment, otherwise much harm may result. Secrecy often breeds suspicion in the minds of employees.

(6) **Judge the Strength or Intelligence of the People Properly:** A knowledge of the strength of its employees will always bring management their co-operation. If proper opportunities are not made available to employees, resentment and frustration may result; or they may leave the organisation or resort to coercion. Therefore, employees should be associated with the decision-making process.

(7) **Sell the Personnel Programme:** Because if employees are not made aware of it, they will learn it from some other source. The selling of a programme should be done either orally or in writing.

(8) **Equal Wage for Equal Work:** All the employees irrespective of their sex or community but doing similar type of work, must be paid equally, and the wages paid must be adequate.

(9) **Set Examples:** Preaching alone will not the desired results, "action are louder than words", and these convince the employee that the management really does not what it says or mean.

Status of Personnel Management

Till recently, personnel managers were considered to be of a low status than other management executives. Their low status was due to certain causes, namely:

(1) **Disrespect for the Function and Those Performing It:** Personnel managers have been viewed as contributing little to the essential functioning of an organisation. This was due to the fact that they were entrusted with such tasks as did not offer challenges; they generally prepared routine plans, programmes and procedures, handled employment details, did wage and salary survey, and handled employee welfare programmes; while the other executives were involved in such challenging tasks as financing and looking after complex production schedules. This lack of involvement on the part of personnel managers often led to frustration; the personnel function itself was placed at a lower level in the oganisational structure and untrained persons, who were not needed anywhere else, were employed on personnel jobs. The inevitable result was the low status and prestige of the personnel manager and his department.

(2) **Low Position in the Organisation:** The personnel function was given a low status in the organisational structure, as a result of which line managers were discouraged from seeking help from the personnel department, mainly because personnel executives were contacted for the solution of a single problem. An ineffective department generally has the following characteristics:

   (i) Personnel functions are not too well co-ordinated;

   (ii) There is no special planning section in the organisation; and

   (iii) There is no justification, written or stated, for using the existing organisational structure.

(3) **Lack of Expertise in Performing the Function:** Frequently, a mediocre line manager was required to perform personnel functions. Sometimes this was done "to kick him upstairs" or "to reward him for his good performance elsewhere." As a result, he did not command the respect of his subordinates or the line personnel. Moreover, incompetent managers could not anticipate the problems of an organisation; and often they underestimated their possible effects. Some did not even have sufficient knowledge or interest in broader organisational matters.

(4) **A Poor Self-image by Personnel Managers:** Since personnel managers felt that they held low level positions, or were not fairly treated by other executives, they did not take any lively interest in their work, and often performed a static role.

These weaknesses influenced the status of personnel managers to a very great extent. But the situation has now changed, and top executives have begun to realise that to meet the changing needs, there should be "human resource experts" well versed in the diverse aspects of personnel management. These experts are knowledgeable, competent and committed personnel specialists who are capable of making meaningful contributions to their organisation and utilising personnel departments very effectively.

In terms of status, "the Personnel Relations Director today often serves as a key member of the top management team. A vice-presidential position is usually assigned to the top personnel man in a large company. He has the ultimate responsibility for all personnel and labour policies. He also assists in decision-making, organisational planning, executives development and community relations policy."

The Future of Personnel Man

In future too, the personnel functions should occupy a significant position in the management area because of the following reasons:

(a) It has a direct bearing on manpower planning, recruitment, career development, management development, training, wage and salary structure and a host of other personnel issues and aspects.

(b) It concerns the dynamics of group behaviour, inter-personal and inter-group relationships.

(c) A large body of knowledge, available as a result of surveys in behavioural sciences, indicates how an organisational structure may be reshaped for a better utilisation of human resources.

(d) In structuring management, the present-day need is to promote a specialisation of the personnel function rather than of the general management function lest we lose a first rate specialist and appoint an indifferent manager who is more concerned about status and position than about the sincere discharge of job responsibilities.

(e) Lastly, the management movement, rapid technological changes, the changes in the thinking of the management itself, and the changes in the political, economic and social climate call for new roles for personnel executives as "catalytic agents of change."

Stages of Change

The needed change can be brought about in three distinct stages, as indicated by Mr. Kamani

In the first stage, "It should be realised that:

- in our traditionally sheltered state of existence, life and living must acquire a new meaning;
- the gap between profession and practice can be bridged if there is a happy amalgam of imagination, determination and ways of service;
- the stewardship of an industrial complex can offer fulfillment of the personnel goal in the coin of love, sympathy and help rather than in favour, prestige and status."

In the second stage, "It should be realised that a new form of organisational structure and process must be a sequel to a philosophy, whereby the management can steadily, but surely move:

- from leadership of authority to leadership of shared autonomy and goals;
- from a state of working under constraint to a state of autonomy and excellence in the temple of work;
- from the primacy of material resources to the primacy of human resources;
- from profit making to growth-achieving;
- from sensation of pleasure to acquisition of happiness; and
- from self-oriented behaviour to a state of working with and through a functional collectivity."

In the final stage, "On the one hand, it should be aware of the enormity of challenge in bringing about the needed quality of transformation and, on the other, the strength that is discovered on oneself and one's colleagues— the patience, humility and the capability of learning from one's failure and disappointments. In order to wear the cap of the agents of social change, one needs, in an equal measures, a challenge of tests and a quiet confidence born out of a sense of humility. A third set of forces needs to be added: the goodwill of those who only 'stand and wait', i.e. the observers."

Human Resources Management

Human resource management (HRM) is an approach to the management of people, based on four fundamental principles. First, human resources are the most important assets an organisation has and their effective management is the key to its success. Second, this success is most likely to be achieved if the personnel policies and procedures of the enterprise are closely linked with, and make a major contribution to the achievement of corporate objectives and strategic plans. Third, the corporate culture and the values, organisational climate and managerial behaviour that emanate from that culture will exert a major influence on the achievement of excellence. This culture must, therefore, be managed which means that continuous effort, starting from the top, will be required to get them accepted and acted upon. Finally, HRM is concerned with integration — getting all the members of the organisation involved and working together with a sense of common purpose.

HRM is a strategic approach to the acquisition, motivation, development and management of the organisation's human resources. It is a specialised field that attempts to develop programmes, policies and activities to promote the satisfaction of both individual and organisational needs, goals and objectives. It is devoted to shaping an appropriate corporate culture, and introducing programmes which reflect and support the core values of the enterprise and ensure its success. HRM is proactive rather than reactive, i.e., always looking forward to what needs to be done and then doing it, rather than waiting to be told what to do about recruiting, paying or training people, or dealing with employee relations problems as they arise. The techniques for the application of HRM will include many familiar functions of personnel managers, such as manpower planning, selection, performance appraisal, salary administration, training and management development. These will be overlaid by special programmes designed to improve communication systems, involvement, commitment and productivity.

In its essence, HRM is the qualitative improvement of human beings who are considered the most valuable assets of an organisation — the sources, resources, and end-users of all products and services. HRM is, no doubt, an outgrowth of the older process and approach. But it is much more than its parent disciplines, viz., personnel management and behavioural science. HRM is also more comprehensive and deep-rooted than training and development. Its approach is multi-disciplinary from the beginning to the end. It is a scientific process of continuously enabling the employees to improve their competency and capability to play their present as well as future expected roles so that the goals of the organisation are achieved more fully and at the same time the needs of the employees are also met to an adequate extent.

HRM is a production model approach to personnel management. The HRM model is characterised as being employee-oriented with an emphasis on the maximisation of individual skills and motivation through consultation with the work force so as to produce high levels of commitment to company strategic goals. It is a resource to be used to be invested in the traditional personnel management in fullest capacity. It is an asset which is non-strategic, separate from the business, reactive, short-term and constrained by a limited definition of its role as dealing with mostly unionised and low level employees. If personnel management is curative, HRM is preventive. The key distinguishing feature of HRM is its evolving strategic role.

HRM essentially emphasises and incorporates the traditional personnel management. It integrates in a meaningful being fulfilled roug way the various sub-systems like performance appraisal, potentiality appraisal and teer lanning training and development, organisation development, developmen', car p, research and systems development, rewards, employee welfare and quality of work life, relations, human resource information, and so on. Under the HRM approah, in us is some basic assumptions about human resource are also different from the traditional approach. The important assumptions of HRM are as follows:

(i) The members of an organisation are reservoirs of untapped resources.

(ii) There is scope for unlimited development of these resources in the nature of self-development than development thrust

(iii) It is not outside.

(iv) The organisation also undergoes development with the overall benefits along with the development of its members.

(v) The organisation further develops a culture in which utmost emphasis is placed on harmonious superior-subordinate relations, team-work, collaboration among different groups of individuals, open communication, and above all, integration of the goals of the organisation with the needs of the employees.

(vi) Top management takes the initiative for HRM, formulates necessary plans and strategies, and creates an overall climate and support for its implementation.

Roots of Human Resource Management

HRM activities have probably been performed since ancient times. As a formal discipline, however, its roots are traceable to the period immediately following the Industrial Revolution.

The pioneering work of Peter Drucker and Douglas McGregor in the 1950s laid its formal foundation.

Drucker in his book "*Practice of Management*" (Heinemann, 1959), writes: "An effective management must direct the vision and effort of all managers towards a common goal." The concept of a visionary goal-directed leadership is fundamental to HRM. Douglas McGregor advocated management by integration and self-control, partly as a form of management by objective, but more importantly as a strategy for managing people which affects the whole business: He believed that a management philosophy needed to be built up, based on attitudes and beliefs about people and the managerial role of achieving integration. He, like Drucker therefore, paved the way to the HRM role philosophy that human resource policies and programmes must be built into the strategic objectives and plans of the business and must also aim to get everyone involved in the achievement of these objectives and plans.

The behavioural science movement came into prominence in the 1960. It was founded by writers such as Maslow whose hierarchy of human needs placed self-fulfillment or self–actualisation at the top pyramid, and Likert, who developed his integrating principal of supportive relationship. Another important figure in the behavioural science movement was Argyris who belived that organisation design should plan for integration and involved and that individual should feels that they have a high degree of self-control over setting their own goals and over the paths to defining those goal.

The most influential member of the behavioural science school, however, was Herzberg who advocated job enrichment as a means of increasing organisational effectiveness claiming that such improvements should centre on the work itself as a source of motivation. If people feel that the job is challenging, they will be moved to perform it well. This school of thought made two useful contributions to HRM. First, it underlined the importance of integration and involvement, and second, it highlighted the idea that management should accept as a basic value the need of consciously improving the quality of working life as a means to obtain increased motivation and improved results.

The philosophy of management by objectives (MBO) can also be traced to this period. MBO mainly refers to: (1) establishment of goals and objectives, (2) formulation of action plans, and (3) reviewing and modifying human behaviour. The concepts of the behavioural scientists provided the impetus for the organisational development (OD) movement of the

60s and 70s, whose beliefs were summarised by Bennis (*Organisational Development*, Addison-Wesely, 1969) as follows:

(i) A new concept of man, based on increased knowledge of his complex and shifting needs which replaces an over-simplified, innocent, push-button idea of man.

(ii) A new concept of power, based on collaboration and reason, which replaces a model of power based on coercion and threat.

(iii) A new concept of organisational values, based on humanistic and democratic ideas, which replaces the mechanistic value system of bureaucracy.

The organisation development specialists attempt to change the attitudes, values, and behavioural patterns of individuals and work in groups in order to promote greater co-operation among organisational members. The OD movement advocated the implementation of programmes designed to improve the effectiveness with which an organisation functions and responds to change, with particular emphasis on how people carry out their work and interact with one another. The management of change and team development are often important parts of an organisation development programme.

Components of Human Resources Management

Human Resource Organisation: Human resource organisation is concerned with achieving success by organisation design and development, motivation, the application of effective leadership, and the process of getting across the message about what the enterprise is setting out to do and how it proposes to do it. The fundamental objective of human resource organisation is to ensure that every aspect of the organisation, employment, motivation and management of people is integrated with the strategic objectives of the business and contribute to the successful achievement of those objectives. The human resource organisation programme has to take account of cultural issues so that the desired corporate culture can be developed or reinforced. Moreover, organisational development programmes and interventions are needed to achieve better integration, improve teamwork, motivate human resource, develop proper leadership, facilitate communication system, manage conflict and change, and obtain commitment.

Human Resource Planning: Human resource planning sets out to define how many people the organisation wants, but with a particular interest in the type of people the organisation needs at present and in the future, in terms of their expertise and how they "fit" the corporate culture.

It involves the forecasting of both the supply and demand for future labour. It provides the base for recruitment programme and for human resource development plans.

Human Resource Systems: Human resource systems are the essential programmes needed to recruit, appraise, pay and look after the health, safety and well-being of the employees in the organisation.

The main key programmes are:

(i) **Recruitment Management:** It is a process of obtaining the required human resource for an organisation.

(ii) **Information Management:** It is a method of ensuring that all policies and practices are well articulated and effectively communicated to the work force.

(iii) **Training Management:** It is a system of identification of training needs, preparation of a training strategy, and an appropriate training system.

(iv) **Performance Management:** It is a technique of appraising performance systematically against defined criteria, reviewing progress to date and assessing the potential for advancement. There are three main appraisal systems such as performance appraisal, potential appraisal, and performance coaching or counselling.

(v) **Reward Management:** This ensures that people are rewarded in accordance with their contribution.

(vi) **Career Management:** It is system of charting special career paths for individual employees for advancement in the organisation.

(vii) **Health and Safety Management:** It is a system of maintaining a healthy and safe system of work in an organisation.

(viii) **Discipline Management:** It is a system of administering discipline to foster positive employee behaviour that will promote organisational objectives.

(ix) **Culture Management:** It is a system of thinking and behaving shaped by the values, attitudes, rituals and sanctions in an organisation.

Human Resources Development (HRD): Lippit (1978) points out that HRD as a system depends on: (a) work itself which generates a higher degree of responsibility for the employees; (b) the individual's personal and professional growth; (c) the improved quality output as a result of increased responsibility; and (d) organisation as an open system. Focus on all these aspects is what HRD is all about.

Rao (1985) defined HRD as "a process by which the employees of an organisation are helped, in a continuous planned way to: (a) acquire or sharpen capabilities required to perform various tasks and functions associated with their present or expected future roles; (b) develop their enabling capabilities as individuals so that they are able to discover and exploit their own inner potentials for their own and/ or organisational development purposes; and (c) develop an organisational culture where superior-subordinate relationship, teamwork. and collaboration among different sub-units are strong and contribute to the organisational health, dynamism and pride of employees."

HRD as a function consists of various activities related to training and development and performance appraisal. All aspects of training and appraisal play a significant role in achieving the individual's growth and development. In this respect HRD is more a proactive and supportive function because the organisation has to take a lead in helping the people to grow and realise their potential.

The primary responsibilities of a HRD manager are:

To act as an internal change agent and consultant.

- To initiate change and act as an expert and facilitator.
- To actively involve himself in the company's strategy formulation.
- To keep communication lines open between the HRD function and individuals and groups both within and outside the organisation.
- To identify and evolve HRD strategies in consonance with overall business strategy.
- To facilitate the development of various organisational teams and their working relationship with other teams of individuals.
- To try and relate people and work so that the organisation objectives are achieved effectively and efficiently.
- To diagnose problems and to determine appropriate solutions particularly in the human resources areas.
- To provide co-ordination and support services for the delivery of HRD programmes and services.
- To evaluate the impact of an HRD intervention or to conduct research so as to identify, develop or test how HRD in general has improved individual or organisational performance.

Human resource development programmes help to ensure that the organisation has the people with the skills and knowledge it needs to achieve its strategic objectives. The thrust of human resource development is on training and development. It is a dynamic process which aims at improving the skills and talents of the personnel. Training fills the gap between what someone can do and what he should be able to do. Development aims at modification of behaviour through experience. It builds on strengths and helps to overcome weakness, and ensures that the organisation has the expertise it needs. Development operates at all level, middle management level and top management level, covering executives and non-executives.

Human Resources Relationships: Human resource relationships deal with the handling of employees individually and collectively as members of trade unions or staff associations. Their aim is to increase co-operation and trust and to involve employees actively in the company's affairs. It also deals with problems-solving techniques, particularly to solve problems relating to disciplinary cases and grievances. There are two sides to a dispute in most organisations; the management and the workers. There is a gap and the means have to be found to bridge that gap. Whether or not unions exist, it is highly desirable for the management to develop methods of dealing with employees collectively. Nonetheless, relationship with unions often involve confrontations. The necessary techniques must be evolved from the encouragement of mutually-working together in the interests of all. Unions have to be managed like everything else in an organisation.

Management normally gets the union it deserves. If it handles unions the wrong way, the results for the organisation can be disastrous. An approach to collective dealing should be: (a) the recognition of the union, (b) the respective role performance of management and union, (c) the type of procedures one can adopt to regularise relationships with unions, (d) the basic techniques of negotiating with unions, and (e) the mechanism of involvement through participation, both traditional forms of joint consultation as well as the more recent Japanese import of quality circles.

Human Resource Utilisation: According to Peters and Waterman, to achieve productivity through people, it is very essential to "treat them as adults, treat them as partners, treat them with dignity, and treat them with respect." These fundamental human relations values provide a base for productivity management programmes, techniques such as method study to improve efficiency. Both managers and workers must be persuaded somehow to realise that they have a common interest in increasing output. The following actions are required to improve the use of human resources: (a) conduct a productivity drive; (b) improve manpower budgeting and control techniques; (c) introduce work measurement; (d) use appropriate payment method by results; bonus and profit-sharing schemes; (e) improve motivation; (f) involve employees in improvement programmes; (g) introduce new technology; (h) negotiate appropriate productivity agreement; and (i) introduce training programmes based on an analysis of productivity needs.

Human Resource Management Approach

Human resource management has received tremendous attention in recent years. lts role in organisations has also undergone a substantial change and many organisations have gradually oriented themselves from the traditional "Personnel Management" to a "Human Resource Management" approach, although many see it as the "old wine in a new bottle". The basic approach of HRM is to perceive the organisation in its totality. Its emphasis is not only on production and productivity but also on the quality of life. It seeks to achieve the fullest development of human resources and the fullest possible socio-economic development.

Broadly, there are three meanings attached to the concept of HRM. ln the first place, persons working in organisations are regarded as a valuable source, implying that there is a need to invest time and effort in their development. Secondly, they are human resources which means that they have their own special characteristics and, therefore, cannot be treated like material resources. The approach focuses on the need to humanize organisational life and introduce human values in the organisation. And thirdly, resources do not merely focus on employees as individuals, but also on other social realities, units and processes in the organisation. These include the role or the job a person has in the organisation, the dyadic unit (consisting of the person and his superior), the various teams in which people work inter-team processes, and the entity of the total organisation.

There has been a great deal of HRM activity in organisations, although most of such HRM systems are designed without understanding the Organisation's structure, tasks, processes and people. It is imperative for any HRM activity to have an organisational climate to stabilise such efforts in reality. It is essential that HRM are designed in the framework of the total organisation. HRM efforts fail miserably such organisations where no attention is paid to these systems.

Human Resource Management in the Indian Context

The Indian economy has become an integral part of the global economy. Total quality management latest technology sophisticated equipment, most up-to-date know-how, high skills, cost consciousness, production with less cost, and customer's satisfaction have become the hallmarks for us to compete with others. In such a fiercely competitive environment, with the liberalisation and globalisation of the economy, the management of the organisation will have to initiate radical changes within the organisation to enable it to compete effectively in a dynamic market. The managers of these organisations will have to become the catalysts of change. The management of organisations has to continually enhance its efficiency and effectiveness for its survival and growth. For many organisations, accustomed to working in a sheltered market and in a monopoly, these changes have been indeed very painful. For some organisations, it has not been easy to adapt and adjust themselves to the economic and technological changes in the Indian environment. In many organisations, surplus workers have refused to accept voluntary retirement, even though very liberal schemes have been offered. In addition, poor performance has made operations in many organisations uneconomic.

Some of the issues and challenges which are confronting the Indian industry are:

- How do we make our organisation dynamic and vibrant?
- How do we ensure an organisation's culture and environment that encourages work commitment and involvement of employees?
- How do we motivate our employees to set and achieve challenging goals?
- How do we ensure team-work which produces synergy and collaborative effort?
- How do we make people productive and result-oriented?

Chapter - 5

Personnel Management in India

Genesis and Growth

The Personnel Function in India has been a product of various factors, labour legislation being one of them. The importance of labour officers in Indian industry was realised as early as 1929, when the Royal Commission on Labour was set up. In 1931, the Commission recommended the appointment of a labour officer in order to "protect the workers from the evils of jobbery and indebtedness, to act as a spokesman of labour and to promote an amicable settlement between the workers and management." The Commission observed that:

(i) The jobber should be excluded from the engagement and dismissal of labour and that, instead, a labour officer be appointed for this purpose;

(ii) The qualities required of a labour officer should be integrity, personality, energy, and the gift of understanding individuals and he should have a linguistic facility. If he is of the right type, the workers will rapidly learn to place confidence in him and regard him as a friend;

(iii) All labour should be engaged by him, and none should be dismissed without consulting him; and

(iv) The labour officer should fulfill many duties, and should particularly initiate and administer welfare measures.

In 1931, the Bombay Millowners' Association appointed labour officers on their own, who were required to attempt to settle grievances and disputes. Similar officers were appointed in the jute industry in Bengal under the directions of the Jute Mills' Association. These officers were entrusted with the responsibility of setting up food shops, promoting sports and welfare activities. Personnel officers in the textile industry came up from the department concerned with recruitment and the settlement of grievances rather than from one administering welfare activities, as in other countries (the USA and the UK). Their functions as Industrial Relations Officers to handle grievances and prevent disputes were stressed from the beginning.

During the Second World War, these officers were generally entrusted with the handling of welfare and labour administration. Their functions were subsequently enlarged and were infuenced by the social reform movement in the country, public concern for improving labour administration and the growth of the modern management movement. Their functions thus included activities relating to welfare, personnel and industrial relations.

The Factories Act 1948 provides for the statutory appointment of a welfare officer in a factory. Section 49 (1) and (2) of the Factories Act lays down that: (1) in every factory wherein 500 or more workers are ordinarily employed the occupier employ in the factory such number of welfare officers as may be prescribed; (2) the state government may prescribe the duties, qualifications and conditions of service of officers employed under sub-section (i). According to the Plantations Labour Act, 1951 every plantation wherein 300 or more workers are ordinarily employed the employer shall employ such number of welfare officers as may be prescribed. The state government may prescribe their duties, qualifications, and conditions of service. The Mines Act, 1952 also provides that every mine wherein 500 or more persons are ordinarily employed, the owner, agent or manager has to appoint a suitably qualified person as welfare officer. These Acts also prescribed the manner of their recruitment, their salaries and conditions, an elaborate list of duties to be performed by them, of service; and also laid including those concerned with welfare, with day-to-day personnel administration and with industrial relations.

In the beginning, personnel management was neither given any particular attention nor place in the organisation system, nor did professionals find themselves involved in the process. Its existence without any apparent assignment or responsibility was the usual picture and the so called champions and protectors of labour welfare used to remain only on the fringe of industrial activities as an appendage to the system. Subsequently, it was entrusted with the policing function within the organisation, i.e., to report on and assist the organisation in dealing with mostly discipline and getting rid of trouble-makers. At this stage, it was mostly engaged in "fire fighting tasks", i.e., going to the forefront at the moments of crisis, without having carried out any preventive or organising action. Incidentally, it was at this stage that, at times, the use of welfare officers for aiding and abetting the exploitation of the working class by certain organisations brought them on the periphery of notoriety. However, by and large, their appointment in industries remained only symbolic, satisfying the statutory requirement, without any specific, constructive role play. The "personnel man" who was initially known as "welfare officer," has moved on to be known as "labour welfare officer", "industrial relation officer" and is now identified as "human resource manager".

Qualifications of Labour Welfare Officer

A welfare officer to be appointed should possess: (i) a university degree; (ii) degree or diploma in social sciences, social work or social welfare from any recognised institution; and (iii) adequate knowledge of the language spoken by the majority of the workers in the area where the factories, mines and plantations are situated.

The National Commission on Labour has stated that "laws were made to ensure that the managements appointed a person exclusively to look after the welfare of their workers and help them in discharging their statutory obligations in respect of welfare measures. Welfare Officers should form part of the administration in order to discharge their responsibilities effectively. Therefore, the eligibility of a Welfare Officer must be ensured before his appointment. The Welfare Officer should not be called upon to handle labour dispute on behalf of the management."

The Committee on Labour Welfare, after going through the views expressed by the State Governments, public sector undertakings, private employers' organisations, workers' organisations and eminent persons in the field of relations and on the role and status of welfare officer, recommended that:

"The management should designate one of the existing officers to their personnel department as welfare officer to fulfill the purpose of the law. The management should ensure that only such officers of the personnel department are designated to look after the welfare activities as are properly qualified to hold these posts and have aptitude for welfare work."

Functions of Labour Welfare Officers

In actual practice, the welfare officer has been entrusted with the following functions:

(a) Supervision of:

- (i) Safety, health and welfare programmes; housing, recreation, and sanitation services;

(ii) looking after the working of the joint committee;
(iii) grant of leave with wages; and
(iv) redressal of workers' grievances.

(b) Counselling Workers on:
(i) Personal and family problems;
(ii) adjusting to work environment; and
(iii) understanding rights and privileges.

(c) Advising the Management on Matters of:
(i) Formulating welfare policies;
(ii) apprenticeship training programmes;
(iii) meeting statutory obligations to workers;
(iv) developing fringe benefits; and
(v) workers' education and use of communication media.

(d) Establishing Liaison with Workers to:
(i) Understand the various limitations under which they work;
(ii) appreciate the need of harmonious industrial relations in the plant;
(iii) interpret company policies to workers; and
(iv) persuade workers to come to a settlement in the event of a dispute.

(e) Establishing Liaison with the Management to:
(i) Appreciate the workers' viewpoint on various matters;
(ii) intervene on behalf of the workers in matters under the consideration of the management;
(iii) help different department heads to meet their obligations;
(iv) maintain harmonious industrial relations in the plant; and
(v) suggest measures for the promotion of the general well-being of workers.

(f) Working with the Management and Workers to:
(i) Maintain harmonious industrial relations in the plant;
(ii) arrange a prompt redressal of grievances and speedy settlement; and
(iii) improve the productivity and productive efficiency of the enterprise.

(g) Working with the Public to:
(i) Secure a proper enforcement of the various provisions of the Acts as applicable to the plant by establishing contact with factory inspectors, medical officers and other inspectors;
(ii) to help workers to make use of community services.

It is obvious that the duties and functions entrusted to a Welfare Officer range from assisting the management in policy formulation and implementation to supervising welfare programme, establishing contacts with workers and the public, solving workers problems and grievances.

The National Commission on Labour has stated, "the care of workers in all matters affecting their well-being, both at the place of work and outside, puts a special responsibility on the welfare officer. He should be a maintenance engineer on human side in many cases he also handles grievances and complaints of workers relating to terms and conditions of service and domestic and other matters which lie in the domain of personnel management. There is thus, virtually no demarcation between personnel management functions answer welfare functions." The Commission recommended that "in order to reduce the hierarchical hiatus in the status of these two officers, there should be an interchange to encourage professional functional mobility and to eliminate the functional monopoly as well the hierarchical status problems.

In the Chart 5.1 are shown the functions of a labour welfare officer. From the chart it will be seen that a Welfare Officer in India is a "multi-purpose personnel officer." He is a mainly concerned with welfare of the staff with list. He is expected to act as an adviser counsellor, mediator and liaison-man between the management and labour, i.e., to act as a "maintenance engineer on the human side."

Chart 5.1: Labour Welfare Officer

Labour Welfare Function	***Labour Administrative Function***	***Labour Relation Function***
Advice and assist in implementing legislative provision relating to:	**These may cover**	**These may consist**
1. Healty and safety	Organisational discipline and non-legislative	Administration of standing orders
2. Working conditions	Safety and medical administrative	Settlement of grievances
3. Sanitation and cleanliness	Wage and salary administration	Settlements of disputes through statutory procedure
4. Recreation	Administration of legislation	Trade union and union management
5. Welfare amenities		Steps to increase productive efficiency
6. Services like co-ops. Grainshops, housing co-ops.		

(*Cond...*)

7. Formation of welfare committees		
8. Housing		
9. Implementations of welfare acts.		

The Central Model Rules, 1957, define the duties of welfare officers so widely (Rule 7) as to comprise:

(1) helping maintain harmonious relation between factory management and workers.

(2) redressal of workers' grievances.

(3) providing feedback to management regarding labours' point of view "to shape and formulate labour policies and to interpret these policies to the workers."

(4) to watch industrial relations and settle disputes by "persuasive efforts."

(5) to advise management on the implementation of health and safety programmes.

(6) to promote productive efficiency.

(7) amelioration of the working conditions and helping workers to adjust and adapt themselves to the working environment, and

(8) personnel counselling - advising workers on individual personal problems, etc.

It will, thus, be observed that practically the whole gamut of personnel management, except disciplinary action, recruitment, and promotion seem to be comprised in this formulation.

Based on these Central Model Rules we give below the duties authority and responsibilities of Labour Welfare Officer in India.

In the United Kingdom, these duties are performed by personnel officers. It may, therefore, be said that the government has unconsciously attempted to develop institution of personnel management through the appointment of welfare officers in industries. However, in the USA and the UK, the personnel manager is an integral part of the top level management and is on a par with the manufacturing and marketing managers. He is clearly defined "staff" and not "line" function. He is in touch with all personnel, enjoys the trust, confidence and respect of all ranks, a position which enables him to advise both management and labour. In that sense the personnel manager is the most powerful bridge connecting the

Chart 5.2: Responsibilities and Authority of Labour welfare officer in India

Name of authority	***Area of responsibility***
(1) Advisory:	
To advices To suggest To encourage To promote To secure	In the formulation of company labour policies (a) should promotes training and apprenticeships progeammes; (b) inductions programmes and improved working condition; (c) welfare programmes, housings, recreational and educational facilities for worker and their families; (d) joint consulations and methods of communications with the workers.
(2) Services: To help To explain	(i) To workers: (a) In personal and family problems (b) In adjusting to work environment (c) In making applications for leave etc. (ii) To management: (a) By helping workers to understand the various limitations under which they have to work.
(3) Supervisory: To inspect To supervise To regulate	(a) Welfare and benefits programmes (b) Health and safety programmes (c) Paid vacations (d) Joint committees.
(4) Functional : To ensure To deal with	(a) Implementation of labour laws (b) Wages and employments.
(5) Policies: To bring To notice To watch To restrain	(a) Factory management the grievances of the workers, individual as well as collective (b) To watch industrial relations with a view to using his influence in the events of a disputes between the factory management and worker (c) To exercise a restraining influence over workers going on an illegal strike and over the management declaring illegal lockouts and to help prevents anti-social activities.
(6) Mediation	(a) To establish contact and hold consultations with a view to maintaining harmonious relation between the factory management and worker (b) To secure an expenditure redressal of the worker grievances and to act as negotiating officers with trade unions (c) To helps bring about a settlements of an industrials disputes by persuasive efforts; To maintain a neutral attitude during a legal strike or lockout and to helps in bringing about a peaceful settlement.

management with labour. He is the central figure in any productivity programme. Contrary to this, the personnel function in India has not made rapid advances. This may be attributed to the impediments in its way.

Impediments to the Progress of Personnel Management In India

There are various factors which have hindered the growth and development of personnel management in India. Some of the important reasons are:

1. The legal status of a Personnel Officer requires him to work in the field of welfare and day-to-day personnel administration and industrial relations. But since the personnel function is a line responsibility and a staff function, it cannot be properly performed by a personnel officer.
2. The attitude of the employees towards personnel officers has not been favourable. Management in India is still traditional and does not take the personnel officer into its confidence. "The line executives are often regarded as those who get the material, cut it up, put it together and ship it out, while staff executives are those who attempt to prevent the line boys from doing their jobs." Such ideas about the role of the personnel managers, generate frustration among them. In the words of Peter Drucker, "the personnel manager tends to conceive his job partly as a file clerk's job, partly as a house-keeping job, partly as a social worker's job and partly as a fire-fighter to head off union trouble or settle it."
3. Personnel officers are even now required to spend a major portion of their time in attending to disputes and the grievances of workers. The plethora of labour laws has encouraged trade unions to keep some matters always under litigation for the advancement of their selfish interests. This factor keeps a personnel officer preoccupied in litigation and away from his more important duties. As a result, he has neither the time nor inclination for long-range planning.
4. Lack of professional training facilities, a sense of insecurity and lack of job satisfaction among a large number of personnel executives drive them away from the profession.
5. The profession has not so far attracted the most meritorious among young persons. Mostly those of ordinary calibre have found place in this profession. One of the reasons being that this profession is still considered by many to be somewhat like a pinjrapole, an abode of useless cows.
6. The educational institutions which supply the 'material', have still the age-old curriculum which falls far short of equipping the incumbents with the desired type of fast changing knowledge and skill — which could enable them to deal with human problems effectively at the first instance.

7. The urge for updating the personnel people themselves is also mostly absent, which keeps them from being developed. The lack of initiative renders them obsolete and incompetent for the challenging jobs.
8. Their pre-occupation with their own personal aspirations make them overlook and, at times, ignore the expectations of all others, including the organisations.
9. By and large such professionals have not been tested in any trying situation and, when actually put in it, have generally emerged as failures succeeding rarely. In their behaviour, tendencies like making false promises for cheap popularity and taking credit for the performance of others make it difficult for them to be acceptable to others.
10. The inability to take decisions and the lack of courage to take responsibility for decisions based on their advice have been their greatest handicaps. The professional courage to disagree is a rare virtue. Absence of such professional courage of conviction and lack of confidence in their own competence often compel them to take the line of least resistance.
11. Many a time, the personnel mean — whether due to professional zeal or personal ambition — have tried to impose their will on other professions. This tendency has been responsible for their alienation. They should shed this trait and make an effort to integrate the expectations of all other professionals in industry without creating the feeling of an imposition.
12. Finally, personnel management has not yet been accorded the totality of acceptance by all concerned. It is because unlike professions such as engineering and medicine, where the result of any faulty action or decision becomes almost immediately obvious, the loss felt and the person responsible identified, the result of faulty decision on the management of human resources is not, by and large felt immediately and the responsibility for it can safely be shifted to someone else. Further, unlike other professions, the acceptance of "man-management" as a profession has to come from employers, trade unions as well as the government. This fact makes the profession an easy prey to politicisation by government machinery, trade unions and even by those within the organisation.

Professionalisation of Personnel Management

The following are some suggestions to improve personnel management profession in India:

1. The employers and the organisation having professional men should give the same status as extended to other professions, and give the personnel man's advice the same weightage as given to others. The areas in man-management should be left to be handled by personnel managers and they must be allowed to contribute their utmost in the formulation of sound personnel policies. It is high time that management of human beings is not made to like anybody's business. The idea, that by virtue of being a man, everybody is capable of handling other human beings, must go. The practice of encroachment by all and sundry in the area of management must stop.
2. The trade unions must recognise is man-management and deal with accordingly. Firmness with fairness must replace the practice of appeasement of the trade unions without creating any misunderstanding.
3. The Government must also professionalise personnel management in the public sector, which is supposed to be the model for others to follow. The Government should and managers, and should reduce its involvement in the day-to-day relationship in its fullness. It should remain the watch dog to encourage bipartism to play its role in its fullnes, it should remain the watch dog to restrain direct and guide the parties as and when required.
4. On the side of the management themselves, it is expected that personnel management should read the writings on the wall. It must be able to identify the goals of the organisation with those of theirs, by appreciating the needs and aspiration of all others.

Future Role of Personnel Manager in India

About the future role of personnel manager in India, Shri Pandey observes:

> "Just as the business of finance men is to manage the finances of the organisation to get the optimum return on investment, just as it is the business of production men to utilise the various resources at their disposal in such manner that optimum output is obtained, so is the business of 'personnel men' to manage human resource ensuring harmony, motivation, satisfaction and commitment".

"The line managers and other functionaries should continue to directly deal with the 'men' under them and, therefore, this relationship must continue. The personnel men's role should be to aid and assist the line managers and others in such a way that the human resource is put to its optimum use. Areas of expertise like wage negotiations, implementation of compensation plans, collective bargaining, recruitment, training in organisational development, management development, manpower planning, manpower audit, employees' service, community development and social welfare and the like are the areas which need professional strategy and skills of personnel men. In these areas they must be given a decisive role to play. By virtue of education and training as well as the time at their disposal, personnel men will be most suited persons to handle these matters.

"The concept of 'line' and 'staff' functions must undergo a change and the word 'adviser' (staff) and 'line' need be redefined. Because in a highly competitive and interdependent process of production, where group dynamics plays significant role, drawing an 'iron-curtain' between these two functions cannot work. It is the teamwork that matters and will matter most in dealing with people. An organisation is an organic system, and management a composite team. The various disciplines in management must be cohesive and given equal importance. From this angle, personnel function should be given appropriate place at all levels of management.

"Status is earned and not asked for. Each personnel man will have to undergo a serious introspection about his role and himself. The power always lies in one's effectiveness and usefulness. It also lies in its capacity to influence other organisational disciplines as well as workers. In a nutshell, personnel man's power and status will depend to a large extent on how pragmatic is his approach.

"In a fast changing society as our own, self-development in professional field is a continuing feature which must be kept up at all levels lest obsolescence would eat our vitalities."

"At present, the personnel officer in India presents a kaleidoscopic picture of his multi-role structure, namely, that of the buffer zone between labour and management; that of the third force in industry; that of the non-aligned professional, of the social worker in an industrial setting, and, above all, of a staff advisor in the organisation and an executive in the personnel and welfare spheres. A clearer perception of the view depends upon four crucial focus-factors, viz., (i) the external conditions generally circumscribing the scope of the role, (ii) the internal environment of the undertaking characterising the motivational analysis and the organisational relations concerning him; (iii) the person's ability to deliver the goods as reflected in the kind of training (in knowledge, acquisition of skills and development of attitudes) received by him for the efficient discharge of his duties; and above all; and (iv) the personality traits and leadership qualities of the individual concerned." The effective discharge of his duties depends upon his capacity and his resilience to meet the challenges of the circumstances as they arise.

The independence of the country and the beginning of a planned economic society, the rapidly developing management movement, rapid technological improvements and the increasing impact of mechanisation, which have brought in their wake changes in organisational structures and group relations; the growing complexity and size of business, the development of employees' associations, the new findings in behavioural science and the changes in political, economic and social climate of the country, together with the changing patterns of industrial relations; the Government's increasing role in promoting this specialised function - all these pose a new challenge to Indian management, which may broadly be described as "a challenge of survival and expansion"- survival because, on account of the increasing costs of production and the creation of increasing competitive conditions, it has become difficult for any business to survive; and expansion because, with a national economic policy geared to rapid economic growth, every business has to make a contribution towards increasing production in its own sphere of activity. To meet this challenge of survival and expansion is an up-hill task for personnel executives. Therefore, the future need of organisations is better management and managerial skills so that they may ably cope with the changing social, economic and industrial environment.

One of the primary responsibilities of the personnel manager is to participate in the process of change and make the acceptance of this change smooth and orderly. This would involve the matching of manpower with the new tasks and new methods of work which, in its turn, calls for a lot of uprooting and re-adjustment in the present functions of the Personnel Department. This may create problems of replacing, not obsolescent plant and machinery, but also men. Their retraining and better mobility would lead to stresses, strains and resistance, for which new approaches will have to be adopted. The personnel manager, therefore, will have to be 'more of a development man' than a 'mere administrator of personnel services.' He would, moreover, need to be equipped with up-to-date knowledge in the fields of industrial engineering, social psychology, behavioural services, law and accountancy etc.

The future personnel officer should be invested with the necessary authority to implement his decisions; and he should be consulted in the framing of labour and industrial relations policies. He should perform the role of an advisory staff in employer-employee relations, industrial relations and management training; and he should have executive authority in the area of employment, health and safety, employee services and benefits, wage and salary administration, productivity, joint consultation, grievance handling, organisation discipline, and maintenance of personnel records and research.

In the selection of unskilled, semi-skilled and skilled employees, the personnel officer should have a more decisive role, while in the highly skilled supervisory and professional categories, his recommendations should be given due weight.

Induction, 'workers' education, apprenticeship training and executive development programme should be his responsibilities and his views taken into consideration while making decisions about training programmes.

The creation of an environment of paper work should be conducive to effective work performance and it must relate to the maintenance of suitable working conditions, the provision of employee services, health, safety, welfare and other benefits, and their administration and supervision. All these should be the sole responsibility of the personnel officer.

The development of a just and reasonable promotion and transfer policy; the placement of employees according to their qualifications, and plans which aim at increasing efficiency, promoting job satisfaction, motivating employees; and finally, the administration and adoption of wage and other incentive plans — all these should be looked after by the Personnel Department.

The maintenance of discipline, the handling of grievances and complaints, consultation in matters of disputes, arrangements for negotiations between the parties at dispute with a view to bringing about an amicable settlement of issues, should be some of the other functions of personnel officers.

Engaging in planning and meaningful personnel research on problems relating to personnel; keeping pace with the changing social, political and economic conditions; stimulating managers to anticipate the employee problems which may arise as a result of the introduction of changes in personnel policies, manufacturing processes and procedures and labour-management agreements; conducting attitude surveys to check on current management agreements; conducting attitude surveys to check on current management practices with a view to assisting line managers to improve upon them; examining and assessing the functions of his own department, pruning obsolete functions, becoming cost-conscious in regard to any personnel proposals he submits to the top management; and bringing home to managers the importance of individual dignity, job satisfaction and social approval with a view to wining the co-operation and building up the morale of workers these, too, are some of the functions of a personnel officer. He should, moreover, be a person who will move, mix and work with all the employees in an organisation, develop an insight into the workings of the human mind, its attitudes and aspirations, improve interdepartmental relations and promote team-work through effective communication.

The future personnel men should keep pace with changes, get very much involved in basic organisational planning, and help the management to gear up human resources to new tasks. In fact, the personnel officer is certainly no less responsible and important in the success of any organisation than one who procures finance, or who produces or who markets the manufactured products. That is why in countries like the USA, the UK and the USSR, his importance has been increasingly recognised. This is equally true of India.

The future role of personnel managers will depend upon:

(i) The responsibilities delegated to personnel managers and their relationship with their bosses, and subordinates;

(ii) Having authority delegated to them for co-operative or service functions;

(iii) Their being able to function unfettered in giving objective advice;

(iv) Their guarding themselves constantly against obsolescence;

(v) Their placing adequate emphasis on personnel research, without which they will turn into corporate refugees;

(vi) Their preparing an adequate training base for the new members of the profession;

(vii) Their ability to slash through procedural brambles in order to achieve results; and

(viii) Their being prepared to accept the full responsibility of their position as senior executives of an enterprise.

Conclusion

In conclusion, it may be said that the future personnel managers should strive hard towards excellence - individually as well as collectively, so that as a body they may occupy a rightful place in the hierarchy of management along with other co-professionals. If they could do it, they would prove worthy of the motto "To Learn to Serve."

Chapter - 6

Organisational Structure

ORGANISATION

Meaning

'Organisation' is a group of people working together co-operatively under 'authority' toward achieving goals and objectives that mutually benefit the participants and the organisation. Kossen states that, "An organisation is a group of individuals co-ordinated into different levels of authority and segments of specialisation or the purpose of achieving the goals and objectives of the organisation". On the other hand, Allen defines an organisation as "The process of identifying and grouping the work to be performed, defining and delegating responsibility and authority, and establishing relationship for the purpose of enabling people to work most effectively together in establishing of objectives.

The essence of this definition is that people who work together require a defined system or structure through which they relate to each other and through which their efforts can be co-ordinate. Every organisation has goals or objectives for its existence. In the case of personnel management, it is to optimize "the effectiveness of human resources." These goals can be achieved more suitably if the behaviour of the workers and the composition of the organisation, can be predicted and integrated co-operatively. The formal organisation structure attempts to give order and unity to the actions and efforts of those who work together.

Organisation Process

The organisation process is the forming of structural inter-personal relationship.

This process involves eight steps, viz., (i) determination of organisational goals or objectives to be strived for; (ii) determination of the task requirements (i.e., the amount of skills, effort and knowledge) necessary to achieve the goals; (iii) division of tasks into different jobs to find out how many personnel will be needed for the complete tasks; (iv) Integration of jobs into departments or other work groups to take advantage of the specialisation and efficiency; (v) selection of personnel to fill jobs; (vi) assignment of work positions to the individuals; (vii) granting the authority to the people to carry out the duties of their jobs; and (viii) determination of superior subordinate relationships for facilitating the performance evaluation.

An 'organisation' is a mechanism with which a management directs, co-ordinates and controls the activities of man. It is distinct from an 'administration'. As Sheldon has said, "An organisation is the formation of an effective machine, the management of an effective executive and the administration of an effective direction. Administration determines the goals; the management strives towards it. Administration determines the organisation; the management uses it. An organisation is a machine of management in its achievement of the ends determined by its administration".

Functions of an Organisation

An organisation tries to establish an effective behavioural relationship among selected employees and in selected work place in order that a group may work together effectively. There are three kinds of work which must be performed whenever an organisation comes into being, viz., division of labour, combination of labour and co-ordination, i.e., the work, the people and the relationship between them. These are known as the fundamentals in every successful organisation. These are now briefly dealt with.

1. **Division of Labour:** Since an organisation is a structure of human association for the achievement of common goals, it involves individuals and groups of individuals. When two or more individuals join together to perform certain tasks, it follows that some division of work is done. Properly or improperly, fairly or unfairly, work is divided among those who participate in a productive organisation. With effective planning and organisation in an enterprise, the division of labour leads to a fixing of responsibility, the delegation of authority, specialisation, and other conceptual schemes which are frequently called the principles of an organisation.
2. **Combination of Labour:** With work divided and assigned to the members of an organisation, their activities are grouped together, forming operations; and operations are arranged to establish

systems and procedures. From a structural point of view, this grouping of activities results in units, departments and divisions of an organisation. The basis for this grouping of activities may be the skills of the workers, the tools and machinery used, the nature of the product, the materials employed, or some other element. Whether it is logical or not, there is always some reason for the arrangement of tasks in a work place.

3. **Co-ordination:** This all-inclusive principle emerges because of the need in every organisation for the integration of activities and the co-ordination of individuals and groups of individuals performing their tasks. Co-ordination is achieved through leadership; in the structural sense, it involves the fixing of responsibility and the delegation of authority. It establishes controls which provide for an efficient scheduling and performance of activities.

Concepts of Organisation Structure

Several fundamental concepts describing the essentials of a sound organisation structure have been presented by the traditional school of thought. These deal with the following essentials:

1. **Task Accomplishment or Personnel Satisfaction:** The emphasis is on organisational accomplishment, i.e., the structuring of work relationship, should be so planned that both the objectives of the organisation and the individual are realised simultaneously.
2. **Delegation of Authority:** It is the delivery by one individual to another the right to act to make decisions, to requisition resources, to direct others to act and to perform other tasks in order to fulfill job responsibilities. Authority is ineffective without ability to exercise it. Individual is given the authority to make it possible for him to his organisational obligations. Authority generally goes hand in hand with responsibility, which may be defined as an obligation or duty that employees have been directed to carry out by someone with authority over them.

   Once the responsibility is identified, the appropriate authority can be extended to the individual by his superiors. However, some personal factors within the superior and his subordinate may interfere with this delegation.

   Beside delegation of authority, the management has also to decide whether to keep most planning, decision-making and controlling activities within their own power or whether to transfer these to their subordinate the authority.

3. **Proper Span of Supervision:** Formal organisation structure determines the breadth of supervisors' responsibilities by indicating the number of individuals who are directly accountable to that supervisor. The span of supervision is important because it determines the amount of attention each supervisor can give to each subordinate, and it affects ease in communicating, methods of decision-making that can be use another superior-subordinate relationships.

   Since managers are accountable for the performance of their subordinates, the span of supervision is made a workable proposition. It is a function of a number of span variables, such as: (i) the similarity or dissimilarity of functions performed by the individuals being supervised; (ii) the physical nearness of workers to each other; (iii) level of complexity or simplicity of functions needed to be performed; (iv) the amount and degree of attention, needed on the part of the supervisor, toward each subordinate; (v) the required to co-ordinate and correlate the actions of subordinates; (vi) the importance and complexity of future programmes and objectives and the time required to review and establish them; and (vii) the amount of support and help the supervisor receives from line and staff assistants. A few more factors have been added, such as: (a) the level of cohesiveness of the workers, (b) the degree of member consensus and identification with common goals, (c) the amount of job satisfaction derived by subordinates from their jobs, and (d) existing levels of performance and productivity'.

   Spans can be narrowed or widened as per the needs of the organisation and the variables.

4. **The Degree of Specialisation:** Under specialisation, limited duties are performed regularly and repetitively. From the individual's point of view, specialisation makes the learning of job routines easier and makes the worker an expert in his job. From the organisation's point of view, it allows proper utilisation of the abilities of the individual workers; and makes co-ordination of activities easier, facilitates the development and implementation of essential controls, encourages the efficient productiveness of workers, quickens the training process. But, too much specialisation often results in making the work monotonous; the worker feeling little pride of accomplishment; and it may also affect a person's opportunity for growth. Therefore, some freedom and flexibility are needed.

5. **Communication Channel should be Proper:** Communication between the subordinates and their bosses should pass through each rung of the ladder without omission as a message is moved upward or downward. No manager in the vertical chain should be bypassed as the communication queue moves its way. When messages are to be conveyed at the horizontal level, they should move upward vertically from the sender to the point where the sender and the receiver have a common superior, then the message can move downward vertically to the receiver.

Merits of Formal Organisation Structure

If the organisational process is carried out properly and the organisation structure is carefully designed the following benefits would occur:

(1) Available resources will be utilised in the most effective way.

(2) Directional and operational goals and procedures will be determined clearly and energies devoted to their achievement.

(3) An orderly hierarchy in which people are related in a meaningful sequence will result. Individual responsibilities will be known clearly and the authority to act would be defined.

(4) Workers will benefit from planned superior-subordinate relationships in which each work receives essential support and direction.

(5) The activities of the individuals and the groups will become more rational, stable and predictable.

(6) Such an organisation may make the treatment of the individual workers more democratic, because patronage and favouritism are reduced.

(7) Individuals will be selected on the basis of ability to perform expected tasks. Simplification and specification of job assignment is possible in a more effective way.

Drawbacks

However, a structured organisation is not free from certain drawbacks, such as:

(1) Very often the fixed relationships and lines of authority seem inflexible and difficult to adjust to meet changing needs.

(2) Individual creativity and originality may be stifled by the rather rigid determination of duties and responsibilities.

(3) Inter-personal communication may be slowed or stopped as a result of strict adherence to formal lines of communication.

(4) Workers may become less willing to assume duties that are not formally a part of their original assignment.

(5) Organisations tend to fail to account for important differences in workers as human beings.

(6) They produce anxiety in individual workers by pressing too heavily for routine and conformity.

(7) They become too costly in terms of time and human dignity in order to implement organisational rules and regulations.

These drawbacks can be reduced through careful planning and efforts by supervisors to be responsive to human problems created by formal organisational structures.

Hierarchy of Formal Organisation

In any organisation there is what is termed a 'hierarchy.' Hierarchy refers to various levels of authority in an organisation, ranging from the Board of Directors at the top to the operating workers at the bottom.

Top management	President Vice- president
Middle management	Superintendents Department heads
First-line management	Superintendent Department heads
Operating employees	Workers

Fig. 6.1: Organisational hierarchy.

The formal organisation structure is usually portrayed in the form of a pyramid. At the base of the pyramid are the operating employees, the workers (i.e., those persons who do not supervise other employees). Moving up the pyramid are found the first line supervisors (usually referred to as Supervisors or Foremen); such persons need both a technical knowledge of their job and skill in human relations since they have direct authority over the operative employees.

Over these people, are found middle management personnel consisting of Superintendents, Plant Managers, and Head of Departments. Individuals at this level sometimes literally feel caught in the middle, both pushed and pulled by other managers on each side of them. Such personnel are responsible for implementation of the policies framed by the top management people. They need leadership abilities and communication skills.

At the apex of the pyramid is top management (which includes the senior executives, Vice-Presidents and the President). They constitute the administrative level, which determines the objectives and policies of the organisation. For them conceptual skill is of utmost importance.

Above them, may be the Board of Directors, elected by the shareholders of a corporate body. They influence over-all policy since they select top management.

Organisation Chart

The superior-subordinate relationships are defined by Organisation charts, which are formal documents that indicate the chain of command and the titles that have been assigned to the managers and other personnel. These charts are somewhat like "road maps" as they are guide to official relationship. Road maps indicate the relationship or roads, culverts and bridges to specific locations on the land. Organisation charts indicate people's locations or positions in the hierarchy and their relationship within a formal organisation. They aid in determining which of the basic types of organisational authority structures a particular enterprise has adopted.

Organisational Authority Structure

This organisational authority structure may be vertical or horizontal. The vertical structure clearly states that the lines of authority pass from top to bottom. At the top, the ultimate power lies in the hands of the top management or other supreme authority, who holds the highest position in the hierarchy. He has subordinates who are directly accountable to him; his subordinates have their own subordinates; and so the hierarchy goes until the lowest level is reached. The structure is based upon two traditional principles. One, the Scalar Principle, which is related to the chain of command and asserts that authority and responsibility in an organisation should flow in a clear, unbroken line from the point of ultimate authority (the boss at the top) to the workers at the bottom of the hierarchy. Two, the Unity of Command, which means that no subordinate shall be responsible to more than one superior, principally because the orders from one may conflict with the orders from another and, thus, place the subordinate in a difficult and awkward situation. This vertical authority structure also determines the social status standing of the individuals, i.e., those at the top usually stand at the upper levels of the social status ladder than those who stand at the bottom.

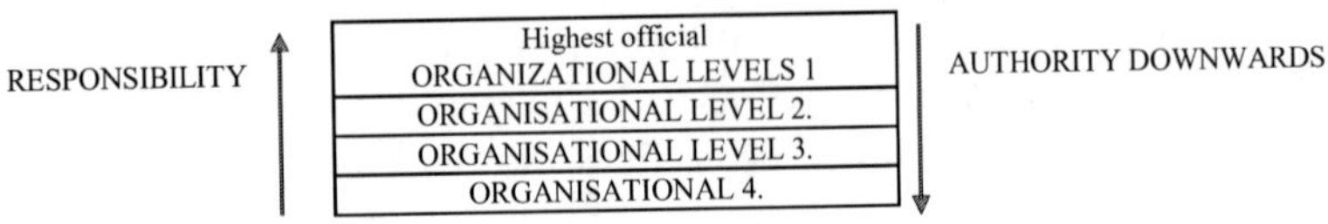

Fig. 6.2: Vertical authority structure.

Horizontal organisation authority structure indicates the relationship between peers, colleagues, and fellow workers across the organisation. Individuals located on the same level normally have no authority over each other. They are rather equal in terms of the amount of authority and formal influence they have. They are more or less equal in social status also. Such structure helps to clarify authority relationships, to understand communication patterns, and to discern more about social interactions. Personnel at this structure often work in a team.

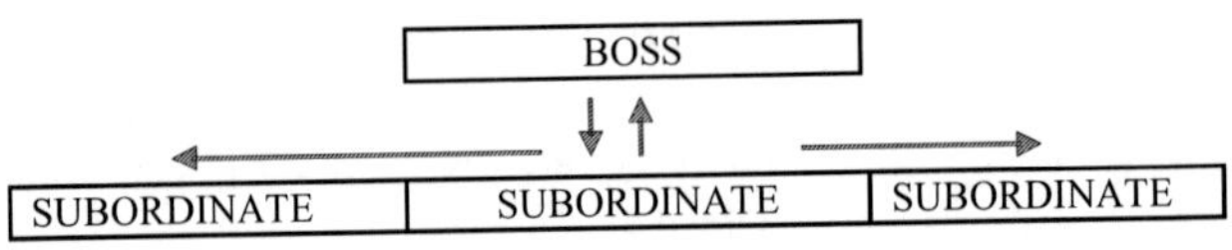

Fig. 6.3: Horizontal Authority Structure.

Line Organisation

In a line organisation, authority descends from the top of the hierarchy to its bottom level (down the channel of command) step by step, through downward delegation of authority, and responsibility runs from bottom to top (up the chain). As a result, all major decisions taken and orders given by the top executives are passed down to their immediate subordinates who, in turn, break up decisions in specific instructions for the purpose of their execution by another set of subordinates. When authority flows from the top to the subordinate at the lowest level in a more or less straight line, it is known as line organisation, and the subordinates under it are responsible to their immediate superiors. A line organisation has a number of common characteristics. First, each manager has direct authority over his subordinates who, in turn, have direct authority over their subordinates, and so on down the organisation. Second, everyone in the organisation reports to only one immediate superior, i.e., "there is one man, one boss." Third, managers have complete authority in their own areas of operation. Fourth, authority flows downward through the organisation and responsibility flows upward.

Merits of a Line Organisation: The following advantages are inherent in this system:

(i) It is the simplest type of organisation which can be easily defined and explained to the rank and file.

(ii) It is economic and effective, for it makes rapid decisions and effective co-ordination possible, as all the activities affecting a department are controlled by one individual.

(iii) Responsibility is fixed and unified at every level; hence each individual knows to whom he is responsible and who is or are, in turn, responsible to him.

(iv) It provides for greater control and discipline in the organisation.

(v) The system is capable of adjusting itself to changing conditions for the simple reason that each executive has sole responsibility in his own sphere.

(vi) It develops all-round officers who are qualified to take over higher positions of line command in a department.

Demerits of Line Organisation: The drawbacks of the system are:

(i) It overloads the executive with pressing activities so that long-range planning and policy formulation are often neglected.

(ii) It does not make for specialisation, for one executive is required to do all the work.

(iii) As it is based on one-man management, the decisions that are taken are rather arbitrary. "The system gives room for arbitrary, opinionated and dictatorial operations."

(iv) The distribution of work may be according to the whims of the executive and not in accordance with any scientific plan.

(v) It does not provide any means by which a good worker may be rewarded and a bad one punished.

(vi) It is likely to encourage nepotism. Every despot is besieged by sycophants and peace-seekers; promotion becomes a matter of attery, and security is a reward for servility.

(vii) It cannot fully develop the co-operative features of group activity.

(viii) Lack of a broad understanding often leads to non-cooperation among departmental line officers; the co-ordination of the activities of various line departments then becomes difficult.

(ix) As the division of the labour is incidental, a crude method for the division of labour and fixation of work prevails because of lack of expert advice.

Moreover, a line organisation cannot function effectively in large enterprises. Prof. Sargent Florence sums up the drawbacks of a line organisation under three heads: "(i) failure to get correct information and to act upon it; (ii) red-tape and bureaucracy; and (iii) lack of the specialised skills of experts... While commands go down the line under the hierarchical system, information is supposed to be coming up the line."

Further, because of the absence of specialised skills each executive is inclined to be a jack of all trades and master of none.

Scope of a Line Organisation

From this discussion, it is obvious that those industries which depend on the ability and ingenuity of workers cannot adopt this type of organisation. However, a line organisation may be adopted:

(i) Where business is carried on a small scale and the number of subordinates and operatives is not very large;

(ii) In industries which have a continuous manufacturing process (such as sugar, oil refining, spinning and weaving);

(iii) Where the work is of a routine nature (i.e., where a large number of processes are easily or simply directed);

(iv) Where the entire work process is automatic and requires little intelligence on the part of a worker; and

(v) Where the relationships between labour and management are cordial.

It is to be noted that most large organisations cannot be managed effectively in a 'pure line authority structure'. Rapid technological changes, as well as the need for breadth and depth of knowledge of legal, financial and labour-management problems, have necessitated the development of a service function usually referred to as 'staff authority'.

Line Managers' Personnel Management Responsibilities

Line managers are authorised to direct the work of subordinates. For example, production managers and sales managers are almost always "line" managers. "The direct handling of people is an integral part of every line manager's responsibility.

Line supervisors' responsibilities for effective personnel management have been given under the following headings:

1. Placing the right man on the right job.
2. Starting new employees in the organisation (orientation).

3. Training men for jobs that are new to them.
4. Improving job performance of each person.
5. Gaining creative co-operation and developing smooth working relationships.
6. Interpreting the company policies and procedures.
7. Controlling labour costs.
8. Developing potential abilities of each person.
9. Creating and maintaining a high level of departmental moral.
10. Protecting health and physical conditions of employees.

In small organisations, line managers may carry out all these personnel management duties unassisted. But in large organisations, they need assistance, specialised knowledge, and advice of a separate personnel staff.

Staff Organisation

Staff managers ordinarily do not have direct authority over the line members. Because of their technical or professional knowledge, staff members, commonly provide assistance or advice to the line members, which helps to free line members from details either not directly related to daily work or requiring specialised knowledge and skills. The staff members provide service for or advice about activities such as planning, research or the determination of executive manpower needs. The staff specialist serving the general manager may be in-charge of purchasing or personnel departments, both of which assist line operations. A personnel manager would not be directly in charge of the operative employees, but would be responsible for assuring that personnel needs are met; personnel managers, however, within their own departments, would be empowered with direct line authority over their subordinates.

Personnel Staff's Personnel Management Responsibilities

In fulfilling the responsibility, the Personnel Manager carries out three major distinct functions, as follows:

1. **A "line" function:** He directs the activities of the people in his own department and in service areas, i.e., he exerts line authority.
2. **A "co-ordinative" function:** He also functions as co-ordinator of personnel activities. He and his department act as, "the right arm of the top executive to assure him that personnel objectives, policies, and procedures which have been approved and adopted by the line organisation are being consistently carried out by line managers".

3. **Staff (service) function:** Service to line management is the "bread and butter" of the personnel manager's job. He assists in the hiring, training, evaluating, rewarding, counselling, promoting, and firing of employees at all levels. He also administers the various benefit programmes (health and accident insurance, retirement, vacation, etc.). He assists the line managers in their attempts to comply with equal employment and occupational safety laws. He plays an important role with respect to grievances of labour relations."

   As a part of his service functions, he also carries out an "innovator" role. He does this by providing up-to-date information on current trends and new methods of solving problems.

Functional Organisation

This system of organisation was evolved by F.W. Taylor. While he was working as a foreman, he experienced difficulty in getting men with sufficient ability, training and adaptability to meet the various requirements of the job he was in charge of. Taylor discovered, through experience and experiments, that "a well-rounded man should possess these qualities: brains, education, special or technical knowledge, manual dexterity or strength, tact, energy, grit, honest judgment or common-sense, and good health." None possessed, in practice, these qualities. Therefore, he evolved his functional organisation system, which consists in "so dividing the work of management that each man, from the assistant superintendent down, shall have as few functions as possible to perform."

Under this form of organisation, each department reports to a man specially qualified for a particular function regarding production, sale, financing, etc. The specialists attend to one function in all the departments; but each workman has to work under four superiors or foreman. These four superiors are the Gang Boss (who procures tools and arranges for set-ups); the Speed Boss who supervises the speed of the machines and feeds the worker performance); the Inspector (who checks the quality); and the Repair Boss (who looks after the maintenance of machinery to see to it that it is in order). These men worked in the shop and were placed as lower level management. At the upper level were placed four other supervisors, viz, the time and cost clerk, instruction card clerk, order-to-work or routine clerk and the disciplinarian. These were primarily office men. The essence of this form of organisation is that the delegation of authority is from the top downward in accordance with the functions to be performed, and the workers have to receive orders from more than one person.

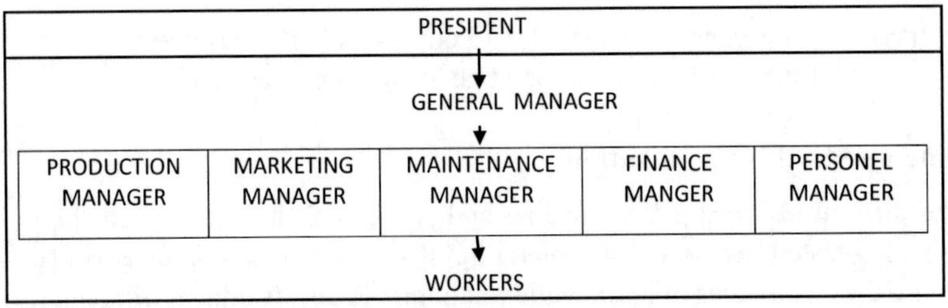

Fig. 6.4: Functional organisation.

Merits of Functional Organisation: The advantages of this type of organisation include:

(i) Intensive utilisation of the principle of specialisation of labour at the managerial level;

(ii) Reduction in the need for men with all-round executive ability;

(iii) Reduction in the need for all-round employees at the non-supervisory level;

(iv) Increase in work satisfaction for specialists who presumably do what they like to do;

(v) Increase in the number of occasions on which co-operative effort along "democratic lines" is called for;

(vi) One man devotes his entire time to doing one thing only;

(vii) Mass production through schemes of standardisation and specialisation is possible;

(viii) It makes possible the principle of undivided responsibility and authority, and at the same time permits staff specialisation.

Demerits of Functional Organisation: The system suffers from the following defects:

(i) Conflicts that arise in determining where one supervisor's responsibility ends and another's begins give rise to confusion and friction;

(ii) The non-supervisory employees are uncertain as to whom they should turn for advice and aid when problems call for analysis;

(iii) Action cannot be taken immediately because of divided control;

(iv) It reduces the opportunities for the training of all-round executives to assume further leadership in the firm;

(v) The staff may be ineffective for lack of authority to carry out its functions or it may not receive intelligent backing in the application of its recommendations;

(vi) The presence of specialists sometimes makes line supervisors feel that their influence and prestige as line men have suffered.

Line and Staff Organisation

The difficulties encountered in line and functional organisation in their form suggested the need for a blending of the two forms in an effort to secure the advantages of both, while retaining the disadvantages of neither. "Line-and-Staff Organisation" refers to and organisational pattern in which individual specialists and groups of specialists to an organ advise 'line officers' on the special aspects of their activities. The staff members concentrate their attention upon the research and planning aspects of business problems, while the line officials are left free to devote their attention to the execution of policy.

In the modern industrial world, almost all giant business enterprises have a line and staff organisation. Through this organisation the goals of an enterprise can be achieved in a systematic and efficient way. The popular concept of line and staff is that functions are those which have a direct responsibility for the accomplishment of the objectives of an enterprise"; and that "staff refers to those elements of an organisation which help the line staff to work most effectively in the accomplishment of the primary objectives of the enterprise. The amalgamation of line and staff organisations gives rise to the Line-and-Staff Organisation, under which the function of the staff is "to guide, advise, counsel and serve line officers." Therefore, there exists a line relationship between a line officer and the staff: Some departments are predominantly in staff position in the entire organisation, while others hold the line position. It is widely held that "staff managers have the authority of ideas, while line managers have the authority to command".

Merits of 'Line-and-Staff' Organisation: This form of organisation offers the following advantages:

(i) Its strength lies in the fact that it can exercise control through a clear-cut and undivided delegation of authority and responsibility and can achieve operating efficiency through specialisation.

(ii) It enjoys the advantages in a pure form.

(iii) As the organisation comprises both line and staff functions, decisions can be easily taken.

(iv) The system is flexible, for new activities may be undertaken by the staff without forcing early adjustments of line arrangements.

(v) It is based upon specialised knowledge. It brings expert knowledge to bear upon managerial and operational problems.

(vi) It provides an adequate opportunity for the advancement of workers.

(vii) It makes possible the principle of undivided responsibility and authority, and, at the same time, makes staff specialisation possible.

Demerits of Line-and-Staff Organisation: The disadvantages of a line-and-staff organisation are:

(i) There is the danger that line and staff officers may misconceive the relationship that should exist between the two types of activities, with consequent friction and ill feeling.

(ii) Certain line officers may place too great a reliance upon staff officers serving as their brains.

(iii) Certain staff officers may act in an irresponsible fashion, for they are not held directly responsible for the operating results brought about by the implementation of their advisory opinions.

(iv) Although expert advice is available, it reaches the workers through line managers. Here, it is liable to create a great deal of misunderstanding and misinterpretation.

(v) The staff is unable to carry out its plans or recommendations because of lack of authority.

(vi) The ability to see each other's viewpoint may cause undue conflict between line and staff personnel.

(vii) The line personnel often resent the activities of staff specialists, feeling that their status and influence are jeopardised in view of the fact that staff enjoys high prestige.

This disadvantages may largely be avoided in an alert and tight-knit.

This form of organisation is very common in modern large enterprises.

Line Versus Staff Organisation Authority

Personnel functions permeate through all the functional departments. These are performed at the operational level by line management, while the staff personnel executive advises, assists, counsels the line management at all levels (the president and his executive staff, the department heads and the foremen) in the performance of personnel functions.

Lawrence Appley clearly expresses the distinction between the line and staff functions in the following words: "The line organisation includes those people who are engaged in the manufacture and distribution of the products or services for which the organisation exists. The staff is engaged in those activities that assist the line in the attainment of its objectives. The line cannot exist without the staff, and the staff and the line frequently deal in the same activities, their relationships to these activities are distinctly different. The staff advises and the line decides." The line executive is directly in charge of persons who are employed in the production line, while the staff executive (work study engineers, industrial engineers, and other service departments) renders the services which are required by other departments in the organisation.

The term staff is best explained as referring to the function of a stick or staff carried by a person for support. In other words, the staff performs a supporting role. It supports the "line" which represents the hierarchical arrangement referred to as the scalar principle of organisation.

According to Dicks, "the staff personnel executive is there to assist, advise, counsel and guide the line executive in the performance of his personnel function. He is responsible for aiding and assisting the line management in the preparation, adoption and continuing evaluation of a programme of personnel administration expressed in terms of definite company written policies." "The personnel department is a specialised department at the executive level, whose function is to encourage, advise, and assist the line management executives, to adopt points of view, develop policies and methods, and apply skills which will release the productive and creative energies of all supervisors and employees."

The staff-line responsibilities in personnel administration are indicated below:

> "The line management has the responsibility and is held responsible for good personnel administration.... The supervisor is the one who actually administers the most essential and important phases of a company's personnel relations programme. By a supervisor we mean every member of the management who assigns work to others, who achieves results through the support, co-operation and effort of others....
>
> "The staff management advises and assists the line management in the fulfillment of the latter's obligations. The staff management, therefore, is only responsible for the reliability of the service, advice and assistance it gives to the line management."

Mooney states that although the staff is auxiliary, it should not lead to an erroneous conception. He states:

> "The structure of an organisation is like a double-track railroad, consisting of line and staff as two co-ordinate functions. The structure

of an organisation is a single track one, and can never be anything else. What is known in military organisation as line is synonymous with what we have called the scalar chain, and there can be but one chain of line authority. Any duty in an organisation, which cannot be identified as an actual link in the scalar process, is an auxiliary function, adhering to the line like siding along the main track. This means that every staff function must adhere to the line in the same dependent relation, and cannot otherwise exist."

Informal Organisation

The organisational structures discussed above are all formal. No business, however, operates, completely "by the book." In a real business setting, the relationship that actually exists amongst the employees does not follow formal lines. Employees in one department know those in other departments. They may need information about the acts of indiscipline in a particular department or some advice on delicate matters regarding the handling of jobs, etc. the associations of persons, in such cases, come under "informal organisation." These associations may be among employees on the same level of the hierarchy or on different levels. They may even cross unit or plant lines.

Informal organisations exist within the confines of the formal authority structure. The informal organisation consists of a group of people who relate to each other spontaneously for various purposes of mutual benefit and achievement. It is a primary source for information and furtherance of social ties. It provides members with useful information and knowledge (through the grapevine), which may supplement or complement formal communication. It also services as a source of protection against threatening oppressive forces. It helps its members to find solutions to mutual and personal problems.

The interactions that occur informally are neither prescribed by the formal structure, nor can they be completely controlled by formal authority. The informal groups sometimes act in support of formal goals and objectives, but it is equally capable of opposing formal guidelines.

The results of various studies indicate that:

(i) informal group dynamics were important;

(ii) informal group norms would develop which could undermine formal working relations;

(iii) informal group norms developed over what was to count as an acceptable day's work despite what management thought;

(iv) such informal group norms were important to the workers even to the extent that an individual worker might refuse promotion if it meant leaving the group;

(v) if management took an interest in the work force and allowed them some control over their environment then the work force would feel less alienated from the workplace;

(vi) where norms of co-operation and high output are established because of a feeling of importance, physical conditions may have little impact.

Organisational Structure of the Personnel Department

The internal organisational structure of the personnel department varies widely in different companies, depending upon their size. For example, in small companies, personnel functions are discharged by line executives. But, in a large company where personal activities are generally of a complex nature, a separate department is where personnel organised for the purpose. This department is variously knows as the Personnel Department the Industrial Relations Department, and is headed by the Personnel Manager or Personnel Director or Vice-President, Personnel, or by the Industrial Relations Director or Labour Relations Officer, Labour Superintendent or Employment, duties assigned to him and the terminology used. His position is upon the nature under the President (or the General Manager) of the organisation. He has under him interviewing Officers Training/Officers, Secretary, Medical Doctor/Welfare Officer, head of cleaners, gatekeepers etc. These subordinates undertake or are entrusted with the responsibility of recruitment and employment, training, industrial relations, employee services and security work.

Personnel Departments or Units may be organised on three basis: (i) Functional basis, (ii) Service basis, and (iii) clientele basis.

(i) Functional Basis

Acording to this basis Departments are grouped into different functions, such as: Procurement (employment), Development (training) Compensation (wage and salary administration), Integration (labour relations), Maintenance (safety), and Separation (employee services, retirement). Such a division would be influenced by such variables as size, abilities of personnel, and top management philosophy towards the role of the personnel.

(ii) Service Basis

The basis takes into consideration the service rendered or the purpose achieved. It tries to prevent dissatisfaction through hygienic maintenance, and promotion of satisfaction through motivators. This basis owes its evolution to Herzbergs' theory.

(iii) Clientele Basis

This basis has been propounded by Soholik whose thesis is that different requirements of different types of employees need specialisation.

Responsibility of Personnel Specialist

According to Richard P. Brown, "the major responsibility of the personnel specialist or staff is that of helping all levels of management to make the company a good place to work in". This naturally means that the responsibility of this specialist is very wide and that his role in developing and administering a personnel programme is a multiple one. Charles Furlog states that "the task of the personnel administrator is to see that sound personnel programmes are installed, not merely conceived".

The responsibility of the personnel specialist lies in the following directions:

(i) Human Resource Planning: His responsibility is to supply qualified employees to the various departments after making a careful screening, recruitment and selection; and to maintain a continuous source of labour force for the organisation. This pre-supposes that he understands and knows the contents and requirements of the job, for no one would think of building an engine without first finding out what the specifications are. Therefore, the work of designing and installing job analysis and job evaluation plans, maintaining suitable records and undertaking wage and salary surveys in the labour market — these, too, are staff responsibilities. The personnel specialist is also responsible for a co-ordination of merit rating schemes and for laying down objective standards for the assessment of performance. However, the decision to improve or change the entire pay schedule or fix the minimum and maximum pay in grades is the responsibility of the top management.

For tasks like transfer, promotion or lay-off, the personnel staff serves primarily in a coordinative capacity. Coaching, performance appraisal, and post-appraisal counselling, job rotation, under studies and special broadening assignments are largely executed by operating managers but co-ordinate by the central personnel staff.

(ii) **Formulation of Programmes and Procedures:** The personnel specialist is also responsible for assisting the top management in the formulation and development of personnel procedures and programmes after taking into consideration the prevailing social, economic, political, local and national policies on the different issues involved. He suggests how these programmes and policies should be implemented and sees to it that they are actually successfully carried out.

(iii) **Employee Health and Safety Programmes:** Employee safety, education and health programmes (pre-employment medical examination, periodic examination of those in service, operation of dispensaries, treatment of first-aid cases and removing health hazards) are a co-operative responsibility of both the staff and line personnel. In fact, the staff acts as a live wire for the promotion of safety consciousness in the plant.

A framing and observance of the rules and regulations pertaining to disciplinary matters, together with the range of penalties for different offences, is also his responsibility.

(iv) **Training and Development of Personnel:** His responsibility is to do the necessary research, plan and organise facilities so that the employee is sufficiently trained to perform his job satisfactorily. There needs to be a separate plug in any organisation to carry on such training. Since the training has to do with people, the responsibility for guiding, developing and co-ordinating it as well as developing programmes and keeping these active is that of the personnel staff.

(v) **Wage and Salary Administration:** The personnel specialist has to see to it that the company's wage and salary structure is sound and well administered. He should provide counselling and training to the supervisory force in the administration of the company's wage policies. He is moreover, required to furnish guidance on performance reviews and merit ratings. He should spearhead the appraisal plan, which may be used by the management to provide an inventory of current and potential human resources in the organisation.

(vi) **Labour-Management Relations:** His responsibility is to see to it that the employee is treated as a human being. He is required to develop a better understanding between the employees and the employers to ensure that a good labour-management relationship is established in the organisation. He is also responsible for bargaining on behalf of the management and for proceeding relating to conciliation, arbitration and adjudication of individual and group disputes. He acts as an advisor and tries to bring understanding between labour and management.

(vii) **Service and Benefits:** The personnel specialist has the responsibility of administering employee benefit programmes - insurance, accident claims, pensions, and provident fund and other fringe benefits. He also operates company medical facilities, fire-fighting and plant protection units, cafeterias, etc. He is responsible for encouraging the formation of clubs, thrift associations and recreational activities, and for arranging social functions. The actual decision to establish or expand these services is taken by the top management on the advice of the personnel staff.

(viii) **Personnel Research:** It is the responsibility of the personnel staff to conduct personnel research on improvement programmes or worthwhile innovations, recommendations or changes in source of employee motivation; on effective supervisory styles, differential illness and accident possibilities in the work force; and on the relative usefulness of alternative safety devices and clothing. These researches will keep the management continually informed so that better decisions and plans can be made. They will also add to the managements knowledge of improved motivation and utilisation of the members of the organisation.

The personnel staff is also responsible for maintenance of accurate and adequate records and statistics of the various personnel problems of the industrial unit. Statistics and data processing equipment are made use of as standard tools in research.

(ix) **Audit and Review Work:** The personnel staff is responsible for a continuing audit and reviewing of the line departments in matters of policies, procedures and programmes, particularly those which relate to accidents, grievances, absenteeism, voluntary quits and disciplinary actions.

Finally, it is the duty of the personnel staff to aid the management in ensuring effective communication throughout the organisation through proper media. In other words, the specialist should be an active force behind the two-way communication programme.

The role and responsibility of personnel men have been very ably and clearly stated in a study by the American Management Association:

"The personnel manager must function as a technical specialist - one who is equipped to perform skilfully the duties which the position entails; as a student who constantly strives for exact knowledge to enable him to recognise and correct the flaws and weaknesses in the programme as it evolves; and as a leader who has the vision and the personal integrity to build an enduring organisation around sound principles, honest convictions and wholesome human relationship."

As Beach has rightly observed: "He creates the environment in which employees can work effectively to accomplish the goal of the enterprise and, at the same time, obtain a substantial satisfaction of their need."

HUMAN RESOURCE MANAGEMENT
PERSONNEL RESEARCH
STAFFING & APPRAISAL
TRAINING & DEVELOPMENT
WAGES & SALARY ADMINISTRATION
BENEFITS & SERVICES
HEALTH & SAFETY

Fig. 6.5: Personnel Administration Department.

The personnel function is essentially a staff function. The aim of personnel management is to develop conditions in a firm which will facilitate the production of goods and services in a manner that will be of optimum benefit to the organisation. However, the decision-making authority in all matters has to be shared with managers outside the personnel department. This sharing occurs both on a vertical basis, with those at the organisational levels above the top personnel executive, and horizontally, with managers of the departments.

Chapter -7

Human Resource Planning

Importance of Human Resource

"Manpower" or "human resource" may be thought of as "the total knowledge, skills, creative abilities, talents and aptitudes of an organisation's work force, as well as the values, attitudes and benefits of an individual involved.... It is the sum total of inherent abilities, acquired knowledge and skills represented by the talents and aptitudes of the employed persons" of all the "Ms" in management (i.e., the management of materials, machines, methods, money, motive power), the most important is "M" for men or human resources. It is the most valuable asset of an organisation, and not the money or physical equipment. It is in fact an important economic resource, covering all human resources — organised or unorganised, employed or capable of employment, working at all levels — supervisors, executives, Government employees, "blue" and "white" collar workers, managerial, scientific, engineering, technical, skilled or unskilled persons, who are employed in creating, designing, developing, managing and operating productive and service enterprises, and other economic activities. Human resources are utilised to the maximum possible extent in order to achieve individual and organisational goals. An organisation's performance and resulting productivity are directly proportional to the quantity and quality of its human resources. Hence, the importance of human resource.

Manpower Planning Defined

"Manpower Planning" and "human resource" planning are synonymous. In the past, the phrase manpower planning was widely used; but now the emphasis is on human resource planning which is more broad based. Human resource or manpower planning is "the process by which a management determines how an organisation should move from its current manpower position to its desired manpower position. Through planning, a management strives to have the right number and the right kind of people at the right places, at the right time, to do things which result in both the organisation and the individual receiving the maximum long-range benefit?

Coleman has defined human resource or manpower planning as "the process of determining manpower requirements and the means for meeting those requirements in order to carry out the integrated plan of the organisation".

Stainer defines manpower planning as "Strategy for the acquisition, utilisation, improvement, and preservation of an enterprise's human resources. It relates to establishing job specifications or the quantitative requirements of jobs determining the number of personnel required and developing sources of manpower.

According to Wickstrom, human resource planning consists of a series of activities, viz.,

(a) Forecasting future manpower requirements, either in terms of mathematical projections of trends in the economic environment and development in industry, or in terms of judgmental estimates based upon the specific future plans of a company;
(b) Making an inventory of present manpower resources and assessing the extent to which these resources are employed optimally;
(c) Anticipating manpower problems by projecting present resources into the future and comparing them with the forecast of requirements to determine their adequacy, both quantitatively and qualitatively; and
(d) Planning the necessary programmes of requirement, selection, training, development, utilisation, transfer, promotion, motivation and compensation to ensure that future manpower requirements are properly met.

Thus, it will be noted that manpower planning consists in projecting future manpower requirements and development manpower plans for the implementation of the projections. This planning cannot be rigid or static; it is amenable to modification, review and adjustments in accordance with the needs of an organisation or the changing circumstances.

Human resource planning is a double-edged weapon. If used properly, it leads to the utilisation of human resources reduces excessive labour turnover and high maximum absenteeism; improves productivity and aids in achieving the objectives of an organisation to disruption in the flow of work lower production, less job satisfaction, high cost of production and constant headaches for the management personnel. Therefore, access of an enterprise human resources planning is a very important function, which can be neglected only at its own peril. It is as necessary as planning for production, marketing, or capital investment.

For an individual, it is important because it helps him to improve his skills and utilise his capabilities and potential to the utmost. For an organisation, it is important because it improves its efficiency and productivity. It is only through initial human manpower planning that capable hands are available for promotion in the future.

Need for Human Resource Planning

Human resource planning is deemed necessary for all organisations for one or the other of the following reasons:

(i) To carry on its work, each organisation needs personnel with the necessary qualifications, skills, knowledge, work experience and aptitude for work. These are provided through effective manpower planning.

(ii) Since a large number of persons have to be replaced who have grown old, or N who retire die or become incapacitated because of physical or mental ailments, there is a constant need for replacing such personnel. Otherwise, the work would suffer.

(iii) Human resource planning is essential because of frequent labour turnover which is unavoidable and even beneficial because it arises from factors which are socially and economically sound such as voluntary quits, discharges, marriage, promotions; or factors such as seasonal and cyclical situations in business which cause a constant ebb and flow in the workforce in many organisations.

(iv) In order to meet the needs of expansion programmes human resource planning is unavoidable. It becomes necessary due to increase in the demand for goods and services with growing population, a rising standard of living - larger quantities of the same goods and services are required.

(v) The nature of the present workforce in relation to its changing needs also necessitates the recruitment of new labour. To meet the challenge of a new and changing technology and new techniques of production, existing employees need to be trained or new blood injected in an organisation.

(vi) Manpower planning is also needed in order to identify areas of surplus personnel or areas in which there is a shortage of personnel. If there is a surplus, it can be redeployed; and if there is shortage, it may be made good.

The objective of human resource planning is to maintain and improve the organisations ability to achieve its goal by developing strategies that will result in optimum contribution of human resources. For this purpose, Stainer recommended the following nine strategies for the manpower planners:

(a) They should collect, maintain and interpret relevant information regarding human resources; (b) They should report periodically manpower objectives, requirements and existing employment and allied features of manpower; (c) They should develop procedures and techniques to determine the requirements of different types of manpower over a period of time from the standpoint of organisation's goals: (d) They should develop measures of manpower utilisation as component of forecasts of manpower requirements along with independent validation; (e) They should employ suitable techniques leading to effective allocation of work with a view to improving manpower utilisation; (f) They should conduct research to determine factors hampering the contribution of the individuals and groups to the organisation with a view to modifying or removing these handicaps; (g) They should develop and employ methods of economic assessment of human resources reflecting its features as income-generator and cost and accordingly improving the quality of decisions affecting the manpower; (h) They should evaluate the procurement, promotion and retention of the effective human resources; and (i) they should analyse the dynamic process of recruitment, promotion and loss to the organisation and control these processes with a view to maximising individual and group performance without involving high cost.

Human resource planning is the responsibility of both the line and the staff manager. The line manager is responsible for estimating manpower requirements. For this purpose, he provides the necessary information on the basis of the estimates of the operating levels. The staff manager provides the supplementary information in the form of records and estimates. The staff manager is expected to (i) report about manpower utilisation in the present and the past; (ii) provide help and advice managers on the assessment of manpower utilisation and to develop sources of information and techniques for purposes of comparison; (iii) administer the procedure of forecasting or objective setting; (iv) present the overall forecasts of departmental managers; and (v) to advise line managers on forecasting techniques.

Benefits of Human Resource Planning

(i) Upper management has a better view of the human resources dimensions of business decisions;

(ii) Personnel costs may be less because management can anticipate imbalances, before they become unmanageable and expensive;

(iii) More time is provided to locate source talent;

(iv) Better opportunities exist to include women and minority groups in future growth plans;

(v) Better planning of assignments to develop managers can be done;

(vi) Major and successful demands on local labour markets can be made.

Human resource planning is practically useful at different levels, as stated by Narayanrao. According to him:

(i) At the national level, it is generally done by the Government and covers items like population projections, programme of economic development, educational facilities, occupational distribution, and growth, industrial and geographical mobility of personnel.

(ii) At the sector level, it may be done by the Government — Central or State — and may cover manpower needs of agricultural, industrial and service sector.

(iii) At the industry level, it may cover manpower forecast for specific industries, such as engineering, heavy industries, consumer goods industries, public utility industries, etc.

(iv) At the level of the individual unit, it may relate to its manpower needs for various departments and for various types of personnel.

Process of Human Resource Planning

The process of human resource planning is one of the most crucial, complex an continuing managerial functions which, according to the Tata Electrical Locomotive Company, "embraces organisation development, management development, career planning and succession planning." The process has gained importance in India with the increase the size of business enterprises, complex production technology, and the adoption of professional management technique. It may be rightly regarded as a multi-step process, including various issues, such as:

(A) Deciding goals or objectives;

(B) Estimating future organisational structure and manpower requirements,

(C) Auditing human resources;

(D) Planning job requirements and job descriptions; and

(E) Developing a human resource plan.

(A) Objectives of Human Resource Planning: Human resource planning fulfils individual, organisational and national goals; but, according to Sikula, "the ultimate mission or purpose is to relate future human resources to future enterprise needs so as to maximise the future return on investment in human resources." In effect, the main purpose is one of matching or fitting employee abilities to enterprise requirements, with an emphasis on future instead of present arrangements." The objectives may be laid down for a short-term (i.e., for one year). For example, the short-term objective may be to hire 25 persons from Scheduled Tribes or Backward Class for purposes of training. The long-term objective may be to start a new industry, to expand the market, to produce a new product, to do its own sales force rather than depend on distributors, or to have minority group members eventually in position of middle and upper management cadres.

ORGANISATION

LONG RANGE OBJECTIVES AND PLANS	OVERALL REQUIREMENTS FOR HUMAN RESOURCES	INVENTORY OF PRESENT HUMAN RESOURCE	NET NEW HUMAN RESOURCE REQUIREMENTS	ACTION PROGRAMMES FOR RECRUITINGS & SELECTING NEEDED PERSONNEL	PROCEDURES FOR EVALUATING EFFECTIVE NESS OF HUMAN RESOURCES PLANNING

SUB-UNITS

SHORT TERM GOALS PLANS PROGRAMMES AND BUDGETS	WORK FORCE REQUIREMENTS BY OCCUPATIONAL CATEGORIES JOB SKILLS, DEMOGRAPHICS CHARECTERISTICS	INVENTORY BY OCCUPATIONAL CATEGORIES, JOB SKILLS, DEMOGRAPHICS, CHARACTERISTICS	NEEDED REPLACEMENTS OR ADDITIONS	PLANS DEVELOPING, UPGRADING, TRANSFERRING. IN RECRUTING AND SELECTING NEEDED PEOPLE

Fig. 6.6: Humans Resources Planning Systems.

(B) Estimating the Future Organisational Structure OR Forecasting the Manpower Requirements: The management must estimate the structure of the organisation at a given point in time. For this estimate, the number and type of employees needed have to be determined. Many environmental factors affect this determination. They include business forecasts, expansion and growth, design and structural changes, management philosophy, government policy, product and human skills mix, and competition.

Forecasting provides the basic premises on which the manpower planning is built. Forecasting is necessary for various reasons, such as:

(a) The eventualities and contingencies of general economic business cycles (such as wages, prices, costs and raw material supplies) have an influence on the short-range and long-run plans of all organisations. (b) An expansion following enlargement and growth in business involves the use of additional machinery and personnel, and a reallocation of facilities, all of which call for advance planning of human resources. (c) Changes in management philosophies and leadership styles. (d) The use of mechanical technology (such as the introduction of automatic controls, or the mechanisation of materials handling functions) necessitate changes in the skills of workers, as well as a change in the number of employees needed. (e) Very often, changes in the quantity or quality of products or services require a change in the organisation structure. Plans have to be made for this purpose as well.

After estimating what the future organisation structure should be the next step is to draw up the requirements of human resources, both for the existing departments and for new vacancies. For this purpose, a forecast of labour force is needed, and requisitions should be obtained from different departments, i.e., forecast has to be made in returns of functional category; the members needed; and the levels at which they are required. Vacancies, occurring in any department, should be notified in writing by different department heads to the personnel department, stating clearly the number of vacancies to be filled, job or category-wise types of personnel needed, their technical qualifications and experience, and the reasons for acquisition (i.e., whether for replacement or addition); a statement of duties, types of jobs, pay scales, age, and previous experience should also be made. Requisitions should be based on accurate job specifications by first line supervisors. They should, as far as possible, be clear-cut about the exact demands of a job.

In determining the requirements of human resources, the expected losses which are likely to occur through labour turnover — quits, retirement, death, transfers, promotions, demotions, dismissals, disability, resignations, lay-offs, and other separations - should be taken into account. Changes in the human quality resulting from the experience gained in the jobs during the period and the training achieved also need to be considered. The addition of new lines of production and new projects also influence the demand estimates of human resources. The basic fact to remember is that the human resource in an organisation constantly changes in terms of its present and future size. Additional human resources are gained through new employment of personnel, promotions, through transfers and demotions, but personnel is lost through voluntary quits, death, dismissals, terminations and retirements.

After making adjustments for wastage, anticipated and expected losses and separations, the real shortage or surplus may be found out. If a shortage is there, efforts are made to meet it either by new recruitment or promotion from within, or by developing the existing staff. If there is a surplus, it is to be decided how it will be dealt with, i.e., whether there should be transfers, lay-offs, retrenchment or reduction in the hours of work of all.

Underestimation of the quality and number of the employees required would lead to shortfalls in performance, while overestimation would result in avoidable costs to the organisation. According to Dr. Ram Taneja, "management can ensure control of labour costs by avoiding both shortages and surpluses of manpower through proper manpower planning".

It may be noted that for purposes of manpower planning, the main dimension be taken into consideration are:

(i) The total number of personnel available, this could be obtained from the pay-rolls and other personnel records, such as the applications for employment. The total number has to be classified on some basis, such as manual workers (i.e., daily-rated, weekly-rated or monthly-rated); clerical employees, ministerial staff, managers and other executives; specialists and skilled and unskilled workers, sex-wise distribution, etc.

(ii) The job-family, i.e., a detailed job-description for each position such as stenographers who may belong to various departments, e.g., finance, marketing, personnel public relations, general administration, etc.

(iii) Age distribution of the employees, available in the present departments, say in the age groups 20-29 years; 30-45 years; 46 years and above.

(iv) Qualification and experience desired, such as a person with five years or 10 years experience in a particular branch/job; and whether under-graduate, post-graduate, or MBAs or graduates in Science,

Commerce, Arts, Engineering or professional diploma holders, etc.; or with specialised knowledge in the field of marketing, finance, computer programming or engineering work.

(v) The salary range, etc.

(C) Auditing Human Resources: Once the future human resource needs are estimate the next step is to determine the present supply of manpower resources. This is done through what is called "Skills Inventory." A skills inventory contains data about each employee's skills, abilities, work preference and other items of information which they indicate his overall value to the company.

(D) Job Analysis: After having decided how many persons would be needed, it is necessary to prepare a job analysis, which records details of training, skills, qualification, abilities experience and responsibilities, etc which are needed for a job. Job analysis includes the preparation of job descriptions and job specifications. This has been discussed in the later section of this chapter.

(E) Developing a Human Resource Plan: This step refers to the development and implementation of the human resource plan, which consists in finding out the sources of labour supply with a view to making an effective use of these sources. The first thing, therefore is to decide on the policy - should the personnel be hired from within through promotional channels or should it be obtained from an outside source. The best policy which is followed by most organisations is to fill up higher vacancies by promotion on lower level positions by recruitment from the labour market.

The labour market is a geographical area from which employers recruit their work force and labour seeks employment. Here, the forces of demand and supply interact. A labour market generally has the following characteristics:

(a) It is highly unstructured and unorganised, for a majority of workers are illiterate and ignorant and do not have any information about available job opportunities.

(b) The procedures by which companies recruit workers and the methods by which workers go about getting jobs are highly variable.

(c) A great range of wage rates for the same occupation exists in the labour market, depending upon the attitude of the management towards wage levels, the employer's ability to pay and the productivity of labour.

(d) Labour is mostly not mobile either because it has incomplete or inaccurate knowledge of job opportunities and available wages or because of lack of job security.

(e) The supply of labour fluctuates and is influenced by the population in the labour market, the attractiveness of a job (benefits, services, wage rates, the reputation of a company), the extent of unemployment, and the particular skills that are in demand.

(f) Manual labour for unskilled jobs has been replaced by activities that require skills, scientific knowledge, technical acumen and professional training.

Various external factors influence the outflow and inflow of manpower resources. At the local level such factors are (i) population density at various distances from the factory or work place; (ii) local unemployment level, particularly of the categories which are relevant for the operation of the organisations; (iii) availability of part-time labour, (iv) current competition for similar categories of manpower from other organisations; (v) output from the educational system (general as well as technical); (vi) pattern of in-migration and out-migration within the area and between it and (vii) transport facilities and communication pattern.

At the corporate level other factors operate, viz., (i) trends in the growth of the working population; (ii) Government training schemes and systems of technical, vocational, professional, and general education, and their out-turn; (iii) impact of social security measures on manpower supply; (iv) mobility of the products of the technical, professional and vocational institutions; (v) cultural factors and customs, social norms, affecting school leaving age, labour force participation of women, children and young persons.

The personnel manager should have a thorough knowledge of the labour market. Which particular source in the labour market will be tapped will depend upon the policy of a firm, the position of labour supply, the arrangements with labour unions, and Govemment regulations. However, it is always safe for the personnel manager to be in close liaison with these different sources and use them as and when the need arises.

Responsibility for Human Resources Planning

Human resource planning is the responsibility of the personnel department. In this task, it is aided by the industrial engineering department, the top management and the team of directors of different departments. It is mostly a staffing or personnel function. The over-all responsibility lies with the

Board of Directors because, as the manpower planning scheme of Hindustan Lever indicates, "these members are in a position to direct the future course of business, set appropriate goals for the management concerned in the formulation of personnel policies." The personnel department's responsibility is "to recommend relevant personnel policies in respect of manpower planning, devise methods of procedure, and determine the quantitative aspects of manpower planning."

The responsibilities of the personnel department in regard to manpower planning have been stated by Geisler in the following words:

(i) To assist, counsel and pressurise the operating management to plan and establish objectives;

(ii) To collect and summarise data in total organisation terms and to ensure consistency with long-range objectives and other elements of the total business- plan;

(iii) To monitor and measure performance against the plan and keep the top management informed about it; and

(iv) To provide the research necessary for effective manpower and organisational planning.

Job Analysis

Developing an organisation structure results in jobs which have to be staffed. "Work" is an organisation's primary function. The 'basic work activities' may relate to three categories — Data, People and Things. Under Data are included synthesising, co-ordinating, analysing, compiling, computing, copying and comparing activities. People relate to monitoring negotiating instructing supervising, diverting, persuading, speaking, signalling, serving and taking instructions. Things are concerned with setting up, precision working operating-controlling driving-operating, manipulating, feeding-off bearing and handling.

While manpower inventory is concerned with telling 'what employees can do,' 'job assesses' what employees are doing.' From job analysis, specific details of is being done and the skills utilised in the job, is obtained. Job analysis enables managers to understand jobs and job structures to improve to work flow or develop techniques to improve productivity. It also involves job design or redesign, co-ordinating demands on available time, individual psychological needs, technical procedures, and desire performances.

Before we proceed to discuss job analysis in detail, certain terms relating to job need be understood. These terms are:

Job: A job may be defined as a "collection or aggregation of tasks, duties and responsibilities which as a whole, are regarded as a regular assignment to individual employees and which is different from other assignments". In other word, work to be done is divided and grouped into packages, we call it a "job". Each job has a definite title based upon standardised trade specifications within a job; two or more grades may be identified where the work assignments may be graded according to skill, the difficulty of doing them, or the quality of workmanship. Further, a job may include many positions, for a position is a job performed by, related to, a particular employee.

Thus, it may be noted that a position is a "collection of tasks and responsibilities regularly assigned to one person" while a job is a "group of positions, which involve regular essentially the same duties, responsibilities, skill and knowledge." A position consists of a set of duties assigned to an individual. There may be, say five persons, all whom are classified under the same job; and yet each may perform a slightly different- work. Therefore each may perform a slightly different work. Therefore, each person would have a different position — position of a secretary, for example. It may be noted that while a "job is impersonal the position is personal."

Job Analysis: It is a procedure by which pertinent information is obtained about job, i.e., "it is a detailed and systematic study of information relating to the operations and responsibilities of a specific job." An authority has defined job analysis as "the process of determining, by observation and study, and reporting pertinent information relating to the nature of a specific job. It is the determination of the tasks which comprise the job and of the skills, knowledge, abilities and responsibilities required of the worker for a successful performance and which differentiate one job from all other."

Job Description: It is a written record of the duties, responsibilities and requirements of a particular job. It "is concerned with the job itself and not with the work." "It is a statement describing the job in such terms as its title, location, duties, working conditions and hazards". In other words, it tells us 'what is to be done' and 'how it is to be done' and 'why.' It is a standard of function, in that it defines the appropriate and authorised contents of a job.

Job Specification: It is a standard of personnel and designates the qualities required for an acceptable performance. It is written record of the requirements sought in an individual worker for a given job. In other words, it refers to a summary of the personal characteristics required for a job. It is a statement of the minimum acceptable human qualities necessary for the proper performance of a job.

Job Design: It is the division of the total task to be performed into the manageable and efficient units positions, departments and divisions - and to provide for their proper integration. The sub-division of work is both on a horizontal scale - with different tasks across the organisation being performed by different people and on the vertical scale, in which higher levels of the organisation are responsible for the supervision of more people, the co-ordination of sub-groups, more complex planning, etc.

Job Analysis (JA): After a job has been defined, it is analysed, i.e., each task is described in detail. JA is a procedure and a tool for determining the specified tasks, operations and requirements of each job. "It is the process of getting information about jobs: specially, what the worker does; how he gets it done; why he does it; skill, education and training required; relationship to other jobs; physical demands; environmental conditions." In other words, it refers to the anatomy of the job. It is a complete study of job, embodying every known and determinable factor, including the duties and responsibilities involved in its performance, the conditions under which the performance is carried on, the nature of the task, the qualities required in the worker, and such conditions of employment as pay, hour, opportunities and privileges. It also emphasises the relation to one job to others in the organisation.

Purpose and Uses of Job Analysis

A comprehensive JA programme is an essential ingredient of sound personnel management. It is the major input to forecasting future human resource requirements, job modifications, job evaluation, determination of proper compensation, and the writing of job evaluation, determination of proper compensation, and the writing of job descriptions. It is of fundamental importance to manpower management programmes because of the wider applicability of its results. The information provided by JA is useful, if not essential, in almost every phase of employee relations.

1. **Organisation and Manpower Planning:** It is helpful in organisation planning, for it defines labour needs in concrete terms and co-ordinates the activities of the work force, and clearly divides duties and responsibilities.
2. **Recruitment, Selection:** By indicating the specific requirements of each job (i.e., the skills and knowledge), it provides a realistic basis for the hiring, training, placement, transfer and promotion of personnel. "Basically, the goal is to match the job requirements with a worker's aptitude, abilities and interests. It also help in

charting the channel of romotion and in showing lateral lines of transfer."

3. **Wage and Salary Administration:** By indicating the qualifications required for doing a specified job and the risks and hazards involved in its performance, it helps in salary and wage administration. Job analysis is used as a foundation for job evaluation.
4. **Job Re-engineering:** Job analysis provides information which enables us to change jobs in order to permit their being manned by personnel with specific characteristics and qualifications. This takes two forms: (a) Industrial engineering activitity, which is concerned with operational analysis, motion study, work simplification methods and improvement in the place of work and its measurement, and aims at improving efficiency, reducing unit labour costs, and establishing the production standard which the employee is expected to meet; and (b) Human engineering activity, which takes into consideration human capabilities, both physical and psychological, and prepares the ground for complex operations of industrial administration, increased efficiency and better productivity.
5. **Employee Training and Management Development:** Job analysis provides the necessary information to the management of training and development programmes. It helps it to determine the content and subject matter of in-training courses. It also helps in checking application information, interviewing, weighing test results, and in checking references.
6. **Performance Appraisal:** It helps in establishing clear cut standards which may be compared with the actual contribution of each individual.
7. **Health and Safety:** It provides an opportunity for identifying hazardous conditions and unhealthy environmental factors so that corrective measures may be taken to minimise and avoid the possibility of accidents.

In sum, it may be noted that job analysis is a systematic procedure for securing and it has many uses in the management reporting the information which of personnel. It determines the qualifications required for a job; provides guidance in recruitment and selection; evaluates current employees for transfer or promotion, and job evaluation and helps by means of appraisal and counselling; for establishing improved methods of analysing problems of health, safety and fatigue; it functions as a guide in connection with discipline and grievances and as a basis for transfers, lay-offs and as a basis of comparison of the pay rates obtaining in other organisations; and it establishes workloads and job assignments. It also helps in redesigning the jobs to improve operational performance or to enrich job content and employee improvement. Managers may develop ways of giving their employees an increased sense of personnel accomplishment and control over themselves and their work.

JA produces four kinds of documentation and procedures that are crucial to personnel activities: (i) Job descriptions; (ii) Job specifications; (iii) Job evaluation, and (iv) Personnel assessment. In turn, the procedures and documentation are basic inputs for diverse personnel functions.

Contents of Job Analysis

A job analysis provides the following information:

(i) *Job identification:* Its title, including its code number;

(ii) *Significant characteristics of a job:* Its location, physical setting, supervision, - union jurisdiction, hazards and discomforts;

(iii) *What the typical worker does:* Specific operation and tasks that make up an assignment, their relative timing and importance, their simplicity, routine or complexity, the responsibility or safety of others for property, funds, confidence and trust;

(iv) *Which materials and equipment a worker uses:* Metals, plastics, grains, yams, milling machines, punch presses and micrometers;

(v) *How a job is performed:* Nature of operation — lifting, handling, cleaning, washing, feeding, removing, drilling, driving, setting up and many others;

(vi) *Required personnel attributes:* Experience, training, apprenticeship, physical strength, co-ordination or dexterity, physical demands, mental capabilities, aptitudes, social skills;

(vii) *Job relationship:* Experience required, opportunities for advancement, patterns of promotions, essential co-operation, direction, or leadership from and for a job.

It is obvious from the foregoing that a job analysis is usually a clear indication of a job description and job specification.

The Steps in Job Analysis

There are five basic steps required for doing a job analysis, viz.,

Step 1: *Collection of Background Information:* According to Terry, "the make-up of a job, its relation to other jobs, and its requirements for competent performance are essential information needed for a job evaluation. This information can be had by reviewing available background information such as organisation charts (which show how the job in question relates to other jobs and where they fit into the overall organisation); class specifications (which describe the general requirements of the class of job to which the job under analysis belongs); and the existing job descriptions which provide a starting point from which to build the revised job description.

Job Analysis

(at process for obtaining all pertinent job facts)

Job description	Job specification
Statements containing items such as	A statement of the human requirements for doing
(a) Job identifications (job title, location, occupational code, alternative, department and units where it exist	(a) Physical make – up or characteristics.
(b) Job summary (gives a quick capsule explanation of the contents of a job, its hazards and discomfort	(b) Psychological characteristics
(c) Duties performed (says the what, how and why of a job ; also describe a workers responsibility in regards to custody of money, supervision of the other workers, training of subordinate, etc.	(c) Personal characteristics
(d) Relation to other jobs (helps in locating a job in the job hierarchy)	(d) Responsibilities
(e) Supervision given/taken (helps in locating a jobs in the job hierarchy).	(e) Others factors of a demographic nature (sex, age, education, language, ability to read, write and speak).
(f) Machine, tools equipment (what types of tools/equipment materials is used. (g) Materials and forms used.	
(h) Condition of work location – factory/ office /inside/outside/overheads/undergrounds/solitary gang; time – day, night, overtime, peak, loads, uniformity of work; posture – standing, sitting, stopping, clinging, walking, reaching, lifting; speeds –quick, moderate, slow accuracy, coarse, fine exacting, health hazard –ventilation, illumination, nerve strain, eye-strain, moisture, heat, dust, humidity, fumes, acids, exposures to such disagreeable features, as dirt, noise, etc.	
(i) Hazards (accidents hazards)	

Step 2: Selection or Representative position to be analysed: Since the analysis of all jobs would be time-consuming, flow representative positions should be analysed.

Step 3: Collection of Job Analysis Data: Job data on features of the job, required employee qualifications and requirements, should be collected either from the employees who actually perform a job; or from other employees (such as foremen of supervisors) who watch the workers doing a job and thereby acquire knowledge about it; or from the outside persons, known as the trade job analysts who are appointed to watch employees performing a job.

The duties of such a trade job analyst are: (i) to outline the complete scope of a job and to consider all the physical and mental activities involved in determining what the worker does. For this purpose, he studies the physical methods used by a worker to accomplish his task (including-the use of machinery, tools and his own movements and necessary mental facilities); (ii) find out why a worker does a job; and for this purpose he studies why each task is essential for the overall result; and (iii) the skill factor which may be needed in the worker to differentiate between jobs and establish the extent of the difficulty of any job.

Step 4: A Job Description: The information collected is to be developed in the form of a job description. This is a written statement that describes the main features of the job, as well the qualifications/activities which the job incumbents must possess.

Step 5: Developing Job Specification: The last step is to convert the Job Description statements into Job Specifications, i.e., to specifically mention what personal qualities, traits, skills and background is necessary for getting the job done.

Techniques of Job Analysis Data

The determination of job tasks, the concomitant skills and abilities necessary for successful performance, and the responsibilities inherent in the job can be obtained through such methods or approaches as the following:

(i) Personal observation;

(ii) Sending out questionnaires;

(iii) Maintenance of log records; and

(iv) Conducting personal interviews.

(i) Personal Observation: The materials and equipment used, the working conditions and probable hazards, and an understanding of what the work involves are the facts which should be known by an analyst. Direct observation is especially useful in jobs that consist primarily of observable physical ability, like the jobs of draftsman, mechanic, spinner or weaver.

(ii) Sending Out Questionnaires: The method is usually employed by engineering consultants. Properly drafted questionnaires are sent out to job-holders for completion and are returned to supervisors. However, the information received is often unorganised and incoherent. The idea in issuing questionnaire is to elicit the necessary information from job-holders so that any error may first be discussed with the employee and, after due corrections, may be submitted to the job analyst.

(iii) Maintenance of Log Records: The employee maintains a daily diary record of duties he performs, making the time at which each task is started and finished. But this system is incomplete, for it does not give us any desirable data on supervisor relationship, the equipment used, and working conditions. Moreover, it is time-consuming.

(iv) Personnel Interviews: May be held by the analyst with the employees, and answers to relevant questions may be recorded. But the method is time-consuming and costly.

However, it may be noted that the personal observation and interview approach are more or less complete and accurate. If a particular job is simple and repetitive, observation may be the only technique required. Otherwise, in most cases, interviews coupled with observation constitute the desirable approach.

Caroll L. Shartle, Otis and Lenhert have provided the following suggestions for making the job analyst's task simple:

(i) Introduce yourself so that the worker knows who you are and why you are there;

(ii) Show a sincere interest in the worker and the job that is analysed;

(iii) Do not try to tell the employee how to do his job;

(iv) Try to talk to the employees and supervisors in their own language;

(v) Do not confuse the work with the workers;

(vi) Do a complete job study within the objectives of the programmes; and

(vii) Verify the job information obtained.

Position or Job Description (JD)

"Job description" is an important document which is basically descriptive in nature and contains a statement of job analysis. It provides both organisational information (location in structure, authority, etc.) and functional information (what the work is). It approved by defines the scope of job activities, major responsibilities, and positioning of the job in the organisation. It provides the worker, analyst, and supervisor with a clear idea of what the worker must do to meet the demands of the job.

"Job description" is different from "performance assessment". The former concern such functions as planning, co-ordinating, and assigning responsibility; while the latter concerns the quality of performance itself. Though job description is not assessment, it provides an important basis for establishing assessment standards and objectives.

Job description describe 'jobs,' not 'job holders'. The movement of employees due to promotion, quits, etc. would create instability to job descriptions if people rather than jobs are described.

Uses of Job Description

Job description has several uses, such as:

(i) Preliminary drafts can be used as a basis for productive group discussion, particularly if the process starts at the executive level.

(ii) It aids in the development of job specifications, which are useful in planning recruitment, in training and in hiring people with required skills.

(iii) It can be used to orient new employees toward basic responsibilities and duties.

(iv) It is a basic document used in developing performance standards.

(v) It can be used for job evaluation, a wage and salary administration technique.

A job description enables the manager to frame suitable questions to be asked during an interview. It is particularly helpful when the application form is used as a tool for eliminating the unfit personnel. According to Zerga, who analysed 401 articles on job description about 30 years ago, a job description helps us in:

(i) Job grading and classification;

(ii) Transfers and promotions;

(iii) Adjustments of grievances;

(iv) Defining and outlining promotional steps;

(v) Establishing a common understanding of a job between employers and employees;

(vi) Investigating accidents;

(vii) Indicating faulty work procedures or duplication of papers;

(viii) Maintaining, operating and adjusting machinery;

(ix) Time and motion studies;

(x) Defining the limits of authority;

(xi) Indicating case of personal merit;

(xii) Studies of health and fatigue;

(xiii) Scientific guidance;

(xiv) Determining jobs suitable for occupational therapy;

(xv) Providing hiring specifications; and

(xvi) Providing performance indicators.

Job description helps top executives, especially when they jointly discuss one another's responsibilities. Overlapping or confusion can then be pointed out; questions can be raised about the major thrust of each position, and problems of structure can be identified. A job description becomes a vehicle for organisational change and improvement.

Some companies have more than one job description for each job. A detailed version may be used in training and in evaluating a job, while a shorter version may be used in planning and hiring of management.

Components or Content of Job Description: A job description contains the following data:

1. Job identification, or Organisational Position which includes the job title, alternative title, department, division, plant and code number of the job. The job title identifies and designates the job properly. The department, division, etc., indicate the name of the department where it is situated — whether it is the maintenance department, mechanical shop, etc. The location gives the name of the place. The portion of job description gives answer to two important questions: to what higher level job is this job accountable; and who is supervised directly?
2. Job Summary serves two important purposes. First, it provides a short definition which is useful as an additional identification information when a job title is not adequate. Second, it serves as a summary to orient the reader towards an understanding of detailed

information which follows. It gives the reader a "quick capsule explanation" of the content of a job usually in one or two sentences.

3. Job duties and responsibilities give a comprehensive listing of the duties together with some indication of the frequency of occurrence or percentage of time devoted to each major duty. It is regarded as the heart of a job. It tells us what needs to be done? how it should be done? and why it should be done? It also describes the responsibilities related to the custody of money, the supervision of workers and the training of subordinates.
4. Relation to other jobs: This helps to locate the job in the organisation by indicating the job immediately below or above it in the job hierarchy. It also gives an idea of the vertical relationships of work flow and procedures.
5. Supervision: Under it is given the number of persons to be supervised along with their job titles, and the extent of supervision involved - general, intermediate or close supervision.
6. Machine, tools and equipment define each major type or trade name of –the machines and tools and the raw materials used.
7. Working conditions usually give us information about the environment in which a job holder must work. These include cold, heat, dust, wetness, moisture, fumes, odour, oily conditions, etc. obtaining inside the organisation.
8. Hazards give us the nature of risks to life and limb, their possibilities of occurrence, etc.

Developing Job Descriptions or Guidelines for Writing a Job Description

Opinions differ on how to write job descriptions. Some experts are of the view that these should be written in detail and in terms of work flow. Others feel that these should be written in terms of goals or results to be achieved, in other words as performance standards (or what is popularly known as "management by objectives"). The prevalent thinking is that job descriptions should be written in terms of duties and responsibilities, i.e., in terms of functions performed.

Job descriptions are written by Personnel Department or its representatives.

Although there is no set way of writing a job description, the following pattern is fairly typical, and used by many companies.

(i) A paragraph is allocated to each major task or responsibility.

(ii) Paragraphs are numbered and arranged in a logical order, task sequence or importance.

(iii) Sentences are begun with an active verb, e.g., "types letters," "interviews the candidates," "collects, sorts out, routes and distributes mail."

(iv) Accuracy and simplicity are emphasised rather than an elegant style.

(v) Brevity is usually considered to be important but is largely conditioned by the type of job being analysed and the need for accuracy.

(vi) Examples of work performed are often quoted and are useful in making the job description explicit.

(vii) Job descriptions, particularly when they are used as bases for training, often incorporate details of the faults which may be encountered in operator tasks and safety check-points.

(viii) Statements of opinion, such as "dangerous situations are encountered," should be avoided.

(ix) When job description are written for supervisory jobs, the main factors (such as manning, cost control, etc.) are identified and listed. Each factor is then broken down into a series of elements with a note on the supervisor's responsibility.

The British Institute of Management Publication adds four more guidelines:

(i) Give a clear, concise and readily understandable picture of the whole job;

(ii) Describe in sufficient detail each of the main duties and responsibilities;

(iii) Indicate the extent of direction received and supervision given;

(iv) Ensure that a new employee understands the job if he reads the job description.

Limitations of Job Description

In any use of job descriptions, it should be remembered that these descriptions are not perfect reflections of the job. "The object of a job description is to differentiate it from other jobs and set its outer limits." Further, executives tend to carry work patterns with them into new jobs, thus modifying the job drastically.

To avoid such problems, care must be exercised in writing a job description to make it as accurate as possible, and at the managerial or professional level, it should be reviewed and discussed after the job. Jobs tend to be dynamic, not static and a job description can quickly go out of date. Therefore, jobs should be constantly revised and kept up-to-date, and the personnel and the other departmental heads should be apprised of changes.

Both supervisors and subordinates should understand the uses to which a job description would be put so that appropriate information is recorded by them. The relevant parties should agree that a job description fairly reflects the job; otherwise job evaluation and job performance review would seem to be unfair.

Job Specifications

The job specification takes the job description and answers the question. "What human traits and experience are needed to do the job well?" It tells what kind of person to recruit and for what qualities that person should be tested.

Job specifications translate the job description into terms of the human qualifications which are required for a successful performance of a job. They are intended to serve as a guide in hiring and job evaluation. As a guide in hiring, they deal with such characteristics as are available in an application bank, with testing, interviews, and checking of references.

Job specification are developed with the co-operation of the personnel department and various supervisors in the whole organisation. The personnel department co-ordinates the writing of job descriptions and job specifications and secures agreement on the qualifications required.

These specifications relate to:

(a) Physical characteristics, which include health, strength, endurance, age-range, body size, height, weight, vision, voice, poise, eye, hand and foot co-ordination, motor co-ordination, and colour discrimination.

(b) Psychological characteristics or special aptitudes which include such qualities as manual dexterity, mechanical aptitude, ingenuity, judgement, resourcefulness, analytical ability, mental concentration and alertness.

(c) Personal characteristics or traits of temperament, such as personal appearance, good and pleasing manners, emotional stability, aggressiveness or submissiveness, extroversion or introversion, leadership, co-operativeness, initiative and drive, skill in dealing with others, unusual sensory qualities of sight, smell, hearing, adaptability, conversational ability, etc.

(d) Responsibilities, which include supervision of others, responsibility for production, process and equipment; responsibility for the safety of others; responsibility for generating confidence and trust; responsibility for preventing monetary loss.

(e) Other features of a demographic nature, which are age, sex, education, experience and language ability.

The items to be included in job specifications vary according to the nature of an organisation and the uses to which they are put. However, items like age, sex, experience, skill, education, dexterity and personality are invariably included in job specifications: for example, five years experience; ability to lift 30 kgs; versatility in languages and fluency in speech; ability to type 100 words per minute and take shorthand dictation at 120 words per minute.

Job specifications are mostly based on the educated guesses of supervisors and personnel managers. They give their opinion as to who do they think should be considered for a job in terms of education, intelligence, training etc. One of the most extensive "judgmental" approaches to developing job specifications is contained in a Dictionary of Occupational Titles, published by the U.S. Training and Employment service. Its description for a Personnel Manager's job is as follows:

"Personnel Manager: Director personnel; manager, employee relations; Personnel supervisor.

"Plans and carries out policies relating to all phases of personnel activities:

> "Organisations, recruitment, selection and training procedures, and directs activities of subordinates directly concerned. Confers with company and union official to establish pension and insurance plans, workmen's compensation policies, recreational, and educational activities. Studies personnel records for information, such as educational background, work record and supervisor's reports, to determine personnel suitable for promotions and transfers. May represent — company in negotiating wage agreements with labour representatives. May act as liaison between management and labour within organisation."

Job specifications may also be based on statistical analysis. This is done to determine the relationship between: (1) some predictor or human trait (as height, intelligence, finger dexterity, etc.) and (2) some indicator or criterion of job effectiveness (such as performance as rated by the supervisor).

The statistical analysis comprises five steps: (i) analysing the job and determining criteria of success; (ii) selecting personnel traits which should predict successful performance; (iii) testing candidates for these traits; (iv) measuring these candidates' subsequent job performance; and (v) statistically analysing the relationship between the 'human trait' and job performance.

Performance Standard (Management by Objectives and Results)

Performance standards are the yardsticks by which the actual performance is measured. The purpose may be to encourage more self-direction in the development of personal goals congruent with overall objectives, and to 'enhance creditivity and job commitment'. While job descriptions essentially set what is to be done as a job, performance standards describe how much and how well a job is performed. Job performance induces "goal-consciousness" among superiors and subordinates. It is a means for performance review based on actual accomplishment. Performance standard may be in the form of a job description expanded to include a statement of job goals for some period; or it may be separate statements supplemental to a job description. These should be written in quantitative terms, whenever possible.

The advantage of written job performance standards is that each person knows specifically what is expected of him in terms of goals and targets. But, in actual practice, some job aspects are difficult to reduce to quantitative terms. When this is so, qualitative statements must be made.

Target for safety, reduction in waste, increase in sales, the building of new plants, and the starting of new production are all performance standards implicit in jobs.

Job performance standards should be based on overall objectives and should spread from the top throughout the entire organisation. However, such standards should not be imposed upon members in an autocratic and dictatorial manner, for that would generate resistance. If subordinates participate in setting their own standards, they are likely to set them high and be committed to achieving them.

Standards must be within the capabilities of the person involved in a job; and the motivational system of an enterprise must result in a willingness of a person to attain them. Unrealistically high standards are likely to be a source of friction between supervisors and subordinates, and lead to low performance.

Group discussions of targets and standards do result in getting things done, besides enhancing creativity and team effort. Likert says: "The salesmen in the offices using group methods of supervision sell more on the average than do men in the other offices, and they have more favourable attitudes towards their work."

Recently new programmes termed as "Zero-Defects" programmes have been developed especially in the armed services, jet aircraft, aerospace, the defence industries, etc. where reliable products are needed and for this special programmes are designed to encourage the commitment of employees to high quality standards and to "do it right the first time". Such programmes are also known as PRIDE and Target-Zero. They are based on the basic assumption that most people want to do 'quality' work provided they are given the proper support and recognition. The recognition may be given in the form of plaques, certificates, letters, news items, etc.

Work Rules

Work rules are essential in organisational life. They are pre-determined decisions that a certain course of action will be taken if certain contingencies arise. They are an integral part of the system designed to facilitate all broad operational processes because they are adjuncts of job description and performance standards. They are the minimum standards of conduct or performance which apply to groups of persons. They serve the following purposes:

(i) They canalise the process of an enterprise in the direction of its goals.

(ii) They serve as control devices, since the management uses them as standards against which to apply sanctions in order to ensure a reasonable level of conformity.

(iii) They ensure predictability of behaviour so that an organisation may function without undue disturbance, and its total performance is achieved.

Examples of Work Rules

- Rules pertaining to starting and stopping work;

- Rest periods;
- Insubordination;
- Fighting or drinking on the job;
- Smoking in hazardous areas;
- Report of injuries;
- Time-keeping.

Any violation of rules usually results in punishment or penalty. Offences considered serious enough to warrant immediate discharge are dishonesty, insubordination, drunkenness on duty, and deliberate damage to material or property. Lesser penalties include oral or written warnings, demotions, transfers or disciplinary lay-off.

A partial list of the offences, which may lead to disciplinary action, has been compiled by the American Management Association. These offences are:

- Absence without leave;
- Dishonesty, deception, fraud;
- Drunkenness or possession of liquor on the job;
- Deliberate damage to material or property;
- Fighting on the job;
- Stealing,
- Falsification of accounts;
- Failure to meet work standards;
- Smoking in prohibited or hazardous areas;
- Use of abusive, threatening, or profane language;
- Insubordination;
- Repeated tardiness;
- Carrying concealed weapons;
- Immoral conduct;
- Sleeping on duty;
- Erratic work schedule.

Work rules should be reasonable. If they are irrelevant or unreasonably strict, they are liable to be circumvented, and lead to subterfuge and resentment. If they are too lax they will lead to non-completion of the work in time. Again, if they are arbitrary, they are likely to be resented and ignored. Therefore, rules should be reasonable, and explained clearly to employees. If they are reasonable they assist in the attainment of an organisation's need for security, order, predictability, and avoidance of physical harm. Rules should be periodically evaluated and revised; they should have a definite organisational purpose, and must not coniflict with the employees' interest.

Rules are framed by the chief executive and implemented by the personnel manager. Once these rules are endorsed by the top management or are negotiated into a Labour Agreement, all the managers are responsible for their enforcement.

Chapter - 8

Recruitment and Selection Process

Recruitment

Recruitment forms the first stage in the process which continues with selection and ceases with the placement of the candidate. It is the next step in the procurement function, the first being the manpower planning. Recruiting makes it possible to acquire the number and types of people necessary to ensure the continued operation of the organisation. Recruiting is the discovering of potential applicants for actual or anticipated organisational vacancies. In other words, it is a 'linking activity' bringing together those with jobs and those seeking jobs.

As Yoder and others point out: "Recruitment is a process to discover the sources of manpower to meet the requirements of the staffing schedule and to employ effective measures for attracting that manpower in adequate numbers to facilitate effective selection of an efficient working force." Accordingly, the purpose of recruitment is to locate sources of manpower to meet job requirements and job specifications.

Recruitment has been regarded as the most important function of personnel administration, because unless the right type of people are hired, even the best plans, organisation charts and control systems would not do much good. Flippo views recruitment both as 'positive' and 'negative' activity. He says: "It is a process of searching for prospective employees and stimulating and encouraging them to apply for jobs in an organisation. It is often termed positive in that it stimulates people to apply for jobs to increase the 'hiring ratio,' i.e., the number of applicants for a job. Selection, on the other hand tends to be negative because it rejects a good member of those who apply, leaving only the best to be hired."

Factors Affecting Recruitment

All organisations, whether large or small, do engage in recruiting activity, though not to the same extent. This differs with: (i) the size of the organisation; (ii) the employment conditions in the community where the organisation is located; (iii) the effects of past recruiting efforts which show the organisation's ability to locate and keep good performing people; (iv) working conditions and salary and benefit packages offered by the organisation — which may influence turnover and necessitate future recruiting; (v) the rate of growth of organisation; (vi) the level of seasonality of operations and future expansion and production programmes; and (vii) cultural, economic and legal factors, etc.

Factors governing recruitment may broadly be divided as internal and external factors

The internal factors are:

(i) Recruiting policy of the organisation;
(ii) Human resource planning strategy of the company;
(iii) Size of the organisation and the number of employees employed;
(iv) Cost involved in recruiting employees, and finally;
(v) Growth and expansion plans of the organisation.

The external factors are:

(i) Supply and demand of specific skills in the labour market;
(ii) Political and legal considerations such as reservation of jobs for SCs, STs, and so on.
(iii) Company's image-perception of the job seekers about the company.

Theories Regarding Recruitment

Recruitment is a two-way street: it takes a recruiter and a recruitee. Just as the recruiter has a choice whom to recruit and whom not, so also the prospective employee has to make the decision if he should apply for that organisation's job. The individual makes this decision usually on three different basis, the objective factor, critical contact, and subjective factor.

"The objective factor theory views the process of organisational choice as being one of weighing and evaluating a set of measurable characteristics of employment offers, such as pay, benefits, location, opportunity for advancement, the nature of the work to be performed, and educational opportunities."

"The critical contact theory suggests that the typical candidate is unable to make a meaningful differentiation of organisation's offers in terms of objective or subjective factors, because of his limited or very short contact with the organisation. Choice can be made only when the applicant can readily perceive the factors such as the behaviour of the recruiter, the nature of the physical facilities, and the efficiency in processing paper work associated with the application."

"The subjective factor theory emphasises the congruence between personality patterns and the 'image' of the organisation, i.e., choices are made on a highly personal and emotional basis."

Constraints Limit the Freedom of Manager to Recruit

No employer could ever freely choose the "best" candidate because various forces impinge upon such selection. Such constraints are:

1. **The Image of the Organisation:** The prospective candidate may not be interested in getting job in the particular organisation either because its reputation or goodwill is not good in the community, or because the conditions of work are unsafe or it is indifferent to the need of the community. All such factors reduce its ability to attract the best personnel available.
2. **The Unattractive Job:** If the job is regarded as boring, hazardous, anxiety creating or lacking in promotion potential, people would not be attracted to such an organisation.
3. **Internal Organisational Policies:** If the policy aims at providing promotion to its employee from within, people would be attracted to it, because such a policy enjoys several advantages such as that of creating good public relations, building high morale, encouraging good people who are ambitious and improving the probability of a good selection.
4. **Union Requirements can also Restrict Recruiting Sources:** Some unions emphasise on recruitment to members of the unions only. Where such situation occurs, management has to recruit from a restricted supply.
5. **Governments Influence:** An employer cannot distinguish any individual, on the basis of physical appearance, sex or religious background, for purposes of recruitment.

Steps on Recruitment Process

As was mentioned earlier, recruitment refers to the process of identifying and attracting job seekers so as to build a pool of qualified job applicants. The process comprises five inter-related stages, viz., (i) planning, (ii) strategy development, (iii) searching, (iv) screening, and (v) evaluation and control.

According to Famularo, personnel recruitment process involves five elements, viz., a recruitment policy, a recruitment organisation, a forecast of manpower, the development of sources of recruitment, and different techniques used for utilising these sources, and a method of assessing the recruitment programme.

Recruitment Policy

Such a policy asserts the objectives of the recruitment and provides a framework of implementation of there recruitment programme in the form of procedures. As Yoder and other observe:

"Such a policy may involve a commitment to broad principles such as filling vacancies with the best qualified individuals. It may embrace several issues such as extent of promotion from within, attitudes of enterprise in recruiting its old employees, handicaps, minority groups, women employees, part-time employees, friends and relatives of present employees. It may also involve the organisation system to be developed for implementing recruitment programme and procedures to the employed."

Therefore, a well considered and pre-planned recruitment policy, based on corporate goals, study of environment and the corporate needs, may avoid hasty or ill-considered decisions and may go a long way to man the organisation with the right type of personnel.

A good recruitment policy must contain these elements:

(a) Organisation's objectives -both in the short-term and long-term- must be taken into consideration as a basic parameter for recruitment decisions and needs of the personnel -area-wise, job-family-wise.

(b) Identification of the recruitment needs to take decisions regarding the balance of the qualitative dimensions of the would be recruits, i.e., the recruiters should prepare profiles for each category of workers and accordingly work out the main specifications, decide the sections, departments or branches where they should be placed and identify the particular responsibilities which may be immediately assigned to them.

(c) Preferred sources of recruitment, which would be tapped by the organisation, e.g., for skilled or semi-skilled manual workers, internal sources and employment exchanges may be preferred; for highly specialised categories and managerial personnel, other sources besides the former, may be utilised.

(d) Criteria of selection and preferences: These should be based on conscious thought and serious deliberations. In some cases trade unions may be consulted in working out the recruitment policy. In others, management may take the unilateral decision.

(e) The cost of recruitment and financial implications of the same.

A "recruitment policy," in its broadest sense, "involves a commitment by the employer to such general principles as:

(i) To find and employ the best qualified persons for each job;

(ii) To retain the best and most promising of those hired;

(iii) To offer promising opportunities for life-time working careers; and

(iv) To provide programmes and facilities for personal growth on the job."

According to Yoder, "the recruitment policy is concerned with quantity and qualications (viz., and Q1 and Q2) of manpower." It establishes broad guidelines for the staffing process. Generally, the following factors are involved in a recruitment policy:

(i) To carefully observe the letter and spirit of the relevant public policy on hiring and, on the whole, employment relationship;

(ii) To provide individual employees with the maximum of employment security, avoiding, frequent lay-off or lost time;

(iii) To provide each employee with an open road and encouragement in the continuing development of his talents and skills;

(iv) To assure each employee of the organisation interest in his personal goals and employment objectives;

(v) To assure employees of fairness in all employment relationships, including promotions and transfers;

(vi) To avoid cliques which may develop when several members of the same household or community are employed in the organisation;

(vii) To provide employment in jobs which are engineered to meet the qualifications of handicapped workers and minority sections; and

(viii) To encourage one or more strong, effective, responsible trade unions among the employees.

Prerequisites of a Good Recruitment Policy

The recruitment policy of an organisation must satisfy the following conditions:

(i) It should be in conformity with its general personnel policies;

(ii) It should be flexible enough to meet the changing needs of an organisation;

(iii) It should be so designed as to ensure employment opportunities for its employees on a long-term basis so that the goals of the organisation should be achievable; and it should develop the potentialities of employees;

(iv) It should match the qualities of employees with the requirements of the work for which they are employed; and

(v) It should highlight the necessity of establishing job analysis.

The nature and extent of the recruitment programme depends on a number of factors, including the skills required, the state of the labour market, general economic conditions, and the image of the employer. A company which has a reputation of paying fair wages, providing good employee benefits and taking interest in employee welfare activities would attract a larger number of applicants than it needs without making any extra recruiting effort. Small companies which hire only a few persons each year may not need to do more than spread the word around the plant or office that a vacancy exists. However, as a result of regulations and pressures from society and the government, the recruitment programme now requires the employers to go out and actively seek job applicants from groups of those who may not otherwise apply for employment.

Recruitment Organisation

There is no general procedure for hiring new personnel which is applicable to all business enterprises. Each enterprise has its "tailor-made" procedure which brings it the desired quantity and quality of manpower at the minimum possible cost. The most commonly adopted practice is to centralise the recruitment and selection function in a single office. All employment activity should be centralised if the policies of the top management are to be implemented consistently and efficiently. Only when personnel requisitions go through one central source and all employment records are kept up-to-date is there a possibility of maximum efficiency and success in hiring.

The advantages of centralising of recruitment and selection are:

(i) It reduces the administrative cost associated with selection by consolidating all activities in a single office;

(ii) It relieves line officers of the details involved in hiring workers, which is common under a decentralised plan;
(iii) It tends to make the selection of workers scientifically;
(iv) It makes possible the development of a centralised manpower pool in a company;
(v) It provides a wider opportunity for placing an applicant in several departments of the company;
(vi) It tends to reduce favouritism as a basis for selection.

This centralised department is generally known as the Employee Office, or the Recruitment Section. The staff personnel is attached to it. This enables specialists to concentrate upon the recruitment function; and soon they become very efficient in the use of various recruitment techniques.

This office should be properly equipped with furniture. Its waiting room should be roomy, clean and well ventilated; it should have lighting facilities and drinking water, and it should be comfortable. This room should also have a table or a counter so that candidates may fill in their application blanks conveniently. It is desirable that personnel records be filed in a room accessible to the interviewer.

This office is concerned with the following functions:
(i) Establishing employment standards;
(ii) Making initial contact with prospective employees;
(iii) Testing;
(iv) Conducting physical examinations;
(v) Conducting final interviews;
(vi) Filling out necessary forms and record keeping;
(vii) Introducing the employee to his superior; and
(viii) Following up the employee.

It may be noted that in a small organisation, recruiting procedure is merely informal and generally the "line official" may be responsible to handle this function. But in larger organisations, it is entrusted to a staff unit with Personnel or Industrial Relations Department. However, recruitment remains the line responsibility as far as the personnel requisition forms are originated by the line personnel.

Forecast of Manpower Requirements

This aspect has already been discussed in the previous chapter. It is only to be stated here that a 'requisition' or an 'indent' for recruitment has to be submitted by the line official. Such 'indents' usually specify: (i) the jobs or operations or positions for which the persons should be available; (ii) duration of their employment; (iii) salary to be offered and any other conditions and terms of employment which the indenting officer feels necessary.

The indents are then checked against the posts allotted to the department/branch and also against authorisation for expansion, if already granted. Financial implications of the proposed appointments and additional expenditure are worked out - of course, these would be within the budgetary sanctions of the department concerned. If the indents are found correct, the proposed recruitments are authorised and the initial pay, the scale and other admissible allowances are determined.

Finally, job-specifications and man-specifications are determined, in consultation with the line managers.

Sources of Recruitment

Before an organisation activity begins recruiting applicants, it should consider the most likely source of the type of employee it needs. Some companies try to develop new sources, while most only try to tackle the existing sources they have. These sources, accordingly, may be termed as internal and external.

Internal Sources

Internal sources are the most obvious sources. These include personnel already on the pay-roll of an organisation, i.e., its present working force. Whenever any vacancy occurs, somebody from within the organisation is upgraded, transferred, promoted or sometimes demoted. This source also includes personnel who were once on the pay-roll of the company but who plan to return or whom the company would like to rehire, such as those on leave of absence, those who quit voluntarily, or those on production lay-offs.

Merit: The use of an internal source has some merits:

(i) lt improves the morale of employees, for they are assured of the fact that they would be preferred over outsiders when vacancies occur.

(ii) The employer is in a better position to evaluate those presently employed than outside candidates. This is because the company maintains a record of the progress, experience and service of its employees.

(iii) It promotes loyalty among the employees, for it gives them a sense of job security and opportunities for advancement.

(iv) As the persons in the employment of the company are fully aware of, and well acquainted with, its policies and know its operating procedures, they require little training, and the chances are that they would stay longer in the employment of the organisation than a new outsider would.

(v) They are tried people and can, therefore, be relied upon.

(vi) It is less costly than going outside to recruit.

Demerits: However, this system suffers from certain defects as well.

(i) It often leads to inbreeding, and discourages new blood from entering an organisation.

(ii) There are possibilities that internal sources may "dry up", and it may be difficult to find the requisite personnel from within an organisation.

(iii) Since the learner does not know more than the lecturer, no innovations worth the name can be made. Therefore, on jobs which require original thinking (such as advertising, style, designing and basic research), this practice is not followed.

(iv) As promotion is based on seniority, the danger is that really capable hands may not be chosen. The likes and dislikes of the management may also play an important role in the selection of personnel.

This source is used by many organisations; but a surprisingly large number ignore this source, especially for middle management jobs. In other words, this source is the lode that is rarely mined. It is not only reasonable but wise to use this source, if the vacancies to be filled are within the capacity of the present employees; if adequate employee records have been maintained, and if opportunities are provided in advance for them to prepare themselves for promotion from "blue-collar" to "white-collar" jobs.

External Sources

These sources lie outside the organisation. They usually include:

(i) New entrants to the labour force, i.e., young, mostly inexperienced potential employees — the college students;

(ii) The unemployed - with a wide range of skills and abilities;

(iii) Retired experienced persons such as mechanics, machinists, welders, accountants;

(iv) Others not in the labour force, such as married women and persons from minority groups.

Merits: (i) External sources provide the requisite type of personnel for an organisation, having skill, training and education up to the required standard. (ii) Since persons are recruited from a large market, the best selection can be made without any distinctions of caste, sex or colour. (iii) In the long run, this source proves economical because potential employees do not need extra training for their jobs.

Demerits: However, this system suffers from what is called "brain drain," especially when experienced persons are raided or hunted by sister concerns.

Methods or Techniques of Recruitment

Dunn and Stephens summarise the possible recruiting methods into three categories: direct, indirect and third party".

Direct Methods

These include sending travelling recruiters to educational and professional institutions, employees' contacts with public, and manned exhibits. One of the widely used direct methods is that of sending of recruiters to colleges and technical schools. Most college recruiting is done in co-operation with the placement office of a college. The placement office usually provides help in attracting students, arranging interviews, furnishing space, and providing student resumes. For managerial, professional and sales personnel, campus recruiting is an extensive operation. Persons reading for MBA or other technical diplomas are picked up in this manner. For this purpose, carefully prepared brochures, describing the organisation and the jobs it offers, are distributed among students, before the interviewer arrives. The DCM, TATAs, and other enlightened firms maintain continuing contacts with institutions' placement officials with a view to recruiting staff regularly for different responsible positions.

Sometimes, firms directly solicit information from the concerned professors about students with an outstanding record.

Many companies have found employees' contact with the public a very effective method.

Other direct methods include sending recruiters to conventions and seminars, setting up exhibits at fairs, and using mobile offices to go to the desired centres.

Indirect Methods

Indirect methods involve mostly advertising in newspaper, on the radio, in trade and professional journals, technical magazines and brochures.

Advertising in newspapers and/or trade journals and magazines is the most frequently used method, when qualified or experienced personnel are not available from other sources. Senior posts are largely filled by such methods when they cannot be filled by promotion from within.

Advertising is very useful for recruiting blue-collar and hourly workers, as well as scientific, professional, and technical employees. "Local newspaper can be a good source of blue-collar workers, clerical employees, and lower-level administrative employees."

The main point is that the higher the position is in the organisation, or the more specialised the skills sought, the more widely dispersed advertisement is likely to be. The search for top executive might include advertisements in a national periodical; while the advertisement of blue-collar jobs is usually confined to the daily newspaper or regional trade journals.

The classified advertisement section of a daily newspaper or the Sunday weekly edition of *The Hindustan Times, The Times of India, The Tribune, Bharat Jyoti, The National Herald, The Free Press Journal, The Pioneer, Amrit Bazar Patrika, The Economic Times, The Hindu, The Indian Express* etc., carry advertisements for all types of positions. Such advertisements enable prospective candidates to screen themselves in order to find out whether they are fit for the job for which the advertisement has been issued. In order to be successful, an advertisement should be carefully written. If it is not properly written, it may not draw the right type of applicants or it may attract too many applicants who are not qualified for the job. It should be so framed as to attract attention — for example, by the use of different sizes and types of print. The first line should limit the audience somewhat and the next few lines should further screen out the readers who do not possess the necessary qualifications. It should provide specific information on job requirements and opportunities for advancement, the benefits to be enjoyed by working in the company; and it should emphasise facts related to the dignity of the job and to its professional aspects. "Frilly advertisements, containing exaggerated claims and gimmicky appeals, are to be avoided." Advertising can be very effective if its media are properly chosen.

According to Advertisement Tactics and Strategy in Personnel Recruitment, three points need to be borne in mind before an advertisement is inserted. First, to visualise the type of applicant one is trying to recruit. Second, to write out a list of the advantages a company offers; in other words, why the reader should work for the company. Third, to decide where to run the advertisement, not only in which area but in which newspaper having a local, state or nation-wide circulation."

Many organisations often place what is referred to as a blind advertisement, one in which there is no identification of the organisation. Respondents are asked to reply to a 'Post Office Box Number' or to a consulting firm that is acting as an intermediary between the applicant and the organisation. The large organisations with regional or national reputation do not usually use blind advertisements.

Other methods include advertising in publications, such as trade and professional journals, and radio or television announcements, as is done by many Indian manufacturers. Professional journals are read by people with specialised backgrounds and interests. Therefore, advertisements in these are generally selective.

Third Party Methods

These include the use of commercial or private employment agencies, state agencies, placement offices of schools, colleges and professional associations, recruiting firms, management consulting firms, indoctrination seminars for college professors, and friends and relatives.

Private employment agencies are widely used. They charge a small fee from an applicant. They specialise in specific occupations: general office help, salesmen, technical workers, accountants, computer staff, engineers and executives. These private agencies are brokers who bring employersi and employees together. The specialisation of these agencies enhances their capacity to interpret the needs of their clients, to seek out particular types of persons and to develop proficiency in recognising the talent personnel.

State or public employment agencies also known as Employment or Labour Exchanges, are the main agencies of public employment. They provide a clearing house for jobs and job information. Employers inform them of their personnel requirements, while job-seekers get information for them about the types of jobs that are referred to by employers. These agencies provide a wide range of services — counselling, assistance in getting jobs, information about the labour market, labour and wage rates. Schools, Colleges and Professional Institutions offer opportunities for recruiting their students. They operate placement services where complete bio-data and other particulars of the students are available. The companies that need employees maintain contact with the Guidance Counsellors of Employment Bureaus and teachers of business and vocational subjects. The prospective employers can review credentials and interview candidates for management trainees or probationers. Whether the education sought involves a higher secondary certificate, specific vocational training, or a college background with a bachelor's, master's, or doctoral degree, educational institutions provide an excellent source of potential employees for entry-level positions in organisations. These general and technical/ professional institutions provide blue-collar applicants, white-collar and managerial personnel. Sometimes, the organisations provide Work Study Programme to the students or summer jobs for undertaking a project in the establishment so as to get them interested in the organisation in question, and after completion of this, they may be absorbed by the companies concerned. Professional organisations or recruiting firms or executive recruiters maintain complete information records about employed executives. These firms are looked upon as 'head hunters', 'raiders' and 'pirates' by organisations which lose personnel through their efforts.

However, these same organisations may employ "executive search firms" to help them find executive talent." These consulting firms recommend persons of high caliber for managerial, marketing, and production engineers' posts. Indoctrination seminars for colleges professors are arranged to discuss the problem of companies and employees. Professors are invited to take part in these seminars. Visits to plants and banquets are arranged so that the participant professors may be favourably impressed. They may later speak well of a company and help it getting the required personnel.

Employee Referrals: Friends and relatives of present employees are also a good source from which employees may be drawn. When the labour market is very tight, large employers frequently offer their employees bonuses or prizes for any referrals who are hired and stay with the company for a specific length of time. Some companies maintain a register of former employees whose record was good to contact them when there are new job openings for which they are qualified. This method of recruitment, however, suffers from a serious defect that it encourages nepotism, i.e., persons of one's community or caste are employed, who may or may not be fit for the job.

Trade Unions also provide manual and skilled workers in sufficient numbers. Under agreement, they may agree as to who is to be given preference. But in case of adverse industrial relations, this technique may create difficulties.

Casual Labour or Applicant at the Gate : Most industrial units rely to some extent on the casual labour which presents itself daily at the factory gate or employment office. However, this source is uncertain, and the candidates cover a wide range of abilities. Even then, many of our industries make use of this source to fill up casual vacancies.

Unconsolidated Applications: For positions in which large number of candidates are not available from other sources, the companies may gain in keeping files of applications received from candidates who make direct enquiries about possible vacancies on their own, or may send unconsolidated applications. The information may be indexed and filed for future use when there are openings in these jobs. If necessary, the candidates may be requested to keep the organisation posted with any change in their qualifications, experience or achievements made.

Voluntary Organisations, such as private clubs, social organisations, might also provide employees —— handicapped, widowed or married women, old persons, retired hands, etc. in response to advertisements.

Computer Data Banks: When a company desires a particular type of employee, job specifications and requirements are fed into a computer, where they are matched against the resume data stored therein. The output is a set of resumes for individuals who meet the requirements. This method is very useful for identifying candidates for hard-to-fill positions which call for an unusual combination of skills.

Which particular source is to be tapped will depend on the policy of a firm, the position of labour supply, Government regulations and agreements with labour organisations. However, the personnel manager must be in close touch with these different sources and use them in accordance with his needs. The best management policy regarding recruitment is to look first within the organisation. If that source fails, external recruitment must be tackled.

According to Flippo, the present tendency among most business firms is to "home grow" their executive leaders." Koontz and O' Donnel rightly observe that the policy should be to "raise" talent rather than "raid" for it.

"Recruiting Practices and a Firm's Position in the Labour Market Degree of Tightness in the Sources Used for Area Covered for Labour Market Recruitment.

1. Most loose Direct hiring immediate vicinity
2. Intermediate Unions, friends and relatives, Part of an urban private and public agencies industrial area

3. Tight Advertising, nearby special. The whole urban sources (colleges, private industrial area agencies).
4. Most tight Labour scouting Regional and national.

Chart 8.1: Recruiting Practices and a Firm's Position in the Labour Market

Degree of tightness in the labour market	*Sources used for recruitment*	*Area covered for recruitment*
1. Most loose	Direct hiring	Immediate vicinity
2. Intermediate	Unions, friends and relatives, private and publics agencies	Part of an urban industrial areas
3. Tight	Advertisements, nearly special sources (colleges, private agencies)	The whole urbans industrial areas
4. Most tight	Labour scouting	Regional and national

Recruitment Practices in India

The different sources for recruitment in India have been classified thus (i) Within the organisation; (ii) Badli or temporary workers; (iii) Employment agencies; (iv) Casual callers; (v) Applicants introduced by friends and relatives in the organisation; (vi) Advertisements; and (vii) Labour contractors.

According to a survey of public and private sector employers by Prof. Basavaraj, the following methods were used to recruit employees:

(a) In the public sector (steel units), the major sources of recruitment in order of preference are: (i) Casual callers or employment seekers; (ii) Newspaper advertisements; (iii) Scheduled tribes and scheduled castes; (iv) Employment exchanges; (v) Other public undertakings; (vi) Internal advertisement; (vii) Displaced persons; (viii) Relative and friends; (ix) Employee recommendations; and (x) Institutions in the public sector (heavy engineering), the sources for non-supervisory staff are: (i) Employment exchanges; (ii) External advertisement; (iii) Internal advertisement; (iv) Central training institute; (v) Introduction by the liaison officer of a corporation; (vi) Deputation personnel; and (vii) Transfers from other public undertakings. (b) In the private sector, the survey disclosed that the procedures, though formulated, were not institutionalised in character. In some organisations, preference was given to sons and relatives of employees and to local people. In order of preference, the major sources are: (i) Advertisements; (ii) Employment exchanges; (iii) Relatives and friends; (iv) Casual callers; and (v) Employee recommendations.

The Problem of the "Sons of the Soil"

A controversy has arisen in recent years over giving preference in recruitment to "Sons of the Soil". In this connection the National Commission on Labour has observed the solution has to be sought in terms of the primacy of common citizenship, geographical mobility and economic feasibility of locating industrial units, on the one hand, and local aspiration on the other." It has suggested that:

(a) Young persons from families whose lands are acquired for industrial use should be provided training opportunities for employment in jobs which are likely to be created in new units set up on these lands;

(b) To remove apprehensions among local candidates, the following steps should be taken to supervise the implementation of the directives of the Government of India on recruitment for public sector projects:

   (i) While recruiting unskilled employees, first preference should be given to persons displaced from the areas required for the projects. The next to be preferred should be those who have been living in the same vicinity.

   (ii) The selection of persons to posts in lower scales should not be left entirely to the head of the unit. It should be made through a recruitment committee, with a nominee of the government of the state in which the unit is located.

   (iii) In the case of middle level technicians whose recruitment has to be on an all-India basis, a member of the State Public Service Commission should be associated in making selections in addition to the State Government official on the Board of Directors.

   (iv) Apart from the report sent to the concerned Ministry at the Centre, the undertaking should send a statement to the 'State Government at regular intervals, preferably every quarter, about the latest employment and recruitment position.

Although the Commission has suggested these steps for employment in the public sector, it is of the opinion that they should apply equally to recruitment in the private sector, though the mechanism to regulate this recruitment would necessarily differ from that in the public sector. In India, for recruitment of industrial labour, traditional methods (casual or badli workers on lists maintained by the factory; the use of jobbers, sardars, mukadams, etc., employees' relatives and dependants and undertaking's own labour force, etc., and contract labour) are still used for getting labour in textile industry, for building and construction industry, digging of canals, building of roads and dams, etc.

Besides these, large industrial complexes have developed a more 'committed' labour force. For supplying skilled operators there are a number of Crafts Training Schools (Industrial Training Institutes; Advanced Vocational Training Institutes at Mumbai, Kolkata, Hyderabad, Kanpur, Ludhiana and Chennai; Seven Craft Instructors Training Schools; and an Institute for Training of Foremen at Bangalore).

Recruitment Practices in India and Elsewhere

All public sector enterprises are required to consider candidates sponsored by the Employment Exchanges (over 535) and, in most cases, confine the selection to these candidates. However, the private sector is not under any such formal obligation. Under the Apprentices Act, 1961, young craftsmen having received pre-employment training in Industrial Institutes have to be employed by 'specialised' industries during their training period as a percentage of the total number of regular employees. Reservation of 25 percent of vacancies for Scheduled Castes and Scheduled Tribes candidates and preferential treatment of displaced persons is a part of statutory requirement of Government and public sector employment in India.

The recruitment of supervisory personnel in all organised industries is generally by promotion from within the organisation. Some industries first recruit a number of young person's as management trainees and after two or three years absorb them completely. Executives too are mostly promoted from within. Sometimes good persons are also recruited from Indian Institutes of Technology, All-India Institutes of Management at Kolkata, Institutes of Technology, All-India Institutes of Management at Kolkata, Ahmedabad and Bengaluru; from universities offering MBA courses, etc. Retired military and police personnel also provide an important source of recruitment, particularly for security jobs, and for personnel jobs.

In the USA, four sources of applicants are most used in obtaining hourly workers-direct applications at the company office, public employment sources, recommendations by employees, and newspaper advertising. In the case of blue-collar workers, the sources most successfully used are newspaper advertising, direct application, public employment offices, employee's recommendations, and private employment agencies. In the case of scientific, professional and technical employees, the most productive sources are advertising, on-campus recruiting and employment agencies.

Thus, it may be observed that there is virtually no definite work that develops employer's reasons for selecting various methods of recruitment. No single method is predominant and that recruitment practices are adapted to fill vacancies, employment rates, and other circumstances faced by the employer.

Assessment of the Recruitment Programme

Sources for recruiting should be periodically evaluated. For this purpose, the criteria may be the cost per applicant, the applicant/hiring ratio, tenure, performance appraisals, etc. The organisation should first identify how an applicant was attracted to the firm. A simple way of securing this information is to include in the application blank a question: "How did you learn of the job vacancy for which you have applied?" The next step is to determine whether any one method consistently attracts better applicants. The last step is to use this information to improve the recruiting process. Recruiting should take into consideration ethical practices, such as use of "truth in hiring," i.e., telling an applicant all about the firm and its position, both good and bad, to enable him to decide whether or not to join the firm, if selected.

A successful and effective recruitment programme necessitates a well-defined recruitment policy, a proper organisational structure, procedures for locating sources of manpower resources, suitable methods and techniques for utilising these and a constant assessment and consequent improvement.

SELECTION

Selection Procedure

The selection procedure is concerned with securing relevant information about an applicant. This information is secured in a number of steps or stages. The objective of selection process is to determine whether an applicant meets the qualifications for a specific job and to choose the applicant who is most likely to perform well in that job. Selection is a long process, commencing from the preliminary interview of the applicants and ending with the contract of employment.

The hiring procedure is not a single act but it is essentially a series of methods or steps or stages by which additional information is secured about the applicant. At each stage, facts may come to light which may lead to the rejection to the applicant. A procedure may be compared to a series of successive hurdles or barriers which an applicant must cross. These are intended as screens, and they are designed to eliminate an unqualified applicant at any point in the process. This technique is known as the successive hurdles technique. Not all selection processes include all these hurdles. The complexity of a process usually increases with the level and responsibility of the position to be filled.

According to Yoder, "the hiring process is of one or many 'go, no-go' gauges. Candidates are screened by the application of these tools. Qualified applicants go on to the next hurdle, while the unqualified are eliminated." Thus, an effective selection programme is a non-random process because those selected have been chosen on the basis of the assumption that they are more likely to be "better" employees than those who have been rejected. Chart 8.1 gives the hiring requirements as outlined by Yoder."

Selection processes or activities typically follow a standard pattern, beginning with an initial screening interview and concluding with the final employment decision. The traditional selection process includes: preliminary screening interview; completion of application form; employment tests; comprehensive interview; background investigations, physical examination and final employment decision to hire.

Selection Policy

While formulating a selection policy, due consideration should be given to organisational requirements as well as technical and professional dimensions of selection procedures. Yoder and others have suggested goals, technological issues, cost factors, extent of formality, etc. In other words, an effective policy must assert the "why" and "what" aspects of the organisational objectives.

Essentials of Selection Procedure

The selection procedure adopted by an organisation is mostly tailor made to meet its particular needs. The thoroughness of the procedure depends upon three factors: First, the nature of selection, whether faulty or safe, because faulty selection affects not only the training period that may be needed, but also results in heavy expenditure on the new employee and the loss that may be incurred by the organisation in case the job-occupant fails on his job.

Second, the policy of the company and the attitude of the management. As a practice some companies usually hire more than the actual number needed with a view to removing the unfit persons from the jobs.

Third, the length of the probationary or the trial period. The longer the period, the greater the uncertainty in the minds of the selected candidate about his future.

The hiring process can be successful, if the following preliminary requirements are satisfied:

(i) Some one should have the authority to hire. This authority comes from the employment requisition, as developed by an analysis of the work-load and work force.

(ii) There must be some standard or personnel with which a prospective employee may be compared, i.e., there should be available, beforehand, a comprehensive job description and job specifications as developed by a Job Analysis.

(iii) There must be a sufficient number of applicants from whom the required number of employees may be selected.

Steps in Selection Procedure

There is no shortcut to an accurate evaluation of a candidate. The hiring procedures are, therefore, generally long and complicated. Many employers make use of such techniques and pseudo-sciences as phrenology, physiognomy, astrology, graphology etc., while coming to hiring decisions. However, in modern times, these are considered to be unreliable measures.

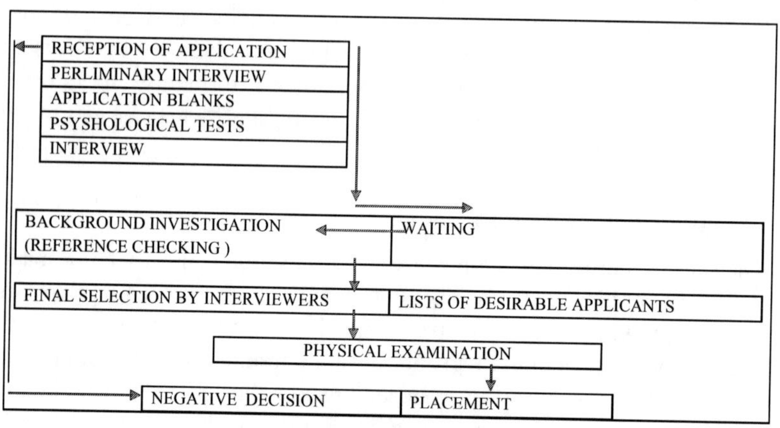

Fig. 8.1: Selection Process Flow Chart.

The following is a popular procedure though it may be modified to suit individual situation:

1. Reception or preliminary interview or screening;

2. Application blank — a fact-finder which helps one in learning about an applicant's background and life history;
3. A well conducted interview to explore the facts and get at the attitudes of the applicant and his family to the job;
4. A physical examination — health and stamina are vital factors in success;
5. Physiological testing to explore the surface area and get an objective look at a candidate's suitability for a job;
6. A reference check;
7. Final selection approval by manager; and communication of the decision to the candidate.

In the paragraphs that follow, we shall be discussing items 1, 2, 4, 5 and 6. The remaining items have been treated in the two subsequent chapters.

Reception, Initial or Preliminary Interview or Screening

The initial screening is usually conducted by a special interviewer or a high caliber receptionist in the employment office. When a large number of applicants are available, the preliminary interview is desirable both from the company's point of view and that of the applicant seeking employment. This interview is essentially a sorting process in which perspective applicants are given the necessary information about the nature of the jobs in the organisation. The necessary information, then, is elicited from the candidates relating to their education, experience, skill, salary demanded, the reasons for leaving their present jobs, their job interests and whether they are available for the job, their physical appearance, age, "drive" and facility in speech. If a candidate meets with the requirements of the organisation, he may be selected for further action. If he does not fit into the organisational structure (because of lack of requisite qualifications, physical disability, weak sight, or poor physique), he is eliminated at the preliminary stage. Such interviews are usually short and may be conducted at a desk, across a counter or railing and they are known as stand-up interviews. The main objective of such interviews is to screen out undesirable/ unqualified candidates at the very outset. Such interviews should be conducted by someone who inspires confidence, who is genuinely interested in people, and whose judgment in the "sizing up" of applicants is fairly reliable. Care is taken to ensure that the "Weeding out" process does not lead to the elimination of desirable workers.

Sometimes, applicants are eliminated because of some feature in the organisation which cannot be adjusted satisfactorily at this stage.

Six biographical items have been suggested as knock-out factors in the preliminary screening programme for salesmen. They include instability of residence, failure in business within two years, divorce or separation within two years, excessive personal indebtedness, too high a standard of living and unexplained gaps in the employment record.

The organisation may fit a job to the person who is available, as when a girl is appointed as a stenographer, telephone operator, secretary or saleswoman. Or jobs may be provided for the blind, the infirm or other handicapped persons. Working hours may be so adjusted as to make it possible for housewives/young girls to get employment. A typical selection programme tries to fit applicants to particular jobs, i.e., match jobs and people. This selection philosophy assumes that the requirements of a given job and the characteristics of a given applicant are sufficiently unique and explicit to make an intelligent match possible between them.

Since the preliminary interview brings about one of the first personal contacts of an individual with a company and since it is the stage at which some candidates must be rejected, it is desirable that the interviewer should be courteous, kind, receptive and informal. Despite the pressure under which he frequently works, he should avoid appearing brusque or impatient. Further, privacy must be maintained in holding interviews.

Chart 9.2: Guideline for preliminary screening

Name of the candidate :...

(a) Personality : grade	A..........	B..............	C................	D.........
(b) Expression (in English) (in hindi)	A............	B................	C.................	D............
(c) Technical knowledge theory : Application	A................	B................	C...........	D...............
(d) General knowledge	A..............	B................	C.............	D............
(e) Any other remarks	A.............	B..................	C................	D.............
Selected for employment test	....	Yes...........	No.......	No......

Date of interview .... Signature of the interviwer ....

Grade A- outstanding; B- goods; C – average; D –poor.

Application Blank or Application Form

An application blank is a traditional, widely accepted device for getting information from a prospective applicant which will enable a management to make a proper selection. The blank provides preliminary information as well as aid in the interview by indicating areas of interest and discussion.

It is a good means of quickly collecting verifiable (and therefore fairly accurate) basic historical data from the candidate. It also serves as a convenient device for circulating information about the applicant to appropriate members of management and as a useful device for storing information for, later reference.

The information required to be given in the applicant's own handwriting is needed to identify him properly and to draw tentative inferences about his suitability for employment. Many types of application forms — sometimes very long and comprehensive and sometimes brief — are used. Information is generally called on the following items:

(a) **Biographical Data:** Name, father's name, date and place of birth, age, sex, nationality, height, weight, identification marks, physical disability, if any, marital status, and number of dependants.

(b) **Educational Attainment:** Education (subjects offered and grades secured- training acquired in special fields and knowledge gained from professional/technical institutes or evening classes or through correspondence courses.

(c) **Work Experience:** Previous experience, the number of jobs held with the same or other employers, including the nature of duties, and responsibilities and the duration of various assignments, salary received, grades, and reasons for leaving the present employer.

(d) **Salary and Benefits:** Present and expected.

(e) **Personal Items:** Association memberships, of NCC or NSS, extra-curricular activities, sports, hobbies, and any other pertinent information supporting a candidates suitability for a post.

(f) **Other Items:** Names and addresses of previous employers, references, etc. An application blank is a brief history sheet of an employee's background and can be used for future reference, in case of need.

The data submitted in an application form should help predict the candidate: chances for making a success of his job. The information sought in it should be relevant to the objective of selection. To ensure that the information given by the applicant is true. The application blank usually carries a threat of discharge at any time after employment if the information furnished in it proves to be false.

The questions included in an application blank should be such as are valid and necessary. Superuous questions should be avoided. They should not by their wording or nature, encourage dishonest answers. In brief, an application form should be complete enough to relieve the interviewer of the burden of recording considerable factual data.

From the analysis of the above Application Blank, four types of information can be gathered:

First, one can make judgments on substantative matters, such as "does the applicant have the education and experience to do the job?"

Second, one can draw conclusions about the applicants previous progress and growth (especially in the case of management candidates).

Third, one can also draw tentative conclusion concerning the applicant's stability based on his previous work record.

Fourth, one may be able to use the data in the application to predict which candidates will succeed on the job and which would not.

In practice, most organisations use different application forms. For technical and managerial personnel, for example, the form may require detailed answers to questions regarding the candidate's education, etc. For blue-collar jobs, the form might stress on tools and equipment the applicant has used.

Weighted Application Blank

Some companies analyse the information on an application blank and determine statistically its relation to later success in the job. The answers are weighted according to the extent of job success. Such application blanks are known as weighted application blanks. Such forms may speed up both recruitment and selection.

A weighted application form should be established and used with a caution. Its objectives should be clearly determined. For example, there may be a selection of more stable employees to decrease labour turnover or increase job efficiency. The factors that bring about success may also be taken into account. For this purpose, the varying conditions in an organisation should be noted. The blank should be continually up-dated. Finally, no firm should try to select an employee solely on the basis of one or two important facts.

Bio-data

Sometimes, when a management wants to appoint an existing employee to a higher position, it may ask him to submit his necessary bio-data for consideration at the time of selection or interview. In such circumstances, an employee need not fill in an application blank. Such bio-data may also be got from different organisations having good employees for whom chances of advancement in their own organisation are very bleak.

Biographical Inventories

These inventories are specially constructed for the purpose of predicting success in a given type of work. The items included are those which a person, who conducts an analysis, believes to have some potential as predictors. A typical inventory contains a large number of items, utilises a multiple-choice format exclusively, and deals with those matters that are normally not covered in an application blank. Such items deal with experiences in early life, hobbies, social relations, values and opinions, etc.

Chapter - 9

Psychological Testing, Interviews, Placement and Induction

Psychological Testing

As organisations become complex and the number of jobs they offer increases, managers have been receptive to the acceptance of any device which would improve their selection decisions. Such decisions are usually arrived at with the help of psychological tests which are more objective and less biased than others. Tests are the most misused, the least understood, yet the most valuable sources of information about applicants. They are probably the most sophisticated tools of measuring human characteristics and individual differences that form the very basis of industrial psychology. But it should not be taken to mean that the tests are infallible and perfect tools. Actually like most other methods of selection they have their limitations.

A test has been defined both in a broad and narrow manner. Broadly, it has been defined as a "systematic procedure for comparing the behaviour of two or more persons." In a narrow sense, "it is a sample of an aspect of an individual's behaviour, performance or attitude." We may define it as a systematic procedure for sampling human behaviour.

Purpose of Tests

Psychological tests are used for more than one purpose. They are used for the purpose of:

(i) Guiding and counselling students seeking admission to schools and colleges;

(ii) Vocational guidance of adults seeking help in their careers;

(iii) Research into human behaviour and personality; and

(iv) Selection of candidates for an organisation.

Tests are also used for the purpose of making a differential placement or assignment of a person to the job for which he is most suitable; for selecting candidates for promotion and transfer within an organisation; for selecting candidates for assignment to a company training programme; and for assisting in individual employee in solving his problems.

According to Wendell, tests are used in business for three primary purposes:

(a) For the selection and placement of new employees;

(b) For appraising employees for promotional potentials; and

(c) For counselling employees. If properly used, psychological tests can be of paramount importance for each of these purposes.

According to Meyer and Bertottle, candidates are judged on the basis of their physical characteristics, their abilities and skills, their interest and personality traits. These are shown in Fig.

Low Accuracy of Act High Degree of Accuracy

Accuracy of Objective Measures

PHYSICAL CHARACTERISITICS {	HEIGHT WEIGHT SENSES VISUAL ACTIVITY HEARING
ABILITIES & SKILLS {	DEXTERITY MATHEMATICAL ABILITY VERBAL ABILITY INTELLIGENCES CLERICAL SKILLS
INTERESTS {	MECHANICAL APTITUDES MECHANICAL INTERESTS SCIENTIFIC INTERESTS ECONOMICAL INTERESTS CULTURAL INTERESTS
PERSONALITY TRAITS {	SOCIALITY DOMINANCE COOPERATIVENESS TOLERANCE EMOTIONAL STABILITY

Fig. 9.1: Measures of Human Characteristics.

Nature and Characteristics of Psychological Tests

Psychological tests are most carefully developed instruments, following certain highly standardised and often intricate procedures discovered by the psychologists as a result of long researches. Such tests usually possess the following characteristics:

1. **Assumption:** The use of tests is based on the assumption that no two persons are equal so far as intelligence, skills, aptitudes and personality are concerned. The different attributes of the individual are revealed when tests are used. Further, people possessing varying skills or other attribute perform differently on a job.
2. **Validity:** Validity refers to the extent to which a test measures what it is designed to measure. A typing or short-hand test, for example, should accurately measure a person's ability to type or take dictation. Validity may be of four specific types, viz., (a) content validity, (b) predictive validity, (c) concurrent validity, (d) construct validity.

   (a) **Content Validity** indicates how well the content of the test, as a sample, represents all the situations that could have been included. For example, in building a test one would seek content validity only in the sense of trying to duplicate the most important classes of activities such as typing financial statements, writing letters, or preparing manuscripts from rough copy. If, in the judgment of those who know the kinds of work is done, the sample tasks are reasonably representative of the probable job assignments, then the test is said to have reasonable content validity.

   (b) **Predictive Validity** is the degree to which there is a relationship between scores on a test and some future behaviour, which is required of a person if he is to perform successfully the job for which he is being tested. This is probably the most important type of validity for personnel selection, since predictive validity tells that there is a strong relationship between a test score and some later outcome, presumably a job performance criterion like production output or managerial effectiveness. For example, when a college recruiter screens candidates based upon their grades, he is assuming a high predictive validity between these grades and actual performance on the jobs for which he is recruiting. These grades, in total, represent a test from which he is estimating future job behaviour.

(c) **Concurrent Validity** is the extent to which test scores are related with a job behaviour measure that is available at the same time. If employees in the organisation are divided into two groups, high performers and low performers, they could be given standardised selection test. If it is found that high performers scored significantly above the low performers, this test could be used in predicting high performance among new applicants. Validity is the most difficult type of validity to understand.

(d) **Construct Validity** is the most difficult type of validity to understand and to prove. It reflects the extent to which the test measures the psychological quality like "intelligence" or "introversion" it is supposed to measure. It is most theoretical type of validity since it is aimed at measuring the relationship between a test and an artificial abstraction or "construct" such as intelligence.

3. **Reliability:** The reliability of a test means the test's ability to give consistent results. Test reliability is "the consistency of scores obtained by the same person when re-tested with the identical test or with an equivalent from the test." Test consistency is very important: if a person scores, say 80 on an intelligence test on Sunday and when retested on Monday, test cannot be relied upon in that case.

   Several ways are used to measure reliability. For example, the same test may be administered to the same people at two different points of time, comparing their performance at time two with that at time one. Or a test may be administered and then another equivalent test may be administered at a later date, which the experts may suggest.

4. **Standardisation:** A test must be standardised — that administered under standard conditions to large group of persons who are represent This is done to obtain norms or standards so that an individual's for whom it is intended score can be compared to the scores of others in the representative sample of people or a defined group like college students, adults, etc.

5. **Objectivity:** To be reliable a test must be constructed in such a fashion that or tasks in the same two or more persons can score the responses to items, questions way.

   Finally, if the subject's test score is to impart any meaningful information, it must be interpretable in relation to scores made by other individuals in a defined group.

Classification or Types of Psychological Tests

It must be noted that there is no one single and complete system of test classification, actually there are a variety of ways in which they are classified. For example,

(A) on the basis of human behaviour,

(B) on the basis of use of tests, or

(C) individual or group tests.

(a) Classification on the Basis of Human Behaviour

On the basis of human behaviour, tests have been generally classified into four categories, as depicted in the Chart 9.1.

Chart 9.1

APTITUDE TEST			ACHIEVEMENT TEST		PERSONALITY TEST			INTEREST TEST
Mental test	Mechanical test	Psycho-motor test	Job knowledge	Work sample test	Objective test	Projective test	Situation test	

(i) **Aptitude or Potential Ability Tests:** Such tests are widely used to measure the latent ability of a candidate to learn new job or skill. They enable us to find out whether a candidate, if selected, would be suitable for a job which may be clerical mechanical. These tests detect peculiarities or defects in a person's sensory or intellectual capacity. They focus attention on a particular type of talent, such as learning, reasoning or a mechanical bent of mind. Some of them measure simply sensory activity, speed and dexterity in motor movements of various types. Aptitude tests for medicine, law, music, painting, clerical and number of other activities are also available. Some of these tests are useful in selection of employees.

Such tests may take one of the following forms: mental or intelligence test, mechanical aptitude test or psychomotor or skills tests.

(a) Mental or Intelligence Tests measure the over-all intellectual activity or the intelligence quotient (IQ) of a person and enable us to know whether he has the mental capacity to deal with new problems. They are useful for selection purposes, and determine the future of a employees word fluency, memory, inductive reasoning, speed of perception and spatial visualisation. The

Wechsler Adult Intelligence Scale (WAIS) is widely used for management appraisal and selection. It is given to only one person at a time. The Wonderlic Personnel Test and the Otis Employment Test are, however, general intelligence tests, which may be given to groups in a relatively short time.

The administration of these tests calls for much preparation on the part of an organisation; and they are expensive and cumbersome as well.

(b) Mechanical Aptitude Tests measure the capacity of a person to leam a particular type of mechanical work- they measure a person's capacity for spatial visualisation, perceptual speed, manual dexterity, visual-motor co-ordination or integration, visual insights, etc. They also measure specialised knowledge and information of techniques, arithmetical problem solving ability and technical vocabulary. Some of these functions are measured by apparatus, others by performance type of materials and still others by paper and pencil tests. They are useful when apprentices, machinists, mechanics, maintenance workers and mechanical technicians are selected. In other words, these tests are generally used for the selection of personnel in lower position, who are entrusted with the jobs of operating machines.

(c) Psychomotor or Skills Tests are those tests which measures a person's ability to do a specific job. They are administered to determine mental dexterity or motor ability and similar attributes involving muscular movement, control and co-ordination. They are of primary importance in the selection of workers who have to perform semi-skilled and repetitive jobs, such as bench assembly work, packing, testing and inspection and watch assembly. Examples of this type of tests are the McQuarril Test for mechanical ability, the Purdue Mechanical Adaptability Test, and the O'Connor Finger and Tweezer Dexterity Tests.

(ii) Achievement Tests: Known also as proficiency tests, they measure the skill or knowledge which is acquired as a result of a training programme and on-the-job experience. They determine admission feasibility of a candidate and measure what he is capable of doing. Examples of such test are: General Aptitude Test Battery; the Abstract Reasoning Test, the Millar Analogies Test, the Standford Binet Scales, the Adaptability Tests. Achievement tests are of two kinds:

(a) Tests for measuring job knowledge, which may be oral or written. These tests are administered to determine proficiency in shorthand and in operating calculators, adding machines, dictating and transcribing machines, and simple mechanical equipment. Such tests are useful for office workers, mill supervisors, stenographers, public utility employees, sales girls, inspector, and so on.

(b) Work Sample Tests demand the administration of the actual job as a test. A typing test provides the material to be typed and notes the time taken and the mistakes committed.

(iii) Personality Tests: These tests aim at measuring those basic make-up or characteristics of an individual, which are non-intellectual in their nature. In other words, they probe deeply to discover clues to an individuals' value system, his emotional reactions and maturity, and his characteristic mood. They assess is motivation interests, his ability to adjust himself to the stresses of everyday life, and his capacity for inter-personal relations and self-image. They are express in term of relative significance of such traits of a person as his self-confidence, his ambition, tact, emotional adjustment, emotional stability, neuroticism, obsessions, delusions, compulsions, or various other traits of human personality as perseverance, cooperativeness, aggressiveness impulsiveness, reflectiveness, thoughtfulness, masculinity or feminity, self-restraints, submissiveness, ascendance, optimism, decisiveness, socialability, conformity, objectivity, patience, fear, distrust, initiative, judgment, dominance, etc. These tests are administered to counsel-individuals, to select supervisors and higher executives. They are pen-and-paper tests. Example of such Tests are: Bell Adjustment Inventory, the California Test of Personality Scale, Minnesola Multiphasic Personality Inventory, Thermatic Appreciation Tests, etc.

Personality tests have a wider use in industry because they provide a well-rounded picture of an applicant's personality, and because managers have to realise the importance of emotional characteristics. Some authorities, however, consider these tests to be superficial, easily faked and misleading. These tests are of three types:

(a) **Objective tests** which measure neurotic tendencies, self-sufficiency, dominance- submission, and self-confidence. These are scored objectively. They are paper-and-pencil tests or Personality Inventories.

(b) **Projective tests** are those in which a candidate is asked to project his own interpretation into certain standard stimulus situations. The way in which he responds to these stimuli depends on his own values, motives and personality. The most widely used tests of this type are the Rorschach Blot Test and the Thematic Appreciation Test.

(c) **Situation tests** measures an applicant's reaction when he is placed in a peculiar situation; his ability to undergo stress and his demonstration of ingenuity under pressure. Such tests usually relate to leaderless group situations, in which some problem is posed to a group, and its members are asked to reach some conclusion without the help of a leader.

(iv) Interest Tests: These tests aim at finding out the types of work in which a candidate is interested. They are inventories of the likes and dislikes of the people of some occupations, hobbies and recreational activities. They are useful in vocational guidance, and are assessed in the form of answers to a well-prepared questionnaire. Examples of such tests are: Kuder Reference Record, The Strong Vocational Interest Blank, etc.

(b) Classification on the Basis of Use of Tests

On the basis of the use to which the tests are put, they may be classified in three broad categories: selection tests, classification tests, and placement tests.

Selection Tests: In making a selection, an organisation may decide to accept some candidate and reject others, for filling its various jobs. Hiring of an employee is a selection test.

Classification Tests: Under such tests, special considerations are given to determine on which of the several possible assignments a person will be able to do his best.

Placement Decision: It concerns with assigning a person to different levels of work, rather than distinctly different types of work. For example, choosing a candidate for officer's cadre from amongst the applicants is a placement decision.

(c) Individual and Group Tests

In Individual Tests, a single individual is given a test at a time usually by a trained examiner who not only scored and interpreted the results but also observed his behaviour carefully throughout the testing period.

Group Tests, on the other hand, are usually presented in a format which allows the individual to record his own responses and can be simultaneously given to a number of individuals, without any special need of observing their behaviour.

In sum, it may be noted that some tests have a very wide application and are used by firms, agencies and educational institutions. These have been standardised. Some firms, however, have developed tests to suit their own requirements; these are known as tailor-made tests, and are developed only when there is a continuing demand for a large number of new employees for a single job.

Advantages of Testing

When used appropriately under a well planned testing programme, tests can and do lead to a number of positive benefits to the company in the long run. For instance:

(i) It is easier to determine the value of a test as a selection device, then it is possible to evaluate interview or application blanks.

(ii) Tests are subject to minimum subjective bias or are much more objective than any other selection device presently available.

(iii) Tests provide a uniform basis for comparing candidates from diverse background. They challenge the interviewers or the supervisors to think through their evaluation more carefully.

(iv) They reduce to a considerable extent the labour turnover and which in turn may result in reduced costs of training (because lesser workers will have to be trained as a result or reduced turnover).

(v) They may increase production because better workers are employed; and may result in increased satisfaction of employees because they are placed on the job for which they are most competent and interested. This may reduce absenteeism, reduce rate of accidents and increase morale of the workers.

(vi) Tests minimise the time of selection and can also be judiciously used in training the workers for appropriate positions by determining their training ability on the basis of the test scores.

(vii) Tests are of great value in selecting people with promotional ability, discovering the various causes of failure at the job by analysing the personality traits for the individuals. It must be admitted that though tests are an extremely sophisticated technique for measuring behavioural characteristics, they have their own limitations. As Tiffin and McCormick point out, "It should be recognised that psychological tests are not infalliable and that sometimes they reveal results which are not a true indication of the potential job success of the candidate."

The use of testing in industry should be done with caution because some highly enthusiastic individuals are likely to be fascinated by the interesting ideas which such testing provide. Unscrupulous people, making use of the tests, make exaggerated claims about effectiveness of their testing programmes. Further tests may be administered by incompetent professionals which give wrong results. Therefore, tests should be developed cautiously, within the organisation to take care of its selection needs. It is better to look upon tests as the good adjuncts of interview, application blanks, and such other devices of selection.

Developing a Test Programme

Developing a testing programme calls for careful planning, analysis, experiment, and technical knowledge. For this purpose, the services of a qualified person such as an Industrial Psychologist or a Personnel Manager who is expert in Psychology, Psychometrics and the use of statistical methods are requisitioned.

The following steps are generally involved in establishing a sound testing programme:

(i) **Deciding the objectives of a testing programme, i.e.,** whether it is meant for hiring personnel or for transfers, promotions, etc. Initially, such a programme may be set up only for some jobs. It may then be expanded to cover all types of jobs in an organisation.

(ii) **Analysing jobs to identify those characteristics which appear necessary for job success, i.e.,** the need for active habits, eye-hand co-ordination, finger-and-arm dexterity, perceptual and sensory abilities and such other specific characteristics. In other words, it has to be decided as to which 'human traits and skills' are necessary for adequate performance of job. Consideration may be given to two criteria: one, production-related criteria, i.e., quantity, quality etc., and two, personnel data, i.e., absenteeism, length of service, etc.

(iii) **Choosing tests to measure characteristics:** These tests may be chosen by keeping in mind such factors as realiability, content or face validity, level of difficulty, ease of administration, and the cost involved. This choice is usually based on experience, previous research, "guesses." Several tests — known as "Battery of Tests" are chosen with the purpose of measuring a variety of possible predictors, such as aggressiveness, extroversion, numerical ability, etc.

(iv) **Administering tests to an experimental group of people, i.e.,** to applicants under consideration for jobs. For purposes of employment, a test is usually administered after an application blank has been examined and there has been a preliminary interview. Many candidates are rejected for a variety of reasons before tests are administered.

(v) **Establishing criteria of job success, i.e.,** the criteria should take into account such factors as the quality and quantity of output, accident frequency, regularity or otherwise in attendance, grades obtained during training, speed of promotion in an organisation, professional achievements (published work, awards received), and formal ratings determined by the supervisor.

(vi) **Analysing the results of tests and taking decisions regarding the applications of tests:** As no single test can be expected to measure all the abilities required for a satisfactory job performance, a number of tests in combination are usually administered.

Basic Testing Guidelines

There are some rules and principles which should be observed while considering the testing alternatives. The general guidelines are:

(i) **Tests are to be used as a supplement rather than as a substitute for any other method.** No test should ever be used as the sole criterion for selection, placement, promotion or transfer. Even valid tests represent a small sample of a person's total pattern of behaviour. Hence, reliance should also be placed on information derived from other procedures — from interviews, application blanks, and background checks.

A reasonably complete picture of a candidate can thus be obtained.

(ii) **Tests are better at predicting failure than success.** Testing procedures often determine which applicants will not or cannot perform a job satisfactorily; they do not necessarily determine who can or will perform such duties in a very effective and efficient manner.

(iii) **Tests are a screening device.** They are useful when it is necessary to pick up a small select group from many applicants. When hundreds of candidates apply for a few jobs, a test can only be a preliminary selection technique.

(iv) **Test scores are not precise measures because they are sample of behaviour.** They, therefore, cannot be totally accurate predictors of anything. A test score of 90 does not precisely reveal a 90 percent grasp of a subject matter. Test subjects with the highest test scores are not always better choices for a job than those who score lower.

(v) **Every test must be validated in the organisation in which it is used.** It is always necessary to test the test itself before it is assumed that it will enable us to predict a successful performance of a job. A test may be validated by undertaking research into the environment in which it is used". Besides, a test must also be reliable. In other words, a person should receive the same score whenever he takes the same test, unless some significant educational development has taken place between testing dates.

(vi) **Test conditions are important.** The place where the tests are administered should be reasonably private as well as quiet, well lighted and ventilated. All applicants should take the test under the same test conditions: this ensures that some do not get high or low scores due to differences in test conditions.

(vii) **Invasion of privacy should be avoided.** Most tests are personal and should, therefore, be held in strict confidence. Where necessary test should be administered and evaluated by experts. The results should be keep confidential till they are declared.

(viii) **Test administration, scoring and interpretation require technical competence and training in testing.** So testing must be done by qualified psychologists.

Chart 9.2: Validity of various test as predictive of job proficiency

		Types of test				
	Job	*Intellectual ability*	*Spatial mechanical ability*	*Perceptual accuracy*	*Motor ability*	*Personality traits*
1.	Executive	Moderate	Moderate +	Moderate	Low	Moderate
2.	Supervisor	Moderate	Moderate	Moderate	Low	Low moderate
3.	Clerical	Moderate	Low	Moderate	Low	Low /moderate +
4.	Sales	Low	Low	Low	Low	Low
5.	Protective	Moderate services	Low	Low	Low	Low
6.	Vehicle	Low operator	Low/	Low	Moderate	Moderate
7.	Trade&	Moderate craft	Moderate	Moderate	Low/moderate	Low/ moderate
8.	Industrial	Moderate	Moderate	Moderate	Moderate	high+

Work Sampling

'Work Sampling' is another technique for screening candidates. This technique is based on the presumption that the best indicator of future performance is past performance. Before selecting an employee, the personnel manager in many cases prefer to inquire about the candidates' "prior work experience" to make his judgement."

The basic procedure involves choosing 'several specific tasks that are crucial to performing the job for which a candidate is being recruited'. The applicants are then tested on these specific tasks, their performance (on these tasks) is then used as a predictor of their performance on the job.

As a screening tool, several advantages have been claimed for this technique. Gary Dessler observes: "The emphasis is on samples of actual behaviour so it is harder to 'fake' answers (as a person might on aptitude or interest tests). The work sample is more clearly relevant to the job you are recruiting for. The content of the work sample is not as likely to be 'unfair' (or to emphasise middle class concepts and values) as some psychological tests might be. And, since you are not delving into the applicants' background and personality, there is almost no chance of the work sample being viewed as an invasion of privacy".

Interviews

Interview is probably the most widely used selection tool. It is most complex selection technique because its scope includes measuring all the relevant characteristics and integrating and classifying all other information about the applicant. In practically all organisations interviewing is used for a variety of purposes, including selection, appraisal, disciplinary action, counselling and general problem solving.

The interview is a selection technique which enables the employer to view the total individual and directly appraise him and his behaviour. It is a method by which an idea about an applicant's personality (including his intelligence, breadth of interests, and general attitudes towards life) can be obtained by a face-to-face contact." By "interviewing" is meant "deliberate, active listing with a purpose to draw the other person out, to discover what he really wants to say, and to give a chance to express himself freely". According to Scott and others, "an interview is a purposeful exchange of ideas, the answering of questions and communication between two or more persons. An eminent author defines an interview as "a conversation with a purpose" and the purpose may be to "Get information," "to give information," and "to make a friend".

In other words, an interview is an attempt to secure maximum amount of information from the candidate concerning his suitability for the job under consideration. It tries to achieve an exacting appraisal of an applicant, his previous experience, education, training and family background. It enables the interviewer to judge certain qualities (manners, neatness and appearance, ability to speak, meet other people pleasantly and make a good impression on others) of the prospective candidate before he is selected.

The interview is used in practically every business and profession. Some activities call for a high degree of proficiency in interviewing; these are the activities of professors, engineers, psychiatrists, clinical psychiatrists, lawyers, social workers, employment managers, industrial relations managers, market analysts, salesmen and supervisors, investigating grievances. The interview is widely used in securing credit information, ranking loans, selling, adjusting complaints, diagnosing physical and mental ills, as well as in personnel administration and management.

When used in personnel selection, some of the objectives of interview are:

(i) To get an opportunity to judge on applicant's qualifications and characteristics a basis for sound selection and placement. On the basis of the information obtained about the family background, training, educational and other qualifications, personality, characteristics, aptitude, interests and skills of an applicant the interviewer tries to arrive at as impartial a decision as possible. He may decide to hire him, to reject him or to pass him on to another step in the interview if it is not the final one. This type of interviews are referred to as selection or placement interviews.

(ii) To give an applicant essential facts about the job and the company (nature and hours of work, medical requirements, opportunities for advancement, special hazards, employee benefits and services, company policies, etc.) in order to enable him to decide intelligently whether he should or should not accept the employment. The interview is generally a non-reciprocal relation between the individuals concerned.

(iii) To establish a rapport, or a feeling of mutual understanding and confidence, between the personnel department and the applicant who is to be employed.

(iv) To promote goodwill towards the company whether the interview culminates in employment or not. The goodwill is generated by unfailing courtesy to the interviewees, by providing them with vocational literature, pamphlets, by offering constructive suggestions, and by showing interest in them.

(v) Interviewing is an invaluable tool of disciplinary action, grievance handling and relations with unions.

(vi) To solve problems as when counselling a student conferring with a career guidance person or discussing a grievance with a superior such interviews are information-gathering or fact-findings meetings; but their main purpose is to solve a problem. Such interviews are also termed as counselling interviews.

(vii) To get a real feel of the candidate, observe his appearance, mannerisms, confidence, typical ways of reacting to questions of various sorts.

(viii) To find out why an employee is leaving the company and seeking job elsewhere. Such interviews are called exit or termination interviews.

(ix) Despite the fact the interviews are often regarded as costly, inefficient and non-valid procedure for selection purposes, they are widely used because the psychological tests and application blanks to not give correct information about the candidate as a real flesh and blood human being.

Richard Calhoon observes: "The interview makes three unique contributions to the selection process. First, it is the only way to see an applicant in action — how he looks, his manner, his bearing. Second, it is the only way to witness how he interacts and how he responds; his way of thinking, the effects of his personality on another. Third, it is perhaps the best way to get at the 'will do' features of a performance-motivation, initiative, stability, perseverance, work, habits, and judgements. The so called 'can do' aspect can be examined by application, test and reference checks. An important by-product, unique to the interview, is the opportunity it affords to the management to identify with the applicant a factor that can be quite helpful for a new employee's ultimate success.

Under the 'can do' factors, Dr. McMurray includes these elements: appearance, manners, education as required by the job, intelligence, ability to solve problems, experience in the field knowledge of the project, physical conditions and health. Under the 'will do' factors are listed character traits, viz., stability, industry, willingness to work, perseverance, ability to get along with others' loyalty - that is, identifying with employer - reliance, that is, standing on one's own feet and making one's own decisions, and leadership.

Besides, 'motivation factors' are also taken into consideration. These are vigorous initiative and drive, need for income, need for security, need for status, need for power, need to investigate, need to excel, need for perfection, even the need to starve. For assessing 'emotional maturity,' the factors to be taken into consideration are: freedom from dependence, regard for consequences, capacity for self-discipline, freedom from destructive tendencies and freedom from wishful thinking.

Thus, in brief selection interviews give a chance to personally "size up" the candidate, and to pursue questioning in a way that tests cannot. They give an opportunity to make judgements on the candidates' enthusiasm, and intelligence and they give an opportunity to assess "subjective aspects" of the candidate — facial expression, appearance, nervousness, etc. Interviews, in other words, are a very patent screening tool.

Types of Interviews

Interviews may be classified in many ways. Their main differences arise from the pattem of interaction by which the interviewer communicates with the interviewee, responds to his answers, asks questions, and forms the structure of the interview. Interviews may be conducted on a planned or patterned and non-directed or non-planning plane. A planned interview is one that follows a definite plan of action, and is, therefore, also known as an action interview, while a non-directed interview is one that is not directed by the interviewer and in which the candidate is given the freedom to speak his mind freely. Generally, interviews fall in six categories:

(i) Patterned or highly organised interviews;

(ii) Non-directive, free or quite unorganised interviews;

(iii) Depth or discussion interviews;

(iv) Situational or problem-type interviews or leaderless group discussion interviews;

(v) Stress interviews.

(i) Patterned or Structured Interview: This is the most common method of interview. It is based on the assumption that, to be most effective, every pertinent detail bearing on what is to be accomplished, what kind of information is to be sought or given, how the interview is to be conducted, and how much time is to be allotted to it, must be worked out in advance. Questions would be asked in a particular order, with very little deviation. If an applicant wants to discuss something else, he is swiftly guided back to the prepared questions. Such interviews are also called standardised interviews for they are pre-planned to a high degree of accuracy and precision. McMurray explains why the patterned interview is likely to improve the judgement of the interviews: First, the interviewer works from definite, job specifications; he knows what qualities and each job requires. Second, he has a plan he knows what questions to ask. Third, he has been trained in the techniques of conducting an interview, i.e., he knows how to put the candidate at ease, how to make him talk, and how to extract pertinent information. Fourth, prior to interview, he has checked with outside sources (previous employers, schools, etc.) and already knows a great deal about the applicant. Fifth, he has a series of clinical concepts, i.e., that of emotional immaturity — which provides him with a yardstick for interpreting and evaluating the information obtained from the candidate. Sixth, the interviewer himself has been carefully selected "to assure that he has adequate intelligence and is emotionally well adjusted."

(ii) **Non-directive or Free interview:** It is unstructured and is relatively non-planned as to format. In such an interview, the applicant is asked some questions, and he may reply to these in any way he likes for a considerable length of time. In other words, the interview is not directed by questions or comments as to what the candidate should be asked. Generally, the candidate is encouraged to express himself on a variety of subjects, on his expectations and motivations, background and upbringing, interests, even political predictions, etc. The interviewers look for traits of character and nature of his aspirations and his strengths and weaknesses, mainfest or potential. The purpose of such interview is to determine what kind of person a candidate really is.

(iii) **Depth or Action Interview:** It is semi-structured in nature and utilities questions in key areas which have been studied in advance by the interviewer. The typical subjects discussed at such interviews include the candidate's home life, education, previous experience, aptitude, recreational interests, and hobbies. The interviewer provides instructional information about his organisation, the nature of work, pay, opportunities for advancement, and demand likely to be made on the employee. The idea of such an interview is to get a true picture of the interviewee by intensively examining his background and thinking so that a correct evaluation and decision may be made.

This type of interview demands more mature understanding of human behaviour and development and, therefore, more careful selection of the interviewer.

(iv) **Group Discussion Interview:** In this type of interview, groups rather than individuals are interviewed. The interviewees are given certain problems and are asked to reach a specific decision within a particular time limit. The applicants enter into group discussions, knowing that the interview is a test, but do not know which qualities are being measured or tested. A few observers watch the activities of the interviewees — those who take a lead in the discussion, those who try influencing others, those who summarise and clarify issues, and those who take a lead in the discussion, those who try influencing others, those who summarise and clarify issues, and those who speak effectively. The assumption underlying this type of interview is that "the behaviour displayed in the solution of the problem is related to potential success in the job. The object is to see how well individuals perform on a particular task or in a particular situation."

In this type of interview, the emphasis is on the analysis of the interviewers from discussions rather than a factual information.

Chart 9.3: Excerpts from Patterned Interview Form

Domestic and Social Situation

1. Married.............Single..................Widowed..................... Separated ....Divorced ....Date of Marriage................
2. Living with spouse? Yes .... Specify.............dependants (Members) ....
3. Age ....What plans do you have for children?
4 Do dependants provide adequate motivation?
5. What difficulties or serious arguments have you with your spouse? ....
6. Have you been married previously? Yes..................No................. how many times?
7. When and what was the reason for the end of the marriage or marriages? Death.....
8. Separation (unless death): What were reasons? ....
9. Do domestic difficulties indicate immaturity?
10. What do you do for recreation? ....What hobbies do you have? ....
11. To what extent do you and your spouse entertain? .... Does applicant seem socially well adjusted?
12. What types of persons do you actively dislike? ....
13. Is applicant biased? ....
14. Tell us about your most recent job. Why did you decide to change?
15. As you look back on your recent job. What did you like most about it? What did you like least about it?

16. What do you feel were your three most significant achievements in your past position?
17. Could you tell us if you have any idea about what an effective manager should do?
18. How do you feel your subordinates would describe you as a supervisor?
19. Were you satisfied with the progress you made on your job? Why? Why not?
20. What plans do you have for self-improvement during the next twelve months?
21. What does success mean to you?
22. What do people criticize about you the most?
23. Many of us improve our ability to relate to people as develop more maturity. In what way would you say you have improved over the past two years?
24. What or who has contributed most to your self-development? Think about a difficult decision you have had to make recently regarding your work. Tell us how you went about making this decision.
25. How do you plan your work?
26. What has been the heaviest pressure situation you have had to face in the past year?
    Describe the circumstances.
27. Give us examples of the types of problems that create the greatest stress or strain for you.
28. What goals you have set for the next three years?

(v) Panel or Board Interview: In this type of interview, a candidate is interviewed by a number of interviewers. Questions may be asked in turn or asked in random order as they arise on any topic.

(vi) Stress Interview: In the stress interview, the interviewer assumes a hostile role toward the applicant. He deliberately puts him on the defensive by trying to annoy, embarrass or frustrate him. Usually, the interviewer, in such circumstances, asks questions rapidly, criticizes the interviewee's answers, interrupts him frequently, keeps the candidate indefinitely and then subjects him to a barrage of interrogations questioning whatever he might state, or too many questions are asked at a time by many interviewers, take derogatory remarks about the candidate or puts him in an awkward situation by ping something on the floor and asking him to pick it up, accusing him that he is and so on. The purpose is to find out how a candidate behaves in a stress situation he loses his temper, gets confused or frightened. Stress interview is a highly dangerous tool in the hands of an unskilled interviewer. Moreover, the stressful interview situation may not necessarily reveal, how a candidate will behave in real stressful life situation may not necessarily reveal, how a candidate will behave real stressful life situations involved on a job. Yet its judicial application may reveal many characteristics of an applicant.

Guidelines for Effective Interview

Interview is most complex of the selection techniques, because the validity of the results achieved by interview is dependent upon several factors, which are related to planning of the interview, practice of interview by the interviewer, and to the personality characteristics of the interviewer. I which should generally be. Therefore, there are certain obvious essential guidelines followed, if interview is to serve as an effective tool of selection. These are:

(i) Interviewers should be of a certain status, standing and experience. They should be in the know of the requirements of the job for which interviews are conducted, and be familiar with the background of the organisation and industry which they represent.

They should possess a working knowledge of such topics as individual personality, and human difference, dynamics, motivation, frustration, attitudes, abilities, traits, and should be sympathetic and impartial.

(ii) Skilful interviewing is an art and like all other arts, requires training and experience. It is learnt better by practice than by reading a book. However, the necessary techniques and knowledge about the subject matter may be collected from current books, periodicals and pamphlets bearing on the larger field of management.

(iii) The interviewers should not begin the interview without thoroughly studying the relevant data about the candidate from the application blank, and the tests and preliminary interviews through which he has gone before. The interviewers should clearly understand what the job entails and what its requirements are. This will help them to avoid putting too much weight on irrelevant information and will help them reduce the chances that all candidates are compared with an erroneous "stereotype." By making available to interviewers extensive information about the job to be filled (such as that provided by detailed job descriptions and job titles) reliability of employment selection decision can be increased.

(iv) The interviewers should know what traits are more accurately interviews and others. These include "intelligence," "personal relations aptitude" and especially "motivation to work." Assessment of personal qualities like sincerity, ability to present ideas, emotional balance, friendliness, responsiveness, courtesy, etc., cannot be checked at all because they are characteristics which can be validated after a long acquaintance with the applicant and not in a few minutes' encounter in an interview.

(v) The coverage of factual information should form the main objective of the interview. Such a coverage is of greater value than any attempt to search for personal qualities. It should emphasise on: (a) reliance of education to the job specifications; (b) reasons for the gap in educational and employment history of the applicant; (c) reasons for choosing special courses in schools and colleges; (d) division or grades obtained and academic achievements; reason for failure; (e) likes and dislikes for each job; (f) information regarding domestic, health, financial and other problems, if any; (g) the condition of the job and work the applicant expects.

(vi) The time of the interview should not be consumed in collecting routine information, which can be conveniently gathered from application blank or verified from the applicant's former employer or from his school, institution, records and documents, certificates, etc.

(vii) The interview should be diligently delimited, for it is often the only feasible way of eliciting the required information about the candidate, and it enables the interviewers to view the total individual and to appraise his personal appearance, comments, attitudes, mannerisms, motivations, interests, adjustments, temperament and other personal attributes.

(viii) An interview should be made more reliable and more valid, i.e., the interviewers should guard against being unduly prejudiced or coloured by their own personality or pet theories. Their own feelings and standards, irrespective of job requirements should not be allowed to influence them, nor should their feelings about religion or community, affect their judgement. It is desirable that the decision should be fair and impartial. Bias, prejudices, personal likes and dislikes, preferences and general impression of the candidate should not be allowed to interfere with the process of decision-making. The interviewers should accentuate the positive qualities in a candidate rather than give undue weight to negative ones.

(ix) The candidate should be allowed to talk extensively so that he may unburden himself to the point at which nothing important or relevant is left unsaid, and a fair assessment can be made of his ability. Generally, 25 to 30 minutes are sufficient for semi-skilled or skilled applicants. For high level jobs — managerial, technical, sales — an hour or more may be required.

(x) An interviewer should avoid too much talking. "A good working ratio for an interviewer is to talk for not more than 25 percent of the time and to listen for 75 percent of the time." The best interview is usually one in which the interviewer talks the least. Information from the applicant can be elicited only when the interviewer gives him a patient, prolonged and skilful hearing.

(xi) The interviewer should refrain from passing too quick a judgement before all the relevant facts have been gathered and evaluated. He should avoid derogatory comments and refrain from any revealing facial or verbal expression, he should not voice criticism or moralise. Rather, he should attempt to show understanding and smoothly pass on to another topic when any unfavourable information is uncovered or if the applicant is unable to answer a question.

(xii) If the interviewer is to be objective in decision-making he must be careful to correct irrational feelings of a negative or positive kind. Hostility or nervousness on the part of the applicant may be minimised if he adopts a healthy attitude that the former has not come for the interview with a "begging bowl" in his hand. It is important for him to realise that his organisation needs a good man just as much as the applicant wants a good job.

(xiii) The interviewer should try to do some selling during the interviews. He should be aware of the fact that the interviewee is also evaluating him. Interviewees form overall impressions of the "goodness" or "badness" of an interviewer and this in turn may affect decision to join or not to join the company. Therefore, the interviewer should try give good impression about himself and of the company he represents.

In the words of Wendell French: "Good interviewers are those which take the many needs of the interviewee into account of security, belonging, esteem, wholeness and self-actualisation. Orderly proceedings, cordial relationships, avoidance of unnecessary, ego-damaging events, and an understanding of the process are ingredients in the best interviews." An applicant who is kept waiting unduly, treated rudely, insulted or given no information is likely to display a defensive behaviour, such as anger or humiliation which would seriously affect the friendly atmosphere at an interview.

Qualities of a Successful good Interviewer

Researches have more or less clearly shown that effectiveness of any interview depends upon several personal qualities of the interviewer. A good interviewer must have abilities to evaluate specific as well as overall abilities of the applicant and this is rather a difficult job as ability to evaluate specific traits may differ from the ability to make overall evaluation. However, a successful interviewer should have the following characteristics?

1. He should usually be an elderly person (say above 40 or 45), more mature in outlook on life, slightly or moderately egostical, and not too much extrovert.
2. He must be socially detached which makes it possible for him to accurate judgement of others.
3. He should have slightly more than average intelligence, emotional maturity, interest in human being and there behaviour, sportsmanship and well adjusted life.
4. He should have extensive acquaintance with people similar in age and occupation to those whom he interviews.
5. He should be a man with a genuine feeling of warmth and affection so that he is able to establish rapport quickly with any individual, however, nervous he may be.
6. He should be a man who has been fully trained in 'the art of interviewee and who knows what are the special weakness of this method and how to avoid them: and also the person who is focused on continually refining his method and asking questions in the light of his experience.

His other qualities are

(i) He should read standard literature and current books, periodicals and pamphlets, bearing on the art of interviewing and on the larger field of personnel management.

(ii) He should be well informed and up-to-date where legislation on employment is concerned.

(iii) He should be a member of one or more professional management organisations which serve as clearing houses for personnel information organisation. At the least, he should attend the conferences sponsored by these groups.

(iv) He should have an experimental and open mind attitude towards tests and other device which are developed to assist the interviewers in the selection of personnel.

(v) If he has little or no formal educational background or training in personnel work, he should cure this deficiency by taking courses/coaching in psychology, personnel management, general management, public relations and other subjects bearing on his work.

(vi) The interviewer must have a thorough understanding of the organisations, of the relationships between departments and jobs, the objectives of the organisation, job content, and worker requirements; and he should have a good understanding of the organisation's employment policies and procedures.

(vii) He should be receptive and sensitive to the way his behaviour affects others.

(viii) He should have a working knowledge of such topics as individual differences, personality dynamics, motivations, frustrations, abilities, attitudes, and other human traits.

By continuing to improve in these and other ways, he not only recognises "the challenges of his art," but goes a long way towards meeting that challenge.

Interview Technique or Conducting Interviews

A successful interview of a candidate is a specialised technique which requires a thorough grounding in the art of conducting interviews. The typical sequence of functions that occur in the course of an interview are: (i) Preparation; (ii) Setting; (iii) Conduct of interview; (iv) Close of interview; and (v) Evaluation. Interviewing Procedures for Recruitment

1. Appraise	(a) First impression. (b) Appearance and manner. (c) Evidence of energy (d) Answer to general
2. Probe	**SUSPENDED JUDGEMENT** (a) Use "why" "what" how, where and when types of questions. (b) continue observation of a person (c) estimate suitability for employment. (d) note degree a rapport with interviewer.

3. Act	**CONFIRMED DECISION** Accept (a) give information about company history, product, opportunities, salary, training programmes. Reject (a) maintain good public relation but do not oversell. (b) answer question Refer (a) give information about company history product opportunities (b) answer question. Encourage (a) give information. (b) indicate interest in further contact when available. (c) answer question. (a) Describe the next steps, such as application form, test, factory visit. (b) arrange time for next contact.
4. Close	(a) Indicate decision to person. (b) avoid specific reasons for rejection. (a) Explain referral procedure. (b) give application blanks (c) give name of person or contact. (a) Suggest ways for maintaining ways for maintaining contact.
5. Rate	(a) Make notes fill out rating forms. Prepare to interview next application.

Fig. 9.2: Interview Procedure for Recruitment.

(I) Preparation for the Interview

Advance preparation by the interviewer is basic to the success of an interview for two important reasons. First, as the interview is generally too short to cover all the items that should be included in it, an advance preparation for it will enable an interviewer to cover all important aspects. Second, an advance preparation is necessary for the interviewer if he wants to remember the facts and the main points which he wants to cover in the interview. A number of decisions have to be taken and arrangements have to be made before the interview begins. These include:

(a) The determination of the specific objective of an interview;
(b) The choosing of an appropriate method of accomplishing the interview objectives;
(c) Acquainting oneself with the known information about the interview so that factors needing emphasis may be pre-determined;
(d) Determining the number of interviewers;
(e) Looking into the administration details, such as the place of interview, its approximate duration, and other arrangements.

(a) Determination of Objectives: According to the American Management Association, the main objectives of interviews are:

(1) To afford the interviewer an opportunity to judge an applicant's qualifications;

(2) To give the applicant the essential facts about the job and the company;

(3) To establish a rapport - a feeling of mutual understanding and confidence between the personnel department and the applicant; there the interview culminates;

(4) To promote goodwill towards the company, where as employment or not. In an interview, adequate information can be had in six broad areas:

(1) Personnel characteristics, such as physical appearance, health, ability to organize thoughts, dress, poise and grooming, self-confidence, alertness, the standard and style of conversation, facial expressions, manners and general working habits. In an interview, it can be found out how an applicant deports himself, whether he is outgoing, an extroverted, or a well-adjusted person or whether he is very shy, introverted, and unresponsive.

(2) Technical competency - information about the examinations he has passed, the grades, divisions obtained, awards and honours won, extracurricular activities. An interview provides an opportunity for a further exploration: why did the applicant choose a particular school or college? What did he do during the vacations? Which of the extra-curricular activities or hobbies gave him most satisfaction? Do his academic results reflect his ability correctly?

(3) Initiative, common sense and a general smartness.

(4) Ability to inspire confidence by sustained effort - without supervision. This can be known at an interview - the extent of the skill or stature of the interviewee, the relevance of such skill to the post under consideration, the level attained in regard to good judgment, decision-making ability, capacity for sustained hard work, and his originality and initiative in work. These facts may be gathered by putting questions in to the jobs previously held, any special features which he likes or dislikes and

why, his reasons for changing the job, his most notable achievement, the circumstances in which the existing job was secured and the kind of boss the applicant would like to work for.

(5) Capacity to work in a team: This can be gathered by knowing about the activities in which the applicant adjusted himself, his leisure-time activities, his hobbies, family circumstances and community interests, his relationship with other members of the family, the kind of persons who are his friends and the kind of people he would keep away from, his use of leisure time, the extent and nature of his general reading, the games and sports he has played and the nature and extent of his interests in these.

(6) Potential for growth: By skillful questioning, the interviewer can find out something about the long-range aspirations of the applicant, whether he is merely after money or has definite career goals; whether he is a drifter or one who would exploit every possible chance to develop his potential to the maximum. The probing areas to be covered may be extended to his reasons for applying for the particular job, his expectations about the job, the expected salary, his plans for realising his expectations, his strong and weak points, etc.

(b) Determination of the Method to be Used: It has to be decided before hand which interview technique will be used while interviewing an applicant. It may be the patterned interview method, which is highly accurate, precise and well-directed; or stress interview method, under which the applicant is placed in a position of stress in various ways; or the discussion interview method, or the background information interview method, which consists of putting a number of questions bearing on the interviewee's experience of the job, his education, health, interests, likes and dislikes, and his activities; or the discussion interview method, which is neither systematic nor comprehensive, in which no set questions are asked and in which the emphasis is on an analysis of expressions, not facts; group performance interview method, in which the entire group is interviewed at one and the same time, and the applicants interact more with one another than with the interviewer. The topic for discussion is given to the group and the individual applicants are keenly observed with a view to determining how they initiate or lead and close a discussion.

(c) **Acquainting Oneself About the applicant:** The interviewer should equip himself with as much information as possible about the interviewee. The necessary information may be gathered from the application blank; or verified from the applicant's former employers or from the school or institutions he attended; from referees; records and documents; certificates and testimonials; from the results of tests, etc. Prior information on various issues will make it possible for the interviewer to guard himself against any prejudices arising out of caste, religion or previous experience.

(d) **Determining the Number of Interviewers:** Generally, a minimum of two interviewers may talk to candidates for a lower level position, while for a higher post as many as eight or even more may be entrusted with the task. In the latter case, persons of different ages and representing different educational background, interests, and field experience may be chosen to hold a multiple interview. Two basic methods may be employed for it - either a panel may jointly interview each applicant or individuals may speak to the applicant one after the other. It is always better that several interviewers should interview a candidate consecutively rather than simultaneously. However, some experts are of the view that simultaneous interviewing is more desirable for it gives an opportunity to the interviewers to observe the candidate's responses to a group situation. Moreover, this method enables one interviewer to watch while the other is asking the questions. If there are, say, three interviewers, one may ask questions on the family and educational background, another may engage the applicant in a general discussion, while the third may test his job knowledge.

In an interview committee, usually there is a Chairman and the Personnel executive, the Department head, one or more subject experts, even a psychologist, and one or more other persons, if so desired by the Selection Committee.

(II) The Physical Setting

The place of interview should be carefully chosen, i.e., the physical setting be both private and comfortable in other words, the place of interview should have cross-ventilation and proper lighting arrangements with cooling and heating devices Such a room is generally at the back of the office building where there would be no disturbance, interruptions or frequent telephone calls or noises outside the room. Properly arranged seating accommodation should also be available. The room should generally vacant and the other as an exit. The candidates have two doors - one to be used as entry should be well-received by the receptionist, who is generally a member of the personnel department and led into the room. Nearby there should be privy and drinking water facilities, and the room should preferably be furnished with sofas and easy chairs. A few magazines and daily newspapers and other reading material should be placed on a properly arranged seating accommodation should also be available. The sitting room is generally kept apart from the place where the actual interviews are held so that the conversation between the interviewer and the interviewee is not overheard by other prospective candidates.

Proper arrangements for receptions and seating give an impression to the interviewee that he is an important person to whom the interviewer will devote unlimited attention. From this point of view, the treatment of the applicant before he meets the interviewer is very important; Dingy surroundings, lack of seating accommodation and privacy, a display of poor manners by the receptionist, the delay in starting the interview at the appointed time - all these produce an unhappy effect on the applicant. It should be remembered that first impressions can never be wiped off; they may make or mar the reputation of an organisation, its executives and interviewers.

The climate of the interview should be such gives the candidate an impression that a certain amount of preparation has been made "in his honour" and that the interviewers do not treat the interview as an interruption of their normal work, and which they would like to get over with as quickly as possible. There should be as little delay as possible in starting the interview, and it would be an excellent thing if a cup of tea or coffee, is offered to the candidate while he is waiting.

The time set for interviewers should be strictly adhered to. If a large number of people are to be interviewed for a number of identical jobs, the interviews should be so staggered that they are not required to report at 9:30 AM in a body. This is just managerial laziness and incompetence that such a large number of a candidate are summoned unnecessarily all together and they get bored or remain tenses for hour.

The usual practice should be to interview 25 to 30 candidates in a day; and these may be called in two batches, one in the forenoon and the other in the afternoon. There no set time limits but how long an interview will last will depend upon several factors like the type of position, the number of applicants the importance attached by the company to interview as a selection device and the personality of the interviewer. Some interviews for high positions may last for an hour or so; while for others they may take 20 to 30 minutes. It is to be noted that the value of interview is not so much dependent upon the time spent but the skills of the interviewer to obtain all necessary information in the shortest possible time without embarrassing the applicant in any way.

(III) Conduct of the Interview

This activity is usually aimed at establishing rapport with the candidate, getting a complete and accurate information from him and recording it properly.

(a) **Establishing Rapport:** A job interview can be a trying experience for the applicant. The interviewer should gain the confidence of the candidate at the very beginning by establishing rapport with him — cheerful initial conversation about something which interests the candidate and bearing on his name, his family history, hobbies, interests, achievements; or talk on general or current topics may help to "break the ice" and establish a friendly relationship. Even a genuine smile on the interviewer's face or an offer of a cigarette or a cup of tea and exchange of pleasantries. "Please take your seat and relax and tell us about yourself so that we may get acquainted" — this would serve the purpose. Without realising it, the applicant will be both physically and mentally less tense than he was before and will talk freely. To begin with, the interview should proceed not on the lines of a cross-examination but in the form of a conversation so that the two may get to know each other, with the specific underlying purpose of getting information in certain areas. Sufficient time should be allowed to enable the candidate to reveal the facts necessary for a fair assessment of him.

(b) **Getting Complete and Accurate Information:** Getting complete and accurate information from the applicant is an art which calls for experience, skill and technique on the part of the interviewer. The purpose is to know in depth the personality of the man to be hired and to evaluate his suitability for the post. For this purpose, the interviewer should see to it that, during the interview, he does not allow his own sense of values, feelings and prejudices to influence unduly the course of the conversation. In the words of a philosopher, J. Krishnamurti, "the tick is to observe the observer."

In other words, "the interviewer splits himself into two distinct persons, the outer man physically present and conversing with the applicant, and the inner man consciously watching behind a sort of one-way glass of his own perpetual screen and listening instantly to what is being said and done."

The interviewer should use the language which is clear to the applicant. He should frame skilful questions. Some general rules may be observed in questioning such as:

1. Leading questions should be avoided as well as those that reveal the interviewer's bias and prejudices. "Closed end" questions, which call for "Yes" and "No" should not be asked, for they offer little scope to the candidate to expand his answers and give more information. Moreover, they not only limit the conversation but definitely tend to make him tense and anxious about the next question. Therefore, preference should be given to open-end questions. These not only start the conversation and keep it going, but also afford an adequate opportunity to the candidate to answer the questions fully.
2. In between these two types of questions, there is variety of ways in which sensitive points can be probed. When one interviewer asks a particular question, which leads to some conversation in depth, another may make a note of the other points which strike him and ask clarifying questions later — such other points being based on the earlier answers, statements and responses of the candidate.
3. The interviewers should not "hog" the conversation they should have talent, experience, natural dexterity and a genuinely sympathetic attitude so that they may draw out the applicant, who may have a considerable potential but who may be shy and to be in with, 'probing' questions may be asked reserved in the beginning. Therefore, to begin with, probing question may be asked to find out on which topics, the applicant is interested and on which he is on defensive. Then the topics which interest the applicant may be picked up first, but not ignoring those topics in which he has shown reluctance because they may reveal some substantial information.
4. Highly personal questions should be omitted until one is sure that rapport has been fully established.

A typical aspect of the technique of interviewing is to present a hypothetical situation based fairly accurately on the circumstances which the candidate is likely to face in the normal course of his job and let him think aloud on the various aspects of the problem and how he would solve it. The way in which he understands and grasps the hypothetical situation, clarifies his replies, perceives the implications of the problem, analyses the various possible approaches and finally comes to a conclusion, whether the conclusion be right or wrong — all these reveal a great deal of the inner personality of the candidate and help the interviewers to assess him for the post.

To get answers from the candidate, the interviewer may apply several devices. He may ask questions on different subjects at the beginning to determine which is the most provocative in getting the answer; he may repeat parts of the key sentences of an answer in a questioning tone to indicate that he wants elaboration; he may ask one question at a time; he may clarify the question without indicating what he thinks the correct answer is; he may ask a wrong question with a view to testing the common sense of the candidate; he may not ask highly personal questions until rapport has been established; he may not bring the applicant back to the point on which he disagrees; and he may use the language which is appropriate for the candidate.

(c) Recording of Impressions: In order to make an accurate review and evaluation of the candidate following the interview, it is necessary that "notes," "observations" and "records" of the interviewers' impressions are briefly written down. This needs to be done for two reasons: One, it indicates to the candidate that the interviewer is interested in what he is saying and, therefore, he may continue to talk freely. Two complete information is available at the end of the interview to arrive at a final judgement. Brief notes are taken down of the correctness or otherwise of his answers, the way in which he behaves during the interview (frankness or nervousness), and the overall general impression he creates on the interviewer.

(IV) Close of the Interview

The close of the interview is as important as its beginning. Because it is a trying situation for the candidate. It should end with the same pleasantness with which it began without creating any awkward or embarrassing situation for the interview. The interview should not normally end without the candidate being finally asked whether he himself would like to say anything on any point concerning the job and the interview. It should be closed diplomatically so that the interviewee may feel satisted that he was given a full hearing.

The close of the interview may be indicated by some overt sign, such as laying down of the pen by the Chairman, or pushing back of his chair or standing up by him or by saying to the candidate, "Thanks, that will be all". Courtesy demands that the candidate should be given some indication of whether he has been accepted or not. Desirable applicants are generally told when they are likely to hear further about their acceptability and arrangements for medical examination, etc. Those who are certain to be rejected are told that they will be informed in due course of time, when "letters of regret" may be sent to them. This is done to avoid unpleasantness or frustration on the part of the candidate.

(V) Final Evaluation of the Candidate

After the interviews are over, the interviewers are required to evaluate a candidate's suitability for the job. For his purpose, his strength and weaknesses are critically balanced. The information collected during the interview needs an over-all synthesis on an intensive deductive basis which is the real significance of the interview. This is so because "neither statistical influence nor computed technology can replace the intensive deductive synthesis that occurs when one human being judges another. Moreover, such important job factors as appearance and poise can be described and appraised only by the cognitive faculties of the perceptive human mind." Weightage is also given to test experience, habits, behaviour and attitudes, and the facts which come to the notice of the interviewers. Form should be possible to know what he has done in the past and gauge fairly accurately what he is likely to do or not to do in future.

The evaluation may be done either by giving grades ranging from A to E by allocating marks. A may indicate excellent or outstanding, B very good, C good, average, and E marginal/poor or below average. B may be given to be considered while reaching a final decision. In the latter system, predetermined marks are allocated for requisite qualifications, in the division obtained at different levels, past experience and training received by the candidate. The marks are added and the position of the candidate determined.

The list of selected candidates may be prepared either in a descending order or alphabetically as may be decided by the interview committee.

Defects and Pitfalls in Interview

Certain common defects have been studied in employment interviews: For instance:

1. Interviewers have difficulty in establishing rapport with the applicants.
2. Interviewers do not have a clearly defined technique developed but tend to pounder looking for clue or opening.
3. Questions are not carefully formulated to elicit from the applicant freely and fully desired information.
4. Many interviewers do too much of the talking in an attempt to put the applicant at ease.
5. Many interviewers lack skill in bringing the interview to a close.

The interviewers often forget the fact that an individual fits into a pattern in one characteristic is no measure that his other interests follow a given pattern. In considering the appointment of personnel the following points should be kept in mind differs from another in his personal aptitudes and special abilities

(i) One in and each contributes to the work of his company in his own way in exchange for his salary.

(ii) Individuals differ in interests and motives and respond best to varying stimuli.

(iii) Different kinds of work require different kinds of personal abilities on the part of persons who are to perform them.

(iv) Granting equal ability, different kinds of work are performed best by persons who temperamentally, are particularly interested in them.

(v) The work in each position changes as time goes on and duties are added or taken away. Sometimes the change is negligible, sometimes it is substantial. To the extent to which it takes place, a similar change is apt to occur in the abilities and interests which a job requires of the worker.

(vi) Environment, working conditions, supervision, relations with the employer and fellow-employees and opportunity — these exercise a tremendous influence on personal efficiency and consequently on group production.

(vii) An individual changes from day-to-day from year-to-year in ability (both in degree and kind) and interest.

With purposeful effort under guidance persons can learn to interview effectively. In order to ensure that all the vital areas have been explored and covered, a guide prepare and utilised. This sheet should contain the information about appearance of the interviewee, his mannerisms, early life and family background, his education, work history, personality, social adjustment, and health. Beach has given a simple guide sheet for the beginner interviewee:

A. **Appearance and Mannerism:** It should take into consideration dress and bearing, speech and voice, facial expression, neatness and cleanliness and nervousness.

B. **Early Home and Family Background:** It places emphasis on father's passion, parents family life, number of family members, attitude towards parents and children, economic condition of the family, activities, hobbies and interests when young and social contacts and friends.

C. **Education:** It deals with matters related to educational qualifications, grades and diplomas, courses attended, extra-curricular activities, and so on.

D. **Work History:** It seeks information on reasons for choice of jobs, relation with an attitude to supervisors in previous jobs, reasons for changing jobs, career goals, type of work liked best method of obtain, the previous job and salary increases, promotions.

E. **Personality and Social Adjustment:** It deals with marital status present interests and sparetime activities, financial responsibility, emotional stability maturity, levels of aspiration, attitude towards work associates and towards authority, sincerity, initiative, and perseverance.

F. **Health:** It deals with past and present health problems, observes physical limitations.

Errors in Interviewing

There are certain common types of interviewing errors which need to be guarded against. Such errors are:

1. **The Halo Effect:** Under this type of error, one marked characteristic of the candidate (either favourale or unfavourable) may be allowed to dominate the appraisal of his entire personality. Physical appearance, his brilliant scholastic record, his fluency or lack of it in language, experience of living abroad, experience as a

sportsman, etc. any one of these qualities may create a halo effect. The interviewers should of the candidate's personality and should not be led away by any one trait or achievement. He should remember that good candidates come in all shape, size, ages, education, religion, caste, regionality, etc.

2. **Leniency:** When a candidate is rated by two raters their ratings may be diffent. One may show consistent leniency by giving him high scores; the other may consistently rate him by giving low scores. Leniency is usually associated with lack of confidence and interest in rating. Toughness may be the result of exaggerated expectation, lack of contact with people, and general rigidity of personality.
3. **Projection:** Error of projection arises when an interviewer expects his own qualities, skills, values in an applicant. And therefore, he may select the candidates who very much resemble him in age, appearance, manners, opinion, voice and background supervisors or managers interview the candidate, there is very possibility of this error being done.
4. **Stereotyping:** This type of error arises when the interviewer have already formed some mental association between a particular trait, culture or communal origin and a particular types of personality. Therefore, objectivity is a desirable quality for a particular type of personality of interviewer.

Interview Guidance for the Interviewees

Below are given a few hints to assist the interviewee in getting successfully:

1. **Preparation of a Resume:** An effective, typed biographical summary resume or vital information — is of prime importance. This summary must be a concise reflection of: (i) demographic data (name, permanent address, date of birth, marital status and telephone numbers, if any); (ii) carrier objective, both for short range (such as staff assistant or labour relation) and long range (e.g. Contract negotiators); (iii) educational background, and academic achievement; (iv) leadership position in club, athletic teams, student union and social organisation, and (v) previous work experience.
2. **Preparation for the Interview Itself:** The applicant should prepare himself fully before attending the interviews. He should study some literature about the company (such as its history and recent annual report) in order to ask specific questions about

product, process, goals or competitions. Questions on items that are related to job duties, the reason for joining the organisation, should be thorughly prepared. These questions demonstrate interest in the organisation. Therefore, the candidate should go in well armed with all necessary facts so that he can start off right, with a concrete, intelligent listing of his reasons. It must be noted that "the interviewer is probably not as interested in what the candidate thinks he will get out of the job as much as what he gets out of hiring him."

3. **During the Interview:** Interviewers frequently form their final judgements within the first few minutes of the interview, and most judgements are made before half the interview is completed. The old maxim "first impressions are important" is apparently sound for the interview process. Therefore, if the interviewee enters making a good impression and starts off well, this first impression may be changed by interview, but very rarely. But if he starts off with an initial unfavourable impression it may be impossible to overcome it during the interview.

To make a good impression and "accentuate the positive" aspect the interviewee must follow these considerations:

(i) appropriate clothing; (ii) good grooming; (iii) a firm handshake; (iv) the appearance of controlled energy; (v) pertinent humour and readiness to smile; (vi) a genuine interest in the employers operations and alert attention when the interviewer speaks; (vii) pride in past performance; (viii) an understanding of the employer's needs and a desire to serve them; (ix) the display of sound ideas; and (x) ability to take control when employers fall down on the interviewing job.

The interviewee should not initiate opening small talk. Response should be weighted, precise and relevant emphasing the interviewees' strong points without appearing pompous or egoistical. Eye contact is important.

Most of the interviewers cannot form an accurate impression of traits other than intelligence, personal relations, aptitude and motivation to work. Therefore, the candidates should emphasise on the letter in the interview. The candidate should try to leave the interviewer with the impression that he is eager and enthusiastic to do a good job. He should show the interviewer that he is motivated to work.

A clear statement of next action should be obtained before concluding the interview and a follow up letter from the interviewee acknowledging the interview should be sent within a few days.

What the Applicant should know about the Employer Organisation?

In most cases, out of sheer shyness or for fear of being misunderstood, the fresh applicants, when selected, join the organisation without getting sufficient information about the organisation and the employer. Such persons run a risk for they may not be able to fit themselves in the organisation. Therefore, it would always be useful for the person selected to get necessary information from different sources — acquaintances or person who work with the organisation, company manuals, brochures, annual reports, discussions with others who may have been interviewed with the same company.

Chart contains a listing of questions that should be answered before accepting positions.

Questions to Answer before Accepting a Positions

I. Promotion Criteria:

1. Does the organisation use a formal evaluation system?
2. How often is a person evaluated?
3. What are the major criteria upon which a person is evaluated?
4. Are evaluation criteria discussed with persons being evaluated?
5. Is career counselling available?
6. Does the organisation encourage publication in professional journals?

II. Professional Development:

1. Does the organisation offer a formal training programme?
2. If so, what is the nature and duration of the programme?
3. Is there any formal training in computers and information systems.
4. Does the organisation support travel to professional conferences/seminars?
5. Is there any form of tuition refund programme for college/professional diploma programmes?
6. What type of responsibility is offered during the first year on the job?

III. Organisational Background:

1. What are the objectives of the organisation?
2. What has been the general trend in sales, growth, employment, earnings, research, expenditures, and leverage?

3. What institutions have the senior officers attended? Foreign? or inside the country?
4. What is the nature of the organisations' affirmative action programme?
5. What is opportunity for women/handicaps/special minority groups in management?
6. How many persons left the staff during the past year?
7. What is the absentee rate for hourly personnel? Is it above the average for the industry?

IV. Financial Considerations (to be discussed and considered last):

1. What are the normal working hours? Is overtime pay granted for staff?
2. Is overnight stay required? If so for what period? What is reimbursement policy?
3. Is there a profit sharing plan? and or employees' stock options scheme.
4. Is retirement plan vested?
5. Vacation policy? Hospitalisation? Medical benefits? Life Insurance? Pension? Provident Fund/Gratuity, etc..
6. What would the starting salary be? What would be the usual allowances available?

Once an offer of employment has been extended and accepted, the final stage in procurement function is to be concluded, namely, that of placement of the individual on the new job and orienting him to the organisation.

"Placement" may be defined as "the determination of the job to which an accepted candidate is to be assigned, and his assignment to that job. It is matching of what the supervisor has reason to think he can do which the job demands (job requirements): it is a matching of what he deserves (as strain, working conditions), companionship with others, promotional possibilities, etc." A proper placement of a worker reduces employee turnover, absenteeism and accident rates, and improves morale.

After selection the employee is generally put on a probation period, ranging from six months to one year, after which his employment may be confirmed, provided, that during this period, his work has been found to be satisfactory. Only in very rare cases when there is the employee, once placed, asked to quit, and even something very serious charges against him or he is found guilty of continued negligence in the performance of his duties.

Orientation, Induction or Indoctrination

Induction is a technique by which a new employee is rehabilitated into his surroundings and introduced to the practices, policies and purposes of the organisation. In other words, it is a welcoming process — the idea is to welcome a newcomer, make him feel at home and generate in him a feeling that his own job, however small, is meaningful and has a significance as a part of the total organisation.

Objectives of Induction

When a newcomer joins an organisation he is a stranger to the people and work-place. When a newcomer joins an organisation and work in new environment, he may feel insecure, shy and nervous. The first few days may be anxious and disturbing ones for him. He may have anxiety caused by not following the usual practices prevalent in the organisation, or the haphazard procedures, and lack of information. These may develop discouragement, disillusionment or defensive behaviour. Induction leads to reduction of such anxieties; dispels the irrational fears of present employees and hold colleagues responsible for assisting feel confident.

There is another reason for effective induction. It helps minimise what might be called the reality shock some new employees undergo. This reality shock is caused by the incompatibility between what the employees expect in their new jobs and the realities they are confronted with. The newcomer may expect: (i) opportunities for advancement; (ii) social status and prestige-the feeling of doing something important and the recognition of this by others; (iii) responsibility; (iv) opportunities to use special aptitudes and educational background; (v) challenge and adventure; (vi) opportunity to be creative and original; and (vii) lucrative salary. But when these expectations are often not filled and, therefore, result in frustrating experiences for new employees, experiences of which include jobs with low initial challenge, inadequate feedback and inadequate performance problem appraisals. This result is "reality shock". Orientation by providing for more realistic expectations on the part of new employees and more understanding on the part of the supervisors.

Finally, the purpose of induction is to introduce the new employee and the organisation to each other, to help them become acquainted, and to help them accommodate each other. The newcomer is explained what is expected of him and for this, he is explained the rules and regulations, policies and procedures that directly affect him. He is made aware of how his job fits into the overall operation of the organisation his own duties and responsibilities, and to whom he should look for when he has any problem.

Shri B. P. Billimoria observes: "induction has a greater significance in a developing country like India, where the percentage of illiteracy is very high. The new worker finds himself completely at sea when by force of circumstances he has to shift from rural surroundings into an industrial unit. It is no use trying to push a handbook of certified rules and regulations into his hands and expecting him to turn out into a loyal and efficient employee. He needs a short and simple induction conducted by someone who speaks his own language. This will go a long way in reducing turnover and, above all, in preventing a worker from the likelihood of falling a prey to subversive elements which thrive on creating labour unrest by misrepresenting employees to illiterate employees.

Induction Procedure

An organisation has no obligation to make integration of the individual into the organisation as smooth and anxiety-free as possible. Whether that is achieved through a formal or informal placement orientation programme depends on the size of the organisation and the complexity of the individuals new environment. Many organisations develop formal orientation programmes. These might include a tour of the offices or plant, a talk about the history of the organisation, and short discussion with a representative of the Personnel Department who will describe the organisation's benefit plans. Other organisations may utilise an informal orientation programme which might include being assigned to another senior employee who will not only introduce the new worker to other workers but show him other things too.

There is no model induction procedure. Each industry develops its own procedures as per its needs. The procedure should basically follow these steps:

First, the new person needs time and a place to report to work.

Second, it is very important that the supervisor or the immediate boss meet and welcome the employee to the organisation.

Third, administrative work should be completed. Such items as vacations, probationary period, medical absences, suggestion systems should be covered.

Fourth, the departmental orientation can be conducted. This should include a get acquainted' talk, introduction to the department, explanation of the functions of the department, and job instruction and to whom he should look for help when he has any problem.

Fifth, verbal explanations are supplemented by a wide variety of printed material, employee handbooks, employee manuals, house-journals, picture stories, comics and cartoons, pamphlets, etc. along with short guided tour around the plant.

Orientation programmes usually cover things like employee compensation benefits, personnel policies, the employee's daily routine, company organisation and operations, and safety measures and regulations. The new employee's supervisor is often given an orientation checklist, personnel policies, the employee's daily routine, company organisation and operations, and safety measures and regulations. The orientation checklist is similar to that given in Chart. This helps to ensure that the supervisor has covered all of the necessary orientation.

It will thus be answered that orientation is generally provided on the following:

(i) The significance of the job with all necessary information training and job hazards;

(ii) The company, its history and products, process of production and major operations involved in his job;

(iii) Structure of the organisation - the geography of the plant and functions of the various departments;

(iv) Employee's own department and job and how they fit into the organisation;

(v) Many programmes include follow-up interviews at the end of three or six months with a view to finding out how the new employee is getting along;

(vi) Relations between foremen and personnel department;

(vii) Company policies, practices, objectives and regulations;

(viii) Personnel policy and sources of information;

(ix) Terms and conditions of service, amenities, and welfare facilities;

(x) Rules and regulations governing hours of work and overtime; safety and accidents prevention, holidays and vacations, methods of reporting, tardiness absenteeism;

(xi) Grievance procedure and rules of discipline;

(xii) Social benefits (insurance, incentive plans, pensions, gratuities, etc.) and recreation services (athletic, social and cultural activities); and

(xiii) Opportunities, promotions, transfers, suggestion schemes and job stabilisation.

Formal programmes of orientation may be spread over periods of time ranging from a day to several weeks or even months.

Typical Techniques of Induction Programmes

A typical induction programme should consist primarily of three steps:

(a) General orientation by the staff of the personnel department;

(b) Specific orientation by the job supervisor, or his representative; and

(c) Follow-up orientation by either the personnel department or the supervisor.

The first phase of the programme should ordinarily be conducted by the personnel department. This type of induction is general, for it gives the necessary general information about the history and operations of the firm — the purpose of which is to help an employee to build up some pride and interest in the organisation. Information is also given on specific employee services, such as pension, health and welfare plans, safety programmes, etc. The better policy is not to give everything in one day, but to administer smaller doses over a long period.

At the second stage, induction should be conducted by the job supervisor. Induction is specific and requires skill on the part of the foreman. The employee is shown the department and his place of work, introduced to other employees, informed of the location of the bathrooms, lavatories, canteens, and time clock; and told about the organisation's specific practices and customs (such as whether the personnel bring their lunch or whether lunch is supplied to them at concessional rates, the timings and length: rest periods, the work dress, etc.). The purpose of specific induction is to enable an employee to adjust himself to his work and environment.

Follow-up induction takes place sometime within one week to six months from the time of the initial hiring and orientation. It is conducted either by a foreman or a specialist. Its purpose is to find out whether the employee is reasonably well-satisfied with. The employee may be asked whether his hours of work and his pay are as represented to him before employment; how he feels about his fellow-workers: how he feels about his boss; and whether he has any suggestions to make for changes in the induction procedure or in other company practices. The interviewer records the answers as well as his own comments on the employee's progress. At the same time, the line supervisor completes an evaluation of the employee, indicating his strong and weak points, indicating also whether he is doing well.

Through personal talks, guidance and counselling, efforts are made to remove the difficulties experienced by the newcomer.

Career Planning

Career planning means helping the employees to plan their career in terms of their capacities with regard to the organisational needs. It includes establishing an organisational system of career movement and growth opportunities from the point of entry an individual in employment to the point of his retirement. It is a kind of management's planning exercise to design the entire career of young employees in higher skilled, supervisory and managerial positions. Thus, it is the discovery and development of talents, and planned deployment and redeployment of these talents. It is also referred to as a process of synthesising and harmonising the needs of the organisation with the innate aspirations of the employees, so that while the latter realise self-fulfilment, the organisational effectiveness is improved. Generally, a career can be defined as a sequence of separate but related work activities that provide continuity, order and meaning to a person's life. It is not only a series of work-related experiences, but also a series of properly sequenced role experiences, leading to an increasing level of responsibility, status, power, and rewards. The following are the advantages of career planning:

1. It increases the utilisation of managerial reserves within the organisation.
2. It ensures satisfactory performance of employees by meeting their needs and aspirations for growth.
3. It reduces the employee turnover for lack of promotional avenues.
4. It improves and maintains motivation and morale of employees.

Career planning has its own limitations. Small organisations cannot have career planning. Its other shortcomings are difficulties in identifying suitable persons for career planning and lack of suitable organisational climate. Despite its limitations, it serves as an integral part of the manpower planning and corporate planning and in the process contributes towards individual development and organisational development, and effective achievement of corporate goals.

Chapter - 10

Promotions, Transfers, Separation, Absenteeism and Turnover

Introduction

Promotion, transfer and separation are activities through which an adjustment in the size of workforce of an enterprise can be made to cope with the situations. Such adjustments in work force may be needed to meet special situations. Such as changes in organisational structure involving regrouping of jobs, changes in the jurisdictions of the departments and relocation of individuals, jobs and departments; fluctuations in volume of production and employment due to introduction of new or complete stoppage of old and products, services, processes, methods. etc. The three functions - promotion, transfer and separation - provide work force flexibility and mobility to suit the requirements of the organisation. These functions can be accomplished informally or formally. Usually formal systems are adopted to secure operative consistency and efficiency.

Promotions

"Promotion" is a term which covers a change and calls for greater responsibilities, and usually involves higher pay and better terms and conditions of service and, therefore, a higher status or rank.

According to Scott and Clothier: "A promotion is the transfer of an employee to a job which pays more money or one that carries some preferred status."

A promotion may be defined as an upward advancement of an employee in an organisation to another job, which commands better pay, wages, better status/prestige, and higher opportunities/challenges, responsibility, and authority, better working environment, hours of work and facilities, and a higher rank.

Promotion is a bit different from upgrading, which is concerned with minor promotions, promotions within grade or horizontal promotions.

Purpose of Promotions

A promotion is a vertical move in rank and responsibility. Involved in a promotion and may be some measure of skill; and responsibility, e.g., it may be from a machinist B grade to a machinist A grade, or it may involve an entirely different type of work, for example, from salesman to a sales manager or from a fitter Grade III to a fitter Grade II, or from a clerk to the post of a section in-charge. Promotions are usually given:

(i) To put the worker in a position where he will be of greater value to the company and where he may derive increased personal satisfaction and income from his work.

(ii) To remove a worker from his job as an alternative to avoid the embarrassment of firing or demoting him;

(iii) To recognise an individual's performance and reward him for his work so that he may have an incentive to forge ahead. Employees will have little motivation if better jobs are reserved for outsiders;

(iv) To increase an employee's organisational effectiveness;

(v) To build up morale, loyalty, and a sense of belonging on the part of the employees when it is brought home to them that they would be promoted if they deserve it;

(vi) To promote job satisfaction among the employees and give them an opportunity for unbroken, continuous service;

(vii) To provide a process of "selective socialisation." Employees whose personalities and skills enable them to fit into an organisation's human relations programme tend to stay on; while those whose personalities with those of the organisation clash tend to leave;

(viii) To attract suitable and competent workers for the organisation;

(ix) To create among employees a feeling of contentment with their present conditions and encourage them to succeed in the company.

Watkins, Dodd and others mention that purposes of promotion are:

(a) To furnish an effective incentive for initiative, enterprise and ambition;

(b) To conserve proved skill, training and ability;

(c) To reduce discontent and unrest;

(d) To attract suitable and competent workers; and

(e) To suggest logical training for advancement.

As Yoder and others observe, "promotion provides incentive to initiative, enterprise, ambition; minimises discontent and unrest; attracts capable individuals; necessitates: logical training of advancement and forms an effective reward for loyalty and co-operation, service, etc.

Promotions have a salutary effect on the satisfaction of the promoted person's needs esteem, belonging and security. They also afford an opportunity for greater self-actualisation through more varied and challenging assignments.

Types of Promotions

Promotions may be multiple chain promotions which provide for a systematic linking of each position to several others. Such promotions identify multi-promotional opportunities clearly defined avenues of approach to and exit from each position in the organisation.

In a up or out promotion, a person must either earn a promotion or seek employment. Many universities and other organisations follow this practice. Such promotions lead to termination of services.

Dry promotions are those which are given in lieu of increases in compensation, i.e., all compensation is adjusted upward to keep pace with the cost of living we have promotions.

Promotion becomes a delicate problem not in the matter of selection of the right incumbent for the right job, but it poses a constant challenge to executives at all levels and impels them to chalk out a well-thought-out programme by which the best and the must an opportunity to go up to the top. The procedure for promotion, therefore, starts right at the bottom from the shop floor and ends with the managing director of a company.

All promotions should be on a trial basis (from six months to one year) for if the promoted person is not found capable of handling his job, he may be reverted to his former post and former pay scale.

Promotion Programme and Procedure

A promotion programme consists of the following basic elements:

Deciding the Policy: The management must provide realistic opportunities which will encourage promising employees to take the risks involved in moving upward. It must not discourage valuable employees from seeking advancement by making service in an unpopular job a prerequisite for promotion. It must provide for employees who do outstanding work but who are unwilling to take on new and additional responsibilities. It must provide alternatives for professionals who are reluctant to assume supervisory responsibilities.

"Organisation that have failed to reward excellence is service or that have relied too heavily on personal relationships or length of service, suffer in terms of both efficiency and morale."

Each organisation needs to strike a balance between the internal sources of personnel promotion and external source (through recruitment) on the one hand and between merit and ability as against length of service on the other. "The organisation that fails to develop a satisfactory procedure is bound to pay a severe penalty in terms of administrative costs, misallocation of personnel, low morale, and ineffectual performance, among both non-managerial employees and their supervisors."

Since promotions mean advancement for some, the promotional process itself must ensure that successful candidates are sufficiently acceptable to their subordinate and others so that leadership in, and effective administrative of organisational progress is hindered and unhampered. A management should frame the policy on the basis of which promotions may be made.

A sound promotion policy must satisfy the following criteria:

(a) It should enjoy consistency, i.e., it will be applied irrespective of the persons concerned. Consistency demands that the policy should be so correlated to career planning that there should not be a sudden spurt of promotion in the organisation conferring premature benefits on a number of persons, followed by a long period of absence of promotion.

(b) It should be fair and impartial, i.e., the management should be able to remove all suspicion of arbitrariness, adhocism, improvisation to suit particular individuals, nepotism, etc.

(c) Promotion should be a planned activity, i.e., the management should make a correct assessment of the requirements or opportunities of promotion within the organisation so that there is no phenomenon of 'bunching' or no period of 'promotional drought', i.e., no over-estimation or under-estimation.

The promotion policy should involve six elements as follows:

1. **Promotion Policy Statement,** which should consider whether vacancies are primarily to be filled up from within an organisation or by recruitment from outside. Is any preferential treatment to be given to direct recruits? Would it be sound to deny promotion

otherwise qualified personnel? Whether an increase in pay is to be given? If so, when and how much? Usually, internal promotions are preferred over external recruitment and increase is given at the time of promotion, otherwise promotion is meaningless.

2. **Establish as Plan of Jobs,** i.e., decide on what basis promotions are to be given. Whether on performance appraisal, or on the basis of confidential records, or job and post-bid system. Which positions are to be filled up? Usually promotions are decided on the basis of performance appraisals. "Job-post and bid system", i.e., positing of job vacancies indicating job titles, duties, pay and qualifications on company notice boards, is also utilised.
3. **Trace Transfer Routes**, i.e., having some type of formal and systematic promotion channels. Ladders giving paths of advancement, promotional charts, opportunity charts or fortune sheets clearly distinguish each job and by lines and arrows, connect various jobs; and show the lines/routes of advancement up to and away from them. Stepping jobs should be clearly identified and recorded on paper. Dead-end jobs should be labeled and the path upward well marked.
4. **Prepare Employees for Advancement,** through the Provision of some training, either on the job in professional/technical institutions, or through job rotation, multiple management, under-study and conferences.
5. **Communicate the Policy,** the organisation should communicate its promotion policy either in the form of a manual or in the agreement signed with the union or in the form of a set of Standing Orders. To have a policy and not to communicate it to the employees will only create suspicions and misgivings. However, for higher level personnel a precise formulation of such a policy may not be effective.
6. **Detailed Personnel and Service Records are Kept Ready** on the basis of which promotions may be made.

The following indices are available for judging whether candidates are suitable for promotion:

The margin of performance on his present job, i.e., does he run it with ease and with margin to spare or is he barely able to manage his job?

Flexibility or versatility, i.e., has been successful on different types of jobs requiring different skills and different abilities, or does he seem to be only interested in a restricted field?

Intelligence, i.e., how does he think? How has he learnt on work he has carried out?

Equipment, i.e., how compatible are his education, literacy, expression and personality with the critical needs of the job?

Motivation, i.e., what are his wants? What is important for him? What are his goals, his objectives in work and life?

Promotion System

Thus, a promotion system involves clear-cut denitions of line of future advancement, detailed personnel records, specific promotion plans, definite allocation of responsibility for identifying promotable individuals and a centralised coordination of promotion function. Beach has very aptly described promotion systems for different categories of personnel in the organisation. He observes: "For unskilled and semi-skilled workers, entry is made into 'labour pool' and thereafter upgrading takes place on the basis of seniority or a combination of both seniority and ability. The skilled craftsmen are recruited as helpers or apprentices and thereafter upward mobility occurs up to position of foremen, inspectors or production co-ordinators. Entry in clerical jobs is through appointment as clerks, typists or stenographers and subsequently promotions are made to higher positions such as that of secretaries or administrative assistants. In professional jobs, entry is made as assistant engineers, engineers, senior engineers, project engineers or even managers. Jobs in managerial positions are filled up by individuals who enter as management trainees or assistant supervisors, finally they are promoted to middle level management positions and ultimately to top management positions."

Promotions may be based on either the "rank-in-the-job" or "rank-in-the-man." In former system, the content of the job including level of skill, efforts and responsibility form the basis. In this system emphasis is laid on job analysis, job evaluation, organisational planning, etc. These determine the pay and status in the organisation. In the latter system, emphasis is put on proficiency of the individuals. It determines the position level in the hierarchy of career pattern.

Promotion Policy

The usual policy is to take merit into consideration. Sometimes length of service, education, training courses completed, previous work history, etc., are factors which are given weight while deciding on a promotion. Although promotions are made on the basis of ability, hard work, co-operation, merit, honesty, many informal influences are powerful determinants of a promotional policy.

For higher posts, persons are picked by the top executives:

(i) Who think and feel just as he does;

(ii) Who value loyalty to him and to the organisation; and

(ii) Who have social political, economic and religious interests similar to his own.

Top executives lend to choose those who are carbon copies of themselves.

Seniority versus Merit: "Seniority" refers to length of service in the company or in its various plants, or in its departments, or in a particular position. Under straight plant-wise seniority in all jobs, promotions go to the oldest employees, provided that he is fit for the job. Occupational seniority may be within a department, within a entire plant.

Seniority offers certain rights and benefits. These are:

(a) Some rights are based on competitive seniority among employee promotion, transfer, lay-off and recall are such examples.

(b) Other benefits have nothing to do with one man relative to another, e.g. man may be entitled to have 15 days' casual leave in a year, a pension after 30 years and a certain amount of sick leave after six months service.

There is a great controversy on the question of whether promotions should be given on the basis of seniority or ability. Trade unions are of the view the promotions should be given on the basis of seniority, while managements favour promotions on the basis of merit and ability.

If promotion is given to a qualified man in recognition of his performance or with a view to creating an incentive for him, then it should be based on his ability.

If, on the other hand, promotion is given to recognize and reward senior employee then it should be on the basis of seniority.

The most widely used basis for promotion combines both ability and seniority. The best policy would be to ensure that whenever there are two employees of equal seniority, ability or merit should be the deciding factor in a promotion. Where, however, there are two employees of almost equal competence, seniority should be the decisive factor. Such a policy would satisfy the management which prefers ability, and trade unions which prefer seniority.

Arguments for and Against Promotion by Seniority Systems

Promotion by seniority is preferred by trade unions and most employees because:

(a) The system is simple to understand and operate. All employees are assured that promotion will come automatically when it is due.

(b) It satisfies the personal aspirations of the employees for growth, builds morale and is conducive to better labour-management relations.

(c) It leads to an optimum utilisation of the existing work force by training and development.

(d) This system is much more economical than open market recruitment or recruitment by negotiation with other candidate belonging to another organisation.

(e) The management will have a known man of good performance in a higher position than take a risk in bringing an unknown outsider.

But this system suffers from certain drawbacks too such as:

(a) The internal sources may be quite inadequate, and possibilities are that people who do not quite come up to the requirements of higher jobs, may be promoted.

(b) Since the working system and technology change very fast, it is necessary that new blood should be infused with new and up-to-date knowledge and ideas which the older persons in organisation may be lacking.

(c) The worth of an individual is not appreciated and given due recognition. This generates frustration and may constrain a good employee to leave the organisation.

(d) When there are wholesale promotions, promotion from within might cause disorganisation and upset the working of the organisation.

On the other hand, the system of promotion by merit enjoys these benefits:

(a) It brings rewards for meritorious work, extra competence, achievement and initiative;

(b) It encourages an employee to work hard so that he may get an opportunity for advancement in the organisation;

(c) It leads to increased productivity, for individuals are satisfied that their merit and competence will be properly appreciated and rewarded.

Practice in India

In India, in some companies, promotions are made on the basis of merit. potential and seniority. Internal promotions are also granted, from the existing lower cadre on the basis of seniority and merit.

In public sector organisations, elaborate rules exist for regulating the seniority of employees in different service cadres. Promotions are made from this list. But often, due to political pressures, the rules are violated and a person standing much lower in the list is given priority over the senior-most men.

In the private sector enterprises, the promotions are generally not based upon any clear-cut rule. Efficiency is the main consideration, unless it is a family enterprise where relationship with the proprietors or patronage might play a part. But even there only a limited number of posts would be filled upon the basis of relationship or by way of patronage. Even in such firms where employees are concerned there is generally a well-defined promotion policy and nepotism is avoided, as far as possible, where the employees are well organised. The rule followed is: "Promote the best man available."

While making promotions, the management must ensure that:

(a) Proper talents are first made available by a correct programme of recruitment;
(b) Employees are enabled to satisfy their own aspirations within the framework of the company's own objectives and projects; and
(c) A programme of career planning, coupled with periodic assessment is followed in accordance with rules.

It is worth noting that in a developing economy like India, with rapid technological advances and need for training and education it is not always possible to promote the older workers who can neither be adequately trained nor are willing to be exposed to new concepts, ideas and methods of work. As for the higher level promotions, only in large organisation can a policy of promotions from within be practicable; but even there such promotions cannot be confined entirely to the existing personnel of the organisation, unless management development and career planning are an essential part of the company's promotion policy.

Demotion

'Demotion' has been defined as "the assignment of an individual to a job of rank and pay usually involving lower level of difficulty and responsibility."

In other words, demotion refers to the lowering down of the status, salary and responsibilities of an employee. It is used as a punitive measure when there are serious breaches of duty on the part of an employee when it is often a preliminary to a dismissal. When an employee is demoted, his pride suffers a more severe jolt than it does when he is superseded by his junior.

Causes of Demotion

Demotions may be caused by factors beyond an employee's control: departments are combined and jobs eliminated, employees:

(i) When department are combined and jobs eliminated, employees are often required to accept lower level position until normalcy is restored. Such demotions are not a black mark against an employee;

(ii) Inadequacy on the part of the employees in terms of job performance, attitude and capability – as happen when an individual find it difficult to meet job requirement standards, following his promotion; and

(iii) When because of a change in technology, methods and practices, old hands are unable to adjust, or when employees, because of ill-health or personal cannot do their job properly.

(iv) Demotion is also used as a disciplinary measure.

Demotion Policy: Yoder, Heneman, Turnbull and Stone have suggested a policy in regard to demotion practice:

(i) A clear and reasonable list of rules should be framed, violations of which would subject an employee to demotion;

(ii) This information should be clearly communicated to employees;

(iii) There should be a competent investigation of any alleged violation;

(iv) If violations are discovered, there should be a consistent and equitable application of the penalty, preferably by the immediate supervisor;

(v) There should be a provision for review.

Demotions serve a useful purpose in the sense that they keep the employees alert and alive to their responsibilities and duties. For persons with a long and meritorious service, there should be no demotion.

However, some of their duties and responsibilities may be taken from them and assigned to others. The other alternative is to create a job for the person at the same pay and status but with lower job demands.

A demotion should never be made as a penalty for a violation of the rules of conduct, poor attendance record, or insubordination because such action will not improve the performance of the individual. Only discipline and training can set the things right.

Demotions have a serious impact on need fulfillment. Needs for esteem and belonging are frustrated, leading to a defensive behaviour on the part of the person demoted; there is complaining, emotional turmoil, inefficiency or resignation. Hence, demotions are made quite infrequently. Many managers prefer to discharge employees rather than face the problems arising from demotion.

Transfer

Yoder and associates have defined transfer as "a lateral shift causing movement of individuals from one position to another usually without involving any marked change in duties, responsibilities, skills needed or compensation."

A transfer is a horizontal or lateral movement of an employee from one job, section, department, shift, plant or position to another at the same or another place where his salary, status and responsibility are the same. It generally does not involve a promotion, demotion or a change in job status other than movement from one job or place to another.

Purposes of Transfers

Transfers are generally effected to build up a more satisfactory work team and to achieve the following purposes:

(a) To satisfy such needs of an organisation as may arise out of a change in the quantity of production, fluctuations in work requirements, and changes in the organisational structure; the introduction of new lines of production, the dropping of existing product lines, the reallocation of, or reduction in the work force due to a shortage or a surplus in the same section so that lay-offs may be avoided; filling in of the vacancies which may occur because of separations or because of the need for suitable adjustments in business operations. Such transfers are known as production transfers, flexibility transfers, or organisational transfers. The purpose of such transfers is to stabilise employment in an organisation. They are generally controlled centrally through and by the personnel department.

(b) To meet an employee's own request, when he feels uncomfortable on the job because of his dislike of his fellow workers, or because better opportunities for his future advancement do not exist there, or because of family circumstances which may compel him to change the place of his residence. Such transfers generally have their root in a faulty selection and erroneous placement, and are known as personal transfers. They enable employees to feel at home in the work of their choice.

(c) To utilise properly the services of an employee when he is not performing adequately and when the management feels that he may be more use or suitable elsewhere where his capacities would be better utilised. Such transfers are called remedial transfers. They act as a follow-up measure of the selection-and-placement procedure and help employees to adjust themselves to suitable jobs.

(d) To increase the versatility of the employee, by shifting him from one job to another so that he may have ample opportunities for gaining a varied and broader work. Such transfers are known as versatility transfers. They make it possible experience for an employee to enjoy the facility of job enrichment, which in turn gives to the management a more effective and experienced employee for a higher job.

(e) To adjust the work force of one plant with that of another particularly when one is closed down for reasons beyond the control of the employer. Such transfers are known as plant transfers and are generally effected on humanitarian ground to ensure that as persons who have been long in service of an organisation are not thrown out of employment.

(f) To replace a new employee by an employee who has been in the organisation a sufficiently long time. Such transfers are known as replacement transferred from night shift to morning shift or from the first to the second shift.

(g) To help employees work according to their convenience so far as timings are concerned, for example, an employee is transferred from night shift to morning shift or the first to the second shift. Such transfers are known as shift transfer.

(h) To penalise the employee transfer are also done, under which either a difficult trade union activist or intriguer or lawyer may be transferred to a remote branch or office where he cannot continue his activities. In Government organisations, this practice is widespread, and is also preferred by the employee to the grim alternative of disciplinary action.

(i) Transfer for the maintenance of a tenure system. In senior administrative services of the Government and also in industries, or where there is a system of annual intake of management trainees such transfers are common. Here the employee holds a certain job for a fixed tenure but he is made to move from job to job with a view to enabling him to acquire a variety of experience and skills and also to ensure that he does not get involved in politicking informal groups.

Scott and others have classified transfers according to:

(i) The convenience of the company:
   (a) Temporary transfers arising from temporary absenteeism; shifts in the work load; vacation;
   (b) Permanent transfers arising out of shifts in the work load; vacancies which need the special skill or ability of the transferred employee.

(ii) The convenience of the employee:
   (a) Temporary transfers arising from the ill-health of, or an accident to an employee; for family reasons or for taking care of some private affair;
   (b) Permanent transfers arising out of ill health or accident; out of outside interest — for example, for the purpose of attending a professional school or similar activities; out of family consideration; out of a desire to learn a particular skill.

Transfer Policy

Every organisation should have a just and impartial transfer policy which should be known to each employee. The responsibility for effecting transfers is usually entrusted to an executive with power to prescribe the conditions under which requests for transfers are to be approved.

For successful transfer policies, it is necessary to have a proper job description and job analysis. Care should be taken to ensure that frequent or large-scale transfers are avoided by laying down adequate selection and placement procedures for the purpose.

(i) Specifically clarify the types of transfers and the conditions under which these will be made;

(ii) Locate the authority in some officer who may initiate and implement transfers;

(iii) Indicate whether transfers can be made only within a sub-unit or also between departments, divisions/plants;

(iv) Indicate the basis for transfer, i.e., whether it will be based on seniority or on skill and competence or any other factor;

(v) Decide the rate of pay to be given to the transferee;

(vi) Intimate the fact of transfer to the person concerned well in advance;

(vii) Be in writing and duly communicated to all concerned;

(viii) Not be made frequently and not for the sake of transfer only.

In making transfers, the usual policy that is followed is to pay to the employee the actual cost of moving the household to the place of transfer.

Procedure for Transfer

Intra-departmental transfers or transfers within the same section of the same department are decided by the foreman or plant manager, and these are effected without the issue of any transfer order to the employee. He may be given oral instructions. The personnel manager, however, must be informed of such transfers. Inter-departmental transfers or transfers from one department to another are decided by mutual consultations among the departmental heads/plant managers when such transfers are of a permanent nature or of long duration. Written orders, signed by the personnel manager are issued to the employee.

Transfers from one place or unit to another place or unit, involving a considerable change in working conditions and cost to the company, have to be made in writing, after giving due notice to the employees. But, as far as possible, such transfers are generally discouraged.

Separations

"Separation" means cessation of service with the organisation for one or other reason. The employee may be separated from the pay roll of a company as a result of:

1. Resignation;
2. Discharge and dismissal;
3. Suspension and retrenchment; and
4. Lay-off.

1. Resignation

Resignations may be put in voluntarily by the employees on grounds of health, disability, better opportunities elsewhere, or maladjustment with company policy and officers, or for reasons of marriage or they may be compulsory when an employees are to put in his resignation if he wants to avoid termination of his service on the ground of gross negligence of duty on his part, or some serious charge against him.

2. Discharge

A discharge involves permanent separation of an employee from the pay-roll for violation of company rules or for inadequate performance.

A discharge becomes necessary:

(i) When the volume of business does not justify the continuing employment of the personal involved;

(ii) When a person fails to work according to the requirements of the job either because of incapacity or because he has deliberately slowed down on work, or because there is no suitable place where he can be transferred.

(iii) When an individual forfeits his right to a job because of his violation of a basic policy often involving the safety of others, the morale and discipline of a group.

Causes of Discharge: A discharge seldom arises from a single impulsive act. Many causes may account for it. Some of these are:

(a) **Frequent Causes:** Inefficiency, dishonesty, drunkenness, carelessness or indifference, violation of rules.

(b) **Infrequent Causes:** Accidents, insubordination, personal conduct, uncleanliness, fraction of rules, destructive negligence, wastefulness, and physical unfitness.

(c) **Other Causes:** Carelessness, lack of co-operation, laziness, tardiness in starting work, frequent absence without leave, dishonesty, lack of specific skills preventing promotion adverse attitude towards the organisation.

Discharge Procedure: To avoid unnecessary grievances arising from discharges, proper rule should be framed to govern them.

To demonstrate that a discharge is justified and does not arise out of unfair discrimination or personal prejudice of the supervisor, following evidence needs be produced:

(i) Permanent records of all merit ratings made by supervisors.

(ii) Permanent records of ratings of the defendands – traits maintain by person other than the foreman;

(iii) A Memorandum bearing on the efforts made by the foreman to help the defendant to overcome his weakness,

(iv) A copy of any warning that had been, sent him.

(v) The letter of discharge, especially if the letter states the cause of the discharge.

Discharge is generally made in accordance with the Standing Orders. The action taken should be bonefide and neither a punitive measures nor a case of victimisation.

The following elements should be present in a discharge programmed:

(i) The reasons for discharge should be clearly stated.

(ii) The individual concerned should be adequately informed about the reasons for his discharge.

(iii) The supervisor, in charge of initiating discharge action, should be fully conversant with rules and regulations of the organisation.

(iv) The facts regarding the violations of the rules and regulations should be carefully analysed.

(v) Line officials should handle the discharge affairs.

(vi) There should be a well-thought-out procedure for setting the discharge case.

(vii) Adequate provision should exist for review of the discharged employee's case.

(viii) A discharged employee needs a reasonable notice or an equivalent of pay in lieu of notice. It carries with it certain penalties, such as difficulty of re-employment, loss of benefits and, in certain cases, the loss of a part of the provident fund, etc.

Dismissal

A dismissal is the termination of the services of an employee by way of punishment for some misconduct, or for unauthorised and prolonged absence from duty. Before his services are terminated, an employee is given an opportunity to explain his conduct and to show cause why he should not be dismissed. The general rule is that in this process, there should be no violation of what is known as the principle of natural justice, which ensures that punishment is not out of all proportion to the offence.

3. Suspension

This is a serious punishment, and is generally awarded only after a proper enquiry has been conducted. For reasons of discipline, a workman may be suspended without prejudice during the course of an enquiry. During suspension, the employee receives a subsistence allowance.

Retrenchment: It means a permanent termination of the services of an employee for economic reasons in a going concern. The Industrial Disputes Act, 1947, defines retrenchment as the "termination by the employer of the services of workmen for any reason."

It must be noted that termination of services as a punishment given by way of disciplinary action, or retirement either voluntarily or on reaching the age of superannuation, continued ill-health, or on the closure and winding up of a business, does not constitute retrenchment. The term is applied to continuing operations where a part of the work force found to be superuous.

A worker can be retrenched if the following conditions are satisfied:

(a) He has been given three months' notice in writing, indicating the reasons for retrenchment, and the period of notice has expired; or he has been paid wages in lieu of such notice for the period of the notice;

(b) The worker has been paid, at the time of retrenchment, compensation which is equivalent to 15 days' average pay for every completed year of continuous service or any part thereof in excess of six months;

(c) Notice has been served on the appropriate movement authority and the permission such authority has been obtained if required.

On retrenchment, an employee is entitled to both retrenchment compensation and gratuity. The former is intended to give a worker some relief and to soften the hardship which retrenchment inevitably causes. The principle in the procedure of retrenchment is that the last person employed in each category must be first person to be retrenched, i.e., "last come, first go'. For this purpose, the employer prepares a list of all the workers in the category where retrenchment is contemplated, arranged according to the seniority of service of the employees in that category. This list is displayed on the Notice Board at least seven days before the actual date of retrenchment.

When vacancies arise after retrenchment, the employer gives an opportunity to the retrenched workers to offer themselves for re-employment; and they are given preference. Such vacancies are generally notified at least 10 days before they are filled up.

4. Lay-off

A lay-off refers to an indefinite separation of the employee from the pay-roll due to factors beyond the control of the employer; the employee is expected to be called back in the foreseeable future. It involves a temporary or permanent removable from the pay roll of persons with surplus skills. The purpose of a lay-off is to reduce the financial burden on an organisation when human resources cannot be utilised profitably.

According to Section 2 (KKK) of the Industrial Disputes Act, a lay-off has been defined as "the failure, refusal or inability of an employer, on account of shortage of coal, power or raw materials, on the accumulations of stocks or breakdown of machinery for any reason, to give employment to a workman whose name is borne on the muster roll of his individual establishment and who has not been retrenched."

Thus, a lay-off means the failure, refusal or inability of an employer to provide employment to a workman whose name is borne on the muster roll of his establishment. It is resorted to as a result of some such bonafide reasons as factors which are beyond the control of the employers:

(a) Breakdown of machinery;

(b) Seasonal fluctuations in markets and loss of sales;

(c) Accumulation of stocks or financial slump;

(d) Shortage of raw material, coal and power;

(e) Production delays; and

(f) Other technological reasons.

Generally, hourly-paid employees are first affected by lay-offs, followed by white-collar salaried employees. In a unionised organisation, the labour contract governs the order of lay-off and the method of recall; it defines what a lay-off is, fixes the maximum period during which a laid-off employee has to be recalled, and mentions the other rights which he has.

Workmen must not be laid off capriciously, nor as a part of a manoeuvre to lower labour costs. "Whom to let go and whom to retain" is decided by the top management.

But the general principle to be followed is to lay-off the juniormost, temporary and probationary employees first — last in, first out (LIFO); and when they are recalled, the principle is LOFI (last out, first in).

Sometimes other criteria may be use, such as ability job performance, age, length of service, number of dependants, financial obligations, etc. Usually, job performance and ability are given the greatest weight, followed next by length of service.

A lay-off policy has to be very cautious, otherwise it will lead to a high labour turnover, affect effective teamwork, destroy morale and increase the cost of unemployment insurance. The best policy is to reduce the work days of all the employees or transfer the excess work force of one department to a department where it is needed. A laid-off worker is paid 50 percent of his basic wages and dearness allowance for every working day on which he reports for work. If there is a previous agreement between the worker and management to this effect, lay-off compensation need not be paid for more than 45 days during any period of 12 months. When a workman is laid-off for more than 45 days, and when the lay-off after the expiry of the first 45 days is a continuous period of one week or more, the workman, unless there is any agreement to the contrary between him and the employer, may be paid at the above rate for all the days of every such subsequent period of one week or more. Where a workman has been paid lay-off compensation beyond 45 days and is retrenched, the employer may deduct the amount so paid, from the retrenchment compensation payable to him.

In order to receive his lay-off compensation, the workman must present himself on each working day at the appointed time. Where it is expedient, he may be required to report a second time during the same day. At the time of this second report, he is paid as if he had been employed for the full day provided that he has not been given employment at either time of report.

During a lay-off period, a workman ceases to be eligible for lay off compensation if:

(i) He refuses to accept alternative employment at a place within 5 miles of the establishment from which he has been Laid-off;

(ii) If he does not present himself for work at the appointed time during normal working hours at least once a day; or

(iii) If the lay-off is due to a strike or slowing down of production on the part of workmen in another part of the establishment.

Re-Deployment: Where a re-deployment of employees becomes necessary on account of a reorganisation of production, modernisation of equipment or the expansion of an enterprise, such re-deployment should be effected with minimum hardship for, and discomfiture of the affected employees. There should be no reduction in remuneration for anyone.

If, an re-deployment, employees need further training, that should be arranged at the employer's cost.

Absenteeism

Absenteeism has been variously defined by different authorities. According to Webster's Dictionary, "absenteeism is the practice or habit of being an 'absentee,' and an 'absentee' is one who habitually stays away." According to the Labour Bureau, Simla, "absenteeism is the total manshifts lost because of absences as a percentage of the total number of manshifts scheduled to work." In other words, it signifies the absence of an employee from work when he is scheduled to be at work; it is unauthorised, unexplained, avoidable, and willful absence from work. For calculating the rate of absenteeism, two facts are taken into consideration —— the number of persons scheduled to work and the number actually present. A worker who reports for any part of a shift is to be considered present. An employee is to be considered scheduled to work when the employer has work available and the employee is aware of it, and when the employer has no reason to expect, well in advance, that the employee will not be available for work at the specified time. Any employee may stay away from work if he has taken leave to which he is entitled or on the ground of sickness or some accident, or without any previous sanction of leave. Thus, absence may be authorised or unauthorised, willful or caused by circumstances beyond one's control.

Magnitude of Absenteeism: It has been observed that the phenomenon of absenteeism does not exist only in Indian industry; it is a universal fact. The difference is only in terms of magnitude. The rate of absenteeism varies from 7 percent to nearly 30 percent. In some occupations, it has risen to the abnormal level of 40 percent in some seasons. The extent of absenteeism may differ from industry to industry, place to place and occupation to occupation. It may also differ according to the make-up of the work force. Absenteeism may be extensive in a particular department of an industry or a concern.

There have been many systematic studies of absenteeism in Western industrialised countries. For example, it has been observed that absenteeism among the younger workmen is extensive on Mondays after the week end, particularly among unmarried men who, after a late night on Sunday perhaps with their girl friends, find it difficult to get up and come on time and concentrate on work; and it is the lowest on pay day.

In the USA, it has been observed that curiously enough, the extent of absenteeism is greater among youngsters than among the older employees, greater among women than men. Young men are generally found to be absent for a variety of reasons, including restlessness and a sense of irresponsibility. In some cases, absenteeism of particular workers is due to reasons connected with the job; a worker, for example, may be absent because he does not like his job for some reason, or because he has unsatisfactory relations with his supervisor or with other employees. Absenteeism may also be due to sickness, real or feigned.

There has been a phenomenal rise in absenteeism in some industries. In the cotton textile industry in Madras, it shot up from 8.9 percent in 1951 to 16.0 percent in 1980. Increased from 12.7 percent to 22.0 percent in Bombay, 8.3 percent to 14.9 percent in Ahmedabad; and 12 percent to 24.8 percent in Kanpur. In the engineering industry, it increased from 13.9 percent to 19.1 percent in Maharashtra; in West Bengal from 10.1 percent to 17.3 percent; and in Karnataka from 9.7 percent to 15.7 percent during the same period. A similar trend was noticed in the woollen industry, where in the same period, the percentage of absenteeism went up from 10.6 to 18.8 in Dhariwal; in gold mining in Karnataka from 10.2 to 18.0; in the plantations industry in Karnataka from 18.3 to 20.7. In the coal mines, the increase ranged between 13.5 to 20.4 percent.

These figures are of unauthorised absenteeism. If to these are added the liberal provisions in awards and settlements for privilege leave, casual leave, sick leave and maternity leave (in case of women), it would be found that the number of non-working days in the year in the industries in India is very large.

Absenteeism in Indian industry is not a new phenomenon. The Royal Commission on Labour reported that "high absenteeism prevails among industrial labour mainly due to their rural orientation." Since then, a number of individual researchers have investigated the problem, and have pointed out that absenteeism in our industries varies from 7 percent to 15 percent. Its incidence is high in plantations and in mines; and it is higher in Northern India than in Southern India.

Peculiar Features of Absenteeism: On the basis of micro studies undertaken in different parts of the country, certain observations may be made.

(a) The rate of absenteeism is the lowest on pay day; it increases considerably on the days following the payment of wages and bonus.

"The level of absenteeism is comparatively high immediately after pay day, when workers either feel like having a good time, or in some other cases return home to their village to make purchases for the family and to meet them. The incidence of absenteeism, both before and after a holiday, has also been found to be higher than that on normal days.

(b) Absenteeism is generally high among workers below 15 years of age and those above 40. "The younger employees are not regular and punctual," presumably because of the employment of a large number of newcomers among the younger age groups; while the older people are not able to withstand the strenuous nature of the work.

(c) The rate of absenteeism varies from department to department within a unit. For example, in the mixing and blow room, and in the bundling and baling jobs in which only a few workers are employed and the physical conditions are better than in other departments, the rate of absenteeism is comparatively low. As the size of a group increases, the rate of absenteeism goes up. This difference in the rate of absenteeism is believed to be due to the peculiar style and practices of management, the composition of the labour force and the culture of the organisation.

(d) The percentage of absenteeism is generally higher in the night shifts than in the day shifts. This is so because workers in the night shift experience greater discomfort and uneasiness in the course of their work than they do during day-time.

(e) The percentage of absenteeism is much higher in coal and mica mining industries than in organised industries. This high percentage of absenteeism is due to the engagement of labourers in the fields, marriages and festivals, which together are estimated to account for about 75 percent of the cases of withdrawals, drunkenness, relaxation or sickness.

(f) Absenteeism in India is seasonal in character. It is the highest during March-April- lay, when land has to be prepared for monsoon sowing, and also in the harvest season (September-October), when the rate goes as high as 40 percent.

Reasons for Absenteeism: The phenomenon of absenteeism has been explained various ways. According to one line of thought, "absenteeism is due to a lack of commitment" on the part of the work force. Clark Kerr and his associates are of the opinion that since "the degree of commitment varies with the degree of a country's industrial growth or maturity, absenteeism is inversely related to industrial development". The worker in the process of the early stages on industrialisation is more prone to absenteeism, prolonged and sporadic withdrawal from industrial work, wildcat stoppages, naked violence, and destruction of machines and property. Absenteeism is due to the factors that influence worker's commitment.

Hone, on the other hand, refutes this contention, and is of the view that "absenteeism related to new values and norms which are developing among the work force as a result of technological developments". Work and leisure are now cherished by the worker, and he wants to enjoy along with the monetary benefits he gets for his services. The economic consideration, therefore, decides whether one would like to be absent from work.

The Royal Commission on Labour observed that "high absenteeism among Indian about is due to its rural orientation and its frequent urge for rural exodus." According to In modern industrial establishments, except, perhaps, in very small ones, the individual personality is more or less irretrievably submerged in the general mass through sheer incidence of being thrown together with other individuals for a certain purpose, during the good bit of each day's life. The individual has no elbow-room and is hammered into a set pattern, while the human spirit clamours for open spaces and unfettered air so that it may kick its legs about for a change. The incidence of industrial fatigue, trying climate, universal malnutrition and the appallingly bad working conditions aggravate the feeling for change among industrial workers and sometimes impel them to visit their village homes frequently for rest and relaxation.

American authors hold the view that absenteeism is due to the "internal administration of an organisation." According to them, "the work milieu is very important since a large part of the worker's daily life is spent there." The atmosphere obtaining in a plant, therefore, affects his attitude to his work, and either persuades him to attend regularly or keeps him away. Irritating uncertainty, irregularity, and confusion in the factory are likely to be important causes of absenteeism.

The attitude and practice of the management also contribute to absenteeism. A traditional management treats workers as hirelings, while an enlightened management treats them as human beings. This difference in behaviour leads, in the former situation, to high absenteeism, and in the latter situation to a close affinity with the organisation, the result being lower absenteeism.

The general causes of absenteeism may now be discussed:

(i) **Maladjustment with Factory Conditions:** As a worker continues to live in the city, urban life becomes distasteful to him because of the insanitary conditions prevailing there. He finds himself caught within great factory walls; he is bewildered by heavy traffic, by jostling, by stranger speaking different languages; he is confused by different religions and tastes; and he is weary of the misery of slums and of toiling for long hours. He is subject to strict discipline and is ordered by complete strangers to do the things which he cannot understand. As a result, he is under constant strain, which causes him serious distress and impairs his efficiency. All these factors tend to persuade him to maintain his contacts with his village.

(ii) **Social and Religious Ceremonies:** Social and religious functions divert workers to social activities. In a large number of cases, the proportion of absenteeism due to sickness, accident or maternity is not as high as it is due to other causes, including social and religious causes.

(iii) **Unsatisfactory Housing Conditions:** The workers who come to towns usually find that they are not wanted and they swell the number of unemployed and casual workers. They also experience housing difficulties. Not less than 95 percent of the industrial workers in India are unsatisfactory for healthful habitation. The houses occupancy A room of about 10'×10' accommodates a large family and occassionally two families; fifteen persons sleep in one room. The housing of migrants combines worst characteristics of both rural and urban slums. Not only are the sites most insanitary but the materials used for erecting huts are also very filthy. Forsaken places like be slopes along the railway lines, banks of open drainages streams, waste land adjoining dirty localities in towns, open space earmarked for dumping the town refuse are chosen by them. Health conditions are naturally bad, leading to high morbidity and consequence ill-health. They, therefore, make frequent visits to their village homes to get relief from such insanitary and unhealthy surroundings.

(iv) **Industrial Fatigue:** Low wages compel a worker to seek some part-time job side income. But this often results in constant fatigue, which compels him to remain absent for the next day; and if fatigue affects him seriously, his absence may continue for quite some time.

(v) **Unhealthy Working Conditions:** Irritating and intolerable working conditions exist in factories. Heat and moisture (which rapidly exhaust the worker), noise and vibrations (which affect his hearing), bad lighting conditions (which cause eye-dust, fumes and over-crowding - all of these affect the worker's health, causing him to remain absent for a long time.

(vi) Absence of Adequate Welfare Facilities: Absenteeism is also due to the inadequate welfare facilities available to workers, for a vast majority of industrialists in India still look upon welfare work as a barren liability rather than a wise investment. They have not been National Commission on Labour observes. The statutory we are amenities had been properly and adequately provided. In several cases, particularly in medium and small sized units, the standards are distinctly poor. The studies made by some States in respect of the different components of welfare include sanitation, washing and bathing facilities, first aid appliances, ambulance rooms, drinking water, canteens, shelters, rest rooms and crèches, which strengthen the general impression that compliance with statutory welfare provisions is half-hearted and inadequate. Fed up with the absence of basic facilities, the worker often migrates to his rural home.

(vii) Alcoholism: The habit of alcoholism among workers is a significant cause of absenteeism, which is high in the first week of each month, when workers receive their wages. They rush to liquor shops and drink to forget their immediate worries. Once indulged in drink, the habit continues. Hangover the next day leads to absenteeism.

(viii) Indebtedness: Most of the workers suffer from a high degree of indebtedness. Premchand and Ramprakash found that "a worker had borrowed more than 11 times his net pay; another more than 9 times; a third more than 8 times; a fourth one more than 7 times; yet another more than 6 times, and so on. This is the general case in Indian industry. Workers are always worried about financial matters." Such workers absent themselves or even resign to escape the Pathan moneylenders. As a result, absenteeism is high.

(ix) Improper and Unrealistic Personnel Policies: In most cases, unskilled, untrained, illiterate and inexperienced workers are recruited who fail to cope with, and adapt themselves to their jobs and to their industrial environment. Favouritism and nepotism are rampant. These factors generate a frustration in the minds of workers which results in low efficiency, low productivity and unfavourable employee-employer relationships which, in turn, lead to long period of absenteeism.

(x) Inadequate Leave Facilities: Negligence on the part of the employer to provide adequate leave facilities compels the workers to fall back on ESI leave. Under ESI scheme, they are entitled to 56 days' leave in a year on half pay. Instead of going without pay, the workers avail themselves of this ESI facility. Supervisors with a work— oriented rather than man-oriented approach are also a factor which compels workers to absent themselves on an ESI certificate rather than avail of leave on bonafide grounds.

Measures for Control of Absenteeism

"Absenteeism is a serious problem for a management because it involves heavy additional expenses. Reserves and understudies are kept in readiness to take the place of the absentees, failing which the overhead cost of idle equipment has to be faced. Industrial employees do not usually ask for leave of absence in advance or even give notice during their absence as to how long they would be away. The management is generally uncertain about the probable duration of an employee's absence and cannot take appropriate measures to fill the gap.

As regards measures to be adopted to remedy the situation, the Labour Investigation Committee, 1946, was of the opinion that "proper conditions of work in the factory, adequate wages, protection from accidents and sickness, and facilities for obtaining leave for rest and recreation constitute the most effective means of reducing absenteeism.

The Encyclopaedia of Social Sciences suggests the following measures to reduce the rate of absenteeism:

(i) The personnel management should encourage notification, especially in cases of sickness when the duration of absences is likely to be long.

(ii) In case of personal and family circumstances, e.g., illness of children in the case of married women employees which make absences unavoidable, leave should be granted liberally.

(iii) To reduce unavoidable absence due to sickness and industrial accidents, programmes of industrial hygiene and safety should be strengthened.

(iv) Regularity in attendance can be encouraged to some extent by the offer of a bonus and other pecuniary inducements.

(v) Absenteeism is probably a natural human reaction to the routine of modern factory life. There is a maladjustment between man's instincts and desires and the regular working habits that are imposed upon him. This routine can be relaxed or modified by grant of leave with pay, by shortening or redistributing scheduled hours, by having employees living nearer to their places of work, and by adjusting the physical condition of the plant, especially noise and ventilation.

It should be noted no single measure can be effective in controlling absenteeism; but a skillful combination of various measures would definitely lead to the desired results. These measures are:

(i) Adoption of a Well Defined Recruitment Procedure;
(ii) Provision of Healthful and Hygienic Working Conditions;
(iii) Provision of Reasonable Wages and Allowances and Job Security for the workers;
(iv) Motivation of Workers: Welfare and Social Measures;
(v) Improved Communication and Prompt Redressal of Grievances:
(vi) Liberal Grant of Leave;
(vii) A Safety and Accident Prevention;
(viii) Cordial Relations between Supervisors and Workers;
(ix) Development of Worker's Education: The system of workers' education should be so designed as to take into account their educational needs as individuals for their personal evaluation; as operatives for their efficiency and advancement; as citizens for a happy integrated life in the community; as members of a trade union for the protection of their interests. This educational programme, according to the National Commission on Labour, should be to make a worker:
    (a) A responsible, committed and disciplined operative;
    (b) Understand the basic economic and technical aspects of the industry and the plant where he is employed so that he may take an intelligent interest in its affairs;
    (c) Aware of his rights and obligations;
    (d) Understand the organisation and functioning of a trade union and develop qualities of leadership, loyalty and devotion to it, work so that he may intelligently participate in its affairs;
    (e) Lead a calm, clean and healthy life, based on a firm ethical foundation; and
    (f) A responsible and alert citizen.
(x) Other Measures:
    (a) There should be clear and definite rules and regulations on authorised and unauthorised leave.

(b) The rules and regulations relating to attendance must be explained to workers.

(c) A proper record of each worker's attendance should be maintained on a special daily attendance card.

(d) A supervisor should not be regarded as "another worker" and should be given definite authority to take action in all cases of absenteeism.

The employer, the employee and the State have a definite role to play. If each performs it properly and harmoniously the problems of inefficiency, undesired conflict, low productivity, dissatisfaction on the part of workers and their low morale resulting in frequent absenteeism can be largely eliminated. Industrial relations in a democracy should be based on an integrated approach aiming at individual satisfaction and group satisfaction, and achievements of the goals of the community and of the nation as wholes.

Labour Turnover

Meaning labour turnover has been defined as "the rate of change in the working staff of a concern during a definite period" in other words, it signifies the shifting work force into and out of an organisation. It is a measure of the extent to which old employees leave and new employees enter into service in a given period it is sometimes defined as measurement of inarticulate labour unrest. Strikes are regarded as articulate expressions of discontent amongst workers; in the case of labour turnover, this discontent is expressed not by striking work but by quitting the job. Labour turnover is the cause and effect of instability of employment, apart from being a measure of the morale and efficiency or otherwise of workers.

The rate of labour turnover is generally expressed in a number of different formulas which involve such forms as accessions (i.e., additions to the pay-roll); separations quits discharges, retirements deaths, etc.) - replacements (i.e., one accession plus separation); and average work force (i.e., number at the beginning of a period plus the number at the end divided by 2).

If in a particular industry, the average workforce per month is 1000, and there are 20 accessions and 25 separations during that period:

(i) The accession rate is: $20/1000 \times 100 = 2$ per cent

(ii) The separation rate is: $25/100 \times 100 = 2.5$ per cent

(iii) The replacement rate is: $20/1000 \times 100 = 2$ per cent

Impact of Turnover

The heavy rate of turnover is a great handicap for workers and industry alike, for it implies a reduction in skill and efficiency on the part of the worker and reduced output for the industry. However, some amount of labour turnover is inevitable even natural, particularly when it stems from the retirement of old employees and the accession of new blood. Such turnover may not only be avoidable but is welcome to some cases, it arises because of resignations and dismissals. This turnover is harmful to the efficiency of and impairs the quality of production. It is a serious obstacle to the full utilisation of a country's human and material resources "From side, they are not only deprived of various advantages of continued employment, viz., opportunities of graded pay, bonus, provident fund and leave, but they have even to engagement; and there is bound to be less solidarity among workers who move from mill to mill.

The following costs are involved when an employee leaves an organisation:

(i) Hiring costs, involving time and facilities for recruitment, interviewing, and examining a replacement;

(ii) Training costs, involving the time of the supervisor, the personnel department and the trainee;

(iii) The pay of the learner is in excess of what is produced;

(iv) Accident rates of new employees are often higher;

(v) The loss of production in the interval between and the replacement by the new;

(vi) The production equipment is not fully utilised during the hiring interval and the training period;

(vii) Scrap and waste rates rise when new employees are involved; and

(viii) Overtime pay may result from an excessive number of separations causing trouble in meeting contract delivery dates.

Causes of Labour Turnover

Labour turnover is the outcome of resignations and dismissals. Resignations may be due to such causes as dissatisfaction with working conditions, insufficient wages, bad health, sickness, old age, family circumstances and exodus to the village for agricultural operations. When workers return from their villages after a long time, they do not find their old jobs and have to seek employment elsewhere.

Dismissals on the other hand, may occur due to participation in strikes or union activities, misconduct, insubordination, and inefficiency. But dismissal is a lesser cause of labour turnover.

The badli system also contributes to a high turnover because, with a view to providing work for badli workers, many workers are forced to leave. Dr. Mukenee has observed: The excessive turnover among the badlis in the different establishments in India is largely due to the fact that jobbers are peculiarly interested in extending their circle of patronages so that badli workers obtain a few days employment in a month in a factory.

Measures to Control Labour Turnover

A high rate of turnover is bad both for the worker and the industry. Hence, efforts should be made to reduce it. The measures to be adopted for the purpose call for a positive policy and concerted action on the part of employers. Besides, any measures conducive to the workers' economic advancement and welfare, as well as measures intended to provide security of employment are bound to mitigate the evils of turnover by reducing their tendency to make frequent visits to their villages and to search for what is often a mirage of better employment and higher remuneration. In this connection, the Bombay Texile Labour enquiry committee observed: "Improvement in the methods of recruitment is one of the principal remedies for excessive labour turnover. But more radical and effective methods... such as the establishment of exchanges, the restriction of the powers of jobbers and the organisations of a personnel department are required. Improvement in working conditions, the adoption of an enlightened policy of management in respect of wages, transfers and leave and holidays, the provision of facilities for education and training, the promotion of welfare work, the introduction of unemployment and sickness insurance, gratuity and pension schemes, will all contribute to make the labour force more stable than it is at present. Not the least important factors contributing to the stability will be the attitude of the employers' and workers' organisations and the provision of an effective machinery of the ventilation and redressal of the grievances of the workers."

Besides a scientific system of recruitment, selection and placement, the provision of vocational guidance facilities, enlightened supervision and the development of a two-way communication system between the management and the employees will help to reduce the rate of labour turnover.

Chapter - 11

Employee Training

Introduction

Every organisation needs to have well trained and experienced people to perform the activity to be done. If the current or potential job occupant can meet this requirement, training is not important. But when this is case, it is necessary to raise the skill levels and increase the versatility and adaptability of employees. Inadequate job performance or a decline in productivity or changes resulting out of job redesigning or a technological breakthrough require some type of training and development efforts.

As the jobs become more complex, the importance of employee development also increases. In a rapidly changing society, employee training and development are not only an activity that is desirable but also an activity that an organisation must commit resources to if it is to maintain a viable and knowledgeable work force.

'Training,' 'education' and 'development' are three terms frequently used. On the face of it, there might not appear any difference between them but when a deep thought is given, there appears some differences between them. In all 'training' there is some 'education' an in all education there is some training. And the two processes cannot be separated from 'development'. Precise definitions are not possible and can be misleading; but different persons have used these activities in different ways.

Three Terms: Training, Development and Education

Training is a process of learning a sequence of programmed behaviour. It is application of knowledge. It gives people an awareness of the rules and procedures to guide their behaviour. It attempts to improve their performance on the current job or an intended job. Development is a related process. It covers not only those activities which improve job performance but also those which bring about growth of the personality; help individuals in the progress towards maturity and actualisation of their potential capacities so that they become not only good employees but also women. In organisational terms, it is intended to equip persons to earn promotion and hold greater responsibility. Training a person for a bigger and higher development. And this may well include not only imparting specific skills and knowledge but also in personality and mental attitudes. In this sense, development is not much different from education. Education is the understanding and intervention of knowledge. It does not provide definitive answers, but rather it develops a logical and rational mind that can determine relationships among pertinent variables and thereby character; and understanding of basic principles and develop the capacities of analysis, synthesis and objectivity. Usually, education is outside the scope of an organisation's functions. It involves a range of skills and expertise which can be provided only by educational institutions. An organisation can and does make use of such institutions in order to support and supplement its internal training and development efforts.

Distinction Between Training and Development

"Training is short-term process utilising a systematic and organised procedure by which non-managerial personnel learn technical knowledge and skills for a definite purpose. Development is a long-term educational process utilising a systematic and organised procedure by which managerial personnel learn conceptual and theoretical knowledge for general purpose."

"Training" refers only to instruction in technical and mechanical operations, while "development" refers to philosophical and theoretical educational concepts. Training is designed for non-managers, while development involves managerial personnel. In the words of Campbell, "training courses are typically designed for a short-term, stated set purpose, such as the operation of some piece of machinery, while development involves a broader education for long-term purposes."

Training and development differ in four ways:

(a) "What" is learned;

(b) "Who" is learning;

(c) "Why" such learning takes place; and

(d) "When" learning occurs.

The difference may be stated thus:

Learning dimension	***Training***	***Development***
Who?	Non-managerial personnel	Managerial personnel
What?	Technical and mechanical operations	Theoretical, conceptual ideas
Why?	Specific job-related purpose	General knowledge
When?	Short-term	Long term

Need for Basic Purposes of Training

The need for the training of employees would be clear from the observations made by the different authorities.

(i) To Increase Productivity: "Instruction can help employees increase their level of performance on their present assignment. Increased human performance often directly leads to increased operational productivity and increased company profit. Again, "increased performance and productivity, because of training, are most evident on the part of new employees who are not yet fully aware of the most efficient and effective ways of performing their jobs."

(ii) To Improve Quality: "Better informed workers are less likely to make operational mistakes. Quality increases may be in relationship to a company product or service, or in reference to the intangible organisational employment atmosphere."

(iii) To Help a Company Fulfil its Future Personnel Needs: "Organisations that have a good internal educational programme will have to make less drastic manpower changes and adjustments in the event of sudden personnel alternations. When the need arises, organisational vacancies can more easily be staffed from internal sources if a company initiates and maintains an adequate instructional programme for both its non-supervisory and managerial employees."

(iv) To Improve Organisational Climate: "An endless chain of positive reactions results from a well-planned training programme. Production and product quality may improve; financial incentives may then be increased, internal promotions become stressed, less supervisory pressure ensure and base pay rate increases result. Increased morale may be due to many factors, but one of the most important of these is the current state of an organisation's educational endeavour."

(v) To Improve Health and Safety: "Proper training can help prevent industrial accidents. A safer work environment leads to more stable mental attitudes on the part of employees. Managerial mental state would also improve if supervisors know that they can better themselves through company-designed development programmes."

(vi) Obsolescence Prevention: "Training and development programmes foster the initiative and creativity of employees and help to prevent manpower obsolescence, which may be due to age, temperament or motivation, or the inability of a person to adapt himself to technological changes."

(vii) Personal Growth: "Employees on a personal basis gain individual from their exposure to educational experiences. Again, "Management development programmes seem to give participants a wider awareness, an enlarged skill, and enlightened altruistic philosophy, and make enhanced personal growth possible."

It may be observed that the need for training arises from more than one reason.

(i) An increased use of technology in production.

(ii) Labour turnover arising from normal separations due to death or physical incapacity, for accidents, disease, superannuation, voluntary retirement, promotion within the organisation and change of occupation or job.

(iii) Need for additional hands to cope with an increased production of goods and services.

(iv) Employment of inexperienced, new or badli labour requires detailed instruction for an effective performance of a job.

(v) Old employees need refresher training to enable them to keep abreast of the changing methods, techniques and use of sophisticated tools and equipment.

(vi) Need for enabling employees to do the work in a more effective way, to reduce learning time, reduce supervision time, reduce waste and spoilage of raw material and produce quality goods and develop their potential.

(vii) Need for reducing grievances and minimising accident rates.

(viii) Need for maintaining the validity of an organisation as a whole and raising the morale of its employees.

A programme of training becomes essential for the purpose of meeting the specific problems of a particular organisation arising out of the introduction of new lines of production, changes in design, the demands of competition and economy, the quality of materials processed, individual adjustments, promotions, career development job and personnel changes and changes in the volume of business. Collectively, these purposes directly relate to and comprise the ultimate purpose of organisational training programmes to enhance overall organisational effectiveness.

O. Jeff Harris, Jr. observe

"Training of any kind should have as its objective the redirection or improvement of behaviour so that the performance of the trainee becomes more useful and productive for himself and for the organisation of which he is a part. Training normally concentrates on the improvement of either operative skills (the basic skills related to the successful completion of a task), interpersonal skills (how to relate satisfactorily to others), decision-making skills (how to arrive at the most satisfactory causes of action), or a combination of these."

Importance of Training

Training is the corner-stone of sound management, for it makes employees more effective and productive. It is actively and intimately connected with all the personnel or managerial activities. It is an integral part of the whole management programme, with all its many activities functionally inter-related.

There is an ever present need for training men so that new and changed techniques may be taken advantage of and improvements affected in the old methods, which are woefully inefficient.

Training is a practical and vital necessity because, apart from the other advantages mentioned above, it enables employees to develop and rise within the organisation, and increase their "market value," earning power and job security. It enables management to resolve sources of friction arising from parochialism, to bring home to the employees the fact that the management is not divisible. It moulds the employees' attitudes and helps them to achieve a better co-operation with the company and a greater loyalty to it. The management is benefited in the sense that higher standards of quality are achieved; a satisfactory organisational structure is built up; authority can be delegated and stimulus for progress applied to employees. Training, moreover, heightens the morale of the employees, for it helps in reducing dissatisfaction, complaints, grievances and absenteeism, reduces the rate of turnover. Further, trained employees make a better and economical use of materials and equipment; therefore, wastage and spoilage are lessened, and the need for constant supervision is reduced.

The importance of training has been expressed in these words: "Training is a widely accepted problem-solving device. Indeed, our national superiority in manpower productivity can be attributed in no small measure to the success of our educational and industrial training programmes. This success has been achieved by a tendency in many quarters to regard training as a panacea. It is almost traditional in America to believe that if something is good, more of the thing is even better. Hence, we take more vitamin pills to solve personal health problems and more training to solve our manpower problems. Over and under-emphasis on training stems largely from inadequate recognition and determination of training needs and objectives. They stem also from lack of recognition of the professional techniques of modern industrial training."

Responsibility for Training

Training is the responsibility of four main groups:

(a) The top management, which frames the training policies;

(b) The personnel department, which plans, establishes and evaluates instructional programmes;

(c) Supervisors, who implement and apply developmental procedure; and

(d) Employees, who provide feedback, revision and suggestions for corporate educational endeavours.

According to Prof. John Mee, "the work of training should be done at two levels," viz.

(i) The training department should assume the primary responsibility for the instruction of trainers in methods of teaching; for normal orientation; for the training of supervisors in human relations; for the development of executives, for co-operative education in schools and colleges; and for the general education of employees.

(ii) Line supervisors and employees should carry the bulk of the teaching the following areas: On-the-job instruction of employees; instruction in the technical and professional aspects of a business; daily development of superiors and executives through counselling; departmental communication and staff meetings as part of an overall training programme. It is needless to say that the top line executive has the responsibility for:

 (a) Authorising basic training policies;

 (b) Reviewing and approving the broad outlines of training plans and programmes; and

 (c) Approving training budgets.

Creation of a Desire for Training

The employees can be persuaded to be interested in training programmes in one of the following three ways:

1. They will respond to programmes involving changed behaviour if they believe that the resulting modification in the behaviour is in their own interest, that they will receive benefits as a result of their new behaviour.
2. Trainees will change their behaviour if they became aware of better was of performing (more productive or otherwise more satisfactory ways) and gain experience in the new pattern of behaviour so that it becomes their normal manner of operation.
3. A trainee may change his behaviour in compliance with the forced demands of his superiors or others with more power than the trainee possesses.

Principles or Concepts of Training

Since training is a continuous process and not a one shot affair, and since it consumes time and entails much expenditure, it is necessary that a training programme or policy should be prepared with great thought and care, for it should serve the purposes of the establishment as well as the needs of employees. Moreover, it must guard against over-training use of poor instructions, too much training in skills which are unnecessary for a particular job, initiation of other company training programmes, misuse of testing techniques, inadequate tools and equipment, and over reliance on one single technique example on slides, pictures or lectures - and not enough on practice.

A successful training programme presumes that sufficient care has been taken to discover area in which it is needed most and to create the necessary environment for discover are a its conduct. The selected trainer should be one who clearly understands his job and has professional expertise has an aptitude and ability for teaching, possesses a pleasing personality and a capacity for leadership, is well-versed in the principles and methods of training, and is able to appreciate the value of training in relation to an enterprise.

Certain general principles need be considered while organising a training programme. For example:

1. Trainees in work organisations tend to be most responsive to training programmes when they feel the need to learn, i.e., the trainee will be more eager to undergo training if training promises

answers to problem or needs he has as an employee. The individual who perceives training as the solution to problems will be more willing to enter into a training programme than will the individual who is satisfied with his present performance abilities."

2. "Learning is more effective where there is reinforcement in the form of rewards and punishments," i.e., individuals do things that give pleasure and avoid things that give pain. In other words, after an action, if satisfaction is receive, the action will be repeated. If no satisfaction is received, the action will not be repeated.
3. In the long run, awards tend to be more effective for changing behaviour and increasing one's learning than punishments.
4. Rewards for the application of learned behaviour are most useful when they quickly follow the desired performance.
5. The large the reward for good performance following the implementation of learned behaviour, the greater will be the reinforcement of the new behaviour.
6. Negative reinforcement, through application of penalties and heavy criticism following inadequate performance, may have a disruptive effect upon the learning experience of the trainee than positive reinforcement.
7. Training that requests the trainee to make changes in his values, attitudes, and social beliefs usually achieves better results if the trainee is encouraged to participate, discuss and discover new, desirable behaviour norms.
8. The trainee should be provided with 'feedback' on the progress he is making in utilising the training he has received. As Miller has stated, "If a person with the required abilities is to improve his performance, he must (i) know how a performance is not up to par; (ii) know precisely what corrective aspect is per actions he must take to improve his performance." The feedback should be fast and frequent, especially for the lower level jobs which are often routine and quickly completed.
9. The development of new behaviour norms and skills is facilitated through practice and repetition. Skills that are practised often are better learned and less easily forgotten.
10. The training material should be made as meaningful as possible, because if the trainee understands the general principles underlying what is being taught, he will probably understand it better than if he were just asked to memorise a series of isolated steps.

Learning and Learning Theories

Training is an organised procedure by which people learn knowledge and acquire the skills they need for a definite purpose. Training is what is done to the trainee. This training is rooted in the learning process; and "learning is that human process by which skills, knowledge, habits and attitudes are acquired and utilised in such a way that behaviour is modified." In other words, training causes learning, a process that takes place within the trainee, in which behavioural changes occur as a result of experience. Learning cannot be measured directly but the changes in behaviour that occur as a result of learning can only be measured.

There exists a number of theories and concepts that describe learning. These may be divided into two major schools, the connectionist and the cognitist. The connectionist stimulus-response approach. For the connectionist, learning involves the operation of laws of association such as assimilation, frequency, contiguity, intensity, duration, context acquaintance, composition, individual differences, and cause effect. The basic theme of these theories is that "when an act produces satisfaction, it will be associated with a particular situation and probably will be repeated when the situation arises again. On the other hand, if an act produces psychological or physical comfort, a person will tend to avoid the behaviour in a similar situation." In other words, a teacher can increase the amount of learning in a training situation significantly by reinforcing correct responses rather than by giving some form of punishing feedback when the task is performed incorrectly.

The congnitist or gestatist theories see all learning as leading toward a goal all human behaviour has a purpose. Cognitists believe in latent, or collateral, earning (i.e., the formulation of enduring attitudes, likes and dislikes) in addition to learning in order to acquire a particular-skill. Additionally, the cognitists suggest training must take into consideration the goals of the trainee. A corollary to this is that trainees should structure learning situations so that relationships among stimuli, responses, and individual goals (motivation) are emphasised.

A stimulus is something that initiates action. When some answer is given to this, a response is there. When it is returned with "Correct - go on," it is reinforcement, i.e., as an action that causes the learner to repeat his behaviour. The drive that maintains this process is defined as motivation, i.e., completion of learning may mean obtaining better employment, a promotion, or a raise in salary, or path to some other desired goal.

Principles of Learning

Learning concepts and theories are based on firmly rooted and well-grounded educational and psychological principles. These are:

1. Every human being is capable of learning. Each has an intellectual capacity and the ability to learn from training.
2. It is easier for the trainee to understand/remember material that is meaningful. Training materials may be made more meaningful at least in six ways: (i) At the start of training, the trainee should be provided with the bird's eye view of the material to be presented. Knowing the overall picture and understanding how each part of the programme fits into it helps make the entire programme meaningful. (ii) When presenting material to the trainees, a variety of similar should be used. (iii) The training material is organised in a logical examples manner and has meaningful units. (iv) The materials should be split up into meaningful chunks rather than presenting it all at once. (v) The terms and concepts that are already familiar to the trainees should be used. (vi) As many visual aids should be used as possible to argument "theoretical" material.
3. The training programme should be planned in a logical manner so that each succeeding step builds upon the previous one — "the probability of success increases because the trainee encounters the steps in sequence. The best course for changing behaviour is to bring about the transition through a progression of small, orderly steps."
4. A new employee may learn in order to please his boss, to get confirmed in his job, to acquire the requisite knowledge and skill to perform it in a much better and more effective manner. Supervisors may go in for training to learn how to delegate responsibility more effectively, how to save their own limited time, how to read reports quickly, how to understand their subordinates better, how to eliminate potential labour troubles, and how to administer the agreements reached between the management and the employees.
5. Different levels of learning exist. Learning may involve awareness, changed attitudes and changed behaviour. It may involve mental processes or physical strength. Different time and method requirements are needed to bring about different levels of learning.

6. The basic principles of training design consist of: (a) identifying the components of tasks of final desired performance; (b) assuring that each component is fully achieved; and (c) arranging the total learning situation in a sequence.
7. Learning objectives should be established for every training programme. The objectives guide the instructor in planning the training, guide the trainee, and provide certain or evaluating how much learning has been achieved. A complete statement of learning objectives clearly specifies the behaviour trainee after the instruction has taken place, the conditions under which the trainee will be required to demonstrate the prescribed behaviour and the standards of acceptable performance. A knowledge of standards of performance makes learning effective and the goals and bench marks enable the learner to judge his educational achievements and progress.
8. An adequate interest in, and motive for, learning are essential because people are goal-oriented. They work to satisfy their needs for self expression. If passion, accomplishment, self-actualisation, and financial incentives. However, most earning is self-motivated and related to the attainment of personal goals. The trainer must explain to the trainee how his training can be instrumental in his success. He should first clarify the goals of the training; then explain how job performance is related to rewards; and explain how the training will improve his performance and thereby boost his rewards.
9. Learning is active and not passive. Effective education calls for action an active involvement on the part of all participants. Researchers have revealed (in America) that people remember 10% of what they read 20% of what they hear, 30% of see, 50% of what they see and hear, 70% of what they, what they say as they perform the task." In other words, people learn best and more by doing than by hearing. When human senses involved, the more complete is the training.
10. Previous experience of the individual trainee affects his learning experience. New material is related to his previous knowledge. New behaviour is formulated using existing foundations as a basis.
11. People learn more and even faster when they are told of their achievements, i.e., they should have Knowledge of Results (KR) or feedback. Such feedback should be specific rather than general

It should be precise and diagnostic rather than evaluative. It should be directed at the behaviour that the learner changed can do something right than at values or individual personality traits. It should be the automatic, immediate and meaningfully related to work that is done. In on-the-job-training, an employee should be informed of his success or failure so that he may adjust his efforts, if necessary or correct his mistakes. The trainer should not wait until the end of the day to tell a trainee that he never has done well. Instead, reinforcement should be frequent, whenever he does something right.

12. Training in one activity can be transferred to another if, there are similar components and principles. Once a general principle has been learned, all problems of similar nature can be solved as they arise. For example, a manager trained in the techniques of contingency leadership theory may be capable of analysing a wide variety of motivational problems and developing solutions to them on the basis of his knowledge of a few basic principles. Transfer of training can be accomplished by: (i) maximising the similarity between the training situation and the work situation; (ii) providing adequate experience with tasks during training; (iii) providing for a variety of examples when teaching, concepts or skills; (iv) identifying important features of the task; and (v) making sure that the trainee understands general principles.
13. The training that involves understanding complex problems and discovering new alternative solutions can be achieved best when the environment is relaxed and free of anxiety and the trainees are not under any immediate pressure to produce.
14. The differences in abilities, backgrounds, experiences, readiness to learn and other factors cause individual trainees to acquire new knowledge, skills, and attitudes at differing rates of speed. Training programmes necessarily must be adapted to the training speeds of the separate trainees.
15. Time must be provided to practice that which has been learned. The learning process requires a great deal of time for assimilation, testing, acceptance, and the development of confidence. Repetition, accompanied by constant efforts towards improvement, makes for an effective development of skills. Practice makes man perfect. Moreover, skills that are practiced often are and easily not forgotten.

16. Learning is closely related to attention and concentration. The learning process is more effective if distractions are avoided.
17. Learning is more effective when one sheds one's half knowledge prejudices bias, likes and dislikes, i.e., when one abandons the "I know attitude" and adopts the "I want to know" approach.
18. Early success increases an individual's chances for effective learning, for "nothing succeeds like success."
19. Trainers are important ingredient in the learning environment. They should know the material, be able to communicate, and be aware of learner's needs. The old saying, "if the student failed to learn, the teacher failed to teach," contains great deal of truth.

Steps in Training Programmes

Training programmes are a costly affair, and a time consuming process. Therefore, they need to be drafted very carefully. Usually in the organisation of training programmes, the following steps are considered necessary:

1. Discovering or identifying the training needs.
2. Getting ready for the job.
3. Preparation of the learner.
4. Presentation of operation and knowledge.
5. Performance try-out.
6. Follow-up and evaluation of the programme.

Training Policy

Every company or organisation should have well-established training policy. Such a policy represents the top management's commitment to the training of its employees, and comprises rules and procedures governing the standard of scope of training. A training policy is considered necessary for the following reasons:

(a) To indicate a company's intention to develop its personnel; to provide guidance in the framing and implementation of programmes and to provide information concerning them to all concerned;

(b) To discover critical areas where training is to be given on a priority basis; and

(c) To provide suitable opportunities to the employee for his own betterment.

Training Courses

Training may range from highly specified instruction in the procedures to be adopted while performing a particular job to every general instruction concerning the economy and society.

Training courses in general areas usually aim at making an employee a rounded individual, a happier worker and a good citizen, and at training him for "larger responsibilities" and future advancement. Such training exerts a remarkable influence on production and labour. From the producer's point of view, output would increase with decrease in scrap, spoilage, waste and the cost of production. From the point of view of labour, the employee's morale would improve; so would the rate of turnover, excessive absenteeism and accidents reduce. Training programmes are no doubt expensive; but their worth to a growing concern cannot be over-emphasised.

Training in general areas is given in such subjects as general and home economics, basic English, instruction in better writing and report drafting, reading using gauges, the operation of machines, fire-fighting and safety devices on the job, shop practices and secretarial practices, elementary mathematics, sociology, industrial psychology, time study, personal hygiene, public speaking and public relations, selling and communication with people.

So far as women employees are concerned, they are given training in telephone etiquette, personal hygiene, good grooming, sales talk and handling of sales and courtesy.

Support Material for Training

A variety of equipments is utilised to impart effective training:

(a) Lectures (learning by hearing supplemented by reading assignments); conferences, seminars and staff meetings (learning by participation); demonstrations (learning by seeing); and short courses, through coaching.

(b) Role-playing (learning by doing) and job rotation (learning by experience).

(c) Case or Project studies and problem solving sessions (learning by personal investigation).

(d) Use of pamphlets, charts, brochures, booklets, handbooks, manuals, etc.

(e) Graphs, pictures, books, slides, movie projectors, film strips, tape recorders, etc.

(f) Posters, displays, notice and bulletin boards
(g) Reading rooms and libraries where specified books and journals are maintained for reference and use.
(h) Under-study and visits to plants.
(i) Correspondence courses under which knowledge about business law, statistics, industrial management, marketing, office procedures, retailing and many other similar subjects may be imparted.
(j) Teaching machines.
(k) Membership of professional or trade associations, which offer new techniques and ideas to their members.

Training material has to be prepared with great care and distributed among the trainees so that they may come well-prepared to a session and are able to understand the operations and/or demonstrations quickly and correctly.

Training Period

The duration of a training varies with the skill to be acquired, the complexity of the subject, a trainee's aptitude and ability to understand, and the training media used.

Generally, a training period should not be unduly long; if it is, trainees may feel bored, uninterested. The ideal session should not go beyond 2 to 3 hours at a stretch, with a break in between two sessions. If convenient, employees may be trained for a week or a fortnight for an hour or two, every day after work hours.

The training period may extend from 3 weeks to 6 months or even more, depending upon job requirements.

The physical location of the programme should be pleasant surroundings away from the noise and tension of the work place.

Training for Different Employees

Employees at different levels require training. Unskilled workers require training in improved methods of handling machines and materials to reduce the cost production and waste and to do the job in the most economical way. Such employees are given training on the job itself; and the training is imparted by their immediate superior officers, sardars or foremen. The training period ranges from 3 weeks to 6 weeks.

Semi-skilled workers require training to cope with the requirements of an industry arising out of the adoption of mechanisation, rationalisation and technical processes. These employees are given training either in their own sections or departments or in segregated training where machines and other facilities are usually available. The training is usually imparted by the more proficient workers, bosses or inspectors and lasts for a few hours or weeks, depending upon the number of operations, and the speed and accuracy required on a job. Training methods include instruction in several semi-skilled operations because training in one operation only creates difficulties in adjustments to new conditions, lends the colour of specialisation to a job and makes work somewhat monotonous for an individual.

Skilled workers are given training through the system of apprenticeship, which varies in duration from a year to three or five years. Such training is also known as tradesmen or craftsmen training, and is particularly useful for such trades in industry which require highly sophisticated skills — as in carpentry, drilling, boring, planing and host of other industrial jobs and operations. While the mass production in industry has considerably reduced the proportion of employees who must be skilled tradesmen, the design, the construction and maintenance of new machines have increased to such an extent that a very high level of skill and capacity is required to become a skilled tradesman.

Any apprentice programme usually takes into consideration the facts of individual differences in abilities and capacities. Such programmes are usually conducted in training centres and industry itself.

Besides the above types of employees, others — typists, stenographers, accounts clerks, and those who handle computers — need training in their particular fields; but such training is usually provided outside an industry.

Salesmen are given training so that they may know the nature and quality of the products, and the routine involved in putting through a deal; they are trained in the art of salesmanship, and in handling customers and meeting their challenges.

The supervisory staff need training most, for they form a very important link in the chain of administration. The training programmes for supervisors must be tailor-made to fit the needs of an undertaking. Their training enables supervisors to cope with the increasing demands of the enterprise in which they are employed and to develop team spirit. Supervisory training aims at:

(i) Helping the present supervisors to improve their performance;

(ii) Helping them to prepare for the greater responsibilities of the higher levels of management;

(iii) Building up the security and status of supervisors; and

(iv) Ensuring their technical competence with a view to enabling them to know and understand all about the processes and operations in which their workers participate.

The courses for supervisors concentrate upon those areas which are closely related to their day-to-day jobs. Accordingly, they are generally given training in:

(a) The organisation and control of production, in maintenance and materials handling at the departmental level;

(b) Planning, allocation and control of work and personnel;

(c) Impact of methods study, time study, job evaluation, and the supervisors' responsibilities and functions in connection therewith;

(d) Company policies and practices for the purchase of stores, the preparation of requisitions, inventories, cost analysis, cost control and shop rules and the preparation of reports and other standard operating procedures;

(e) Personnel procedures, policies and programmes;

(f) Training of subordinates and grievance handling; and techniques of disciplinary procedures;

(g) Communication, effective instruction, report writing;

(h) Appraisal of employees and their rating, and the maintenance of personnel records;

(i) Dealing with the problem of absenteeism, tardiness, indiscipline and subordination;

(j) The handling of human problems — i.e., maintaining good interpersonal relations and morale of the employees;

(k) Evaluating the effects of industrial legislation at the department level;

(l) Leadership qualities;

(m) Industrial law; standing orders, and trade union organisation; and

(n) Principles of administration, safety, health, and welfare regulations.

Supervisors' training may include the supply of necessary reading material, job rotation to give them a wide-plant experience, holding of staff meetings, visits to other industrial units, participation in the work of other departments, lectures and teaching, role-playing, case studies and conferences.

In India, such training is provided by the National Productivity Council, New Delhi and the Central Labour Institute at Mumbai and Delhi.

Training Methods/Techniques

The forms and types of employee training methods are inter-related. It is difficult, if not impossible, to say which of the methods or combination of methods is more useful than the other. In fact, methods are multifaceted in scope and dimension and suitable for a particular situation. The best technique for one situation may not be best or different groups or tasks. Care must be used in adapting the technique/method to the learner and the job. An effective training technique provide motivation to the trainee to improve job performance, develop a willingness to change, provide for the trainee's active participation in the learning process knowledge of results about attempts to improve (i.e., feedback), and permit practice where appropriate.

Chart 10.1: Gives the technique mostly used for training of employee

Classification of training methods

- (a) ON THE JOB
- (b) VESTIBULE
- (c) DEMONSTRATION AND EXAMPLE
- (d) SIMULATION
- (e) APPRENTICESHIP
- (f) CLASSROOM METHODS
  - (a) LECTURE
  - (b) CONFERENCE
  - (c) CASE STUDY
  - (d) ROLE –PLAYING
  - (e) PROGRAMMED INSTRUCTION
- (g) OTHER TRAINING METHODS
  - (a) ASSOCIATIONS
  - (b) AUDIOVISUAL AIDS

On-the-job-training (OJT)

Virtually every employee, from the clerk to company president, gets some "on-the-job-training," when he joins a firm. That is why William Tracly calls it, "the most common, the most widely used and accepted, and the most necessary method of training employees in the skills essential for acceptable for job performance.

Trainees earn as they learn under the watchful eyes of a master mechanic or craftsman, receive immediate feedback, practise in the actual work environment, and associate with the same people they will work with after training. Under this technique, "an employee is placed in a new job and is told how it may be performed. It is primarily concerned with developing in an employee a repertoire of skills and habits consistent with the existing practices of an organisation, and with orienting him to his immediate problems." It is mostly given for unskilled and semi-skilled jobs — clerical and sales jobs.

Employees are coached and instructed by skilled co-workers, by supervisors, by the special training instructors. They learn the job by personal observation and practice as well as occasionally handling it. It is learning by doing, and it is most useful for jobs that are either difficult to stimulate or can be learned quickly by watching and doing.

There are a variety of OJT methods, such as "coaching" or "understudy"; job rotation; and special assignments. Under coaching or understudy method (which is also known as 'internship' and 'apprenticeship' method) the employee is trained on the job by his immediate superior. 'Internship' is usually applied to managerial personnel and provide wide variety of job experience, often involving job rotation, or an "assistant to" "type of position." 'Apprenticeship' is generally used to impart skills requiring long periods of practice as found in trade, crafts and other technical fields. In job rotation, a management trainee is made to move from job to job at certain intervals. The jobs vary in content.

Special assignments or committees are other methods used to provide lower-level executives with first-hand experience in working on actual problems. Executives from various functional areas serve on "boards" and are "required to analyse problems and recommend solutions to top management." On-the-job training is made more effective by the use of a variety of training aids and techniques, such as procedure charts, lecture manuals, sample problems, demonstrations, oral and written explanations, tape-recorders and other aids.

Merits: The main advantage of on-the-job training is that the trainee learns on the actual equipment in use and in the true environment of his job. He, therefore, gets a feel of the actual production conditions and requirements. In this way, a transfer from a training centre or school to the actual production conditions following the training period is allowed. Secondly, it is highly economical since no additional personnel or facilities are required for training. Thirdly, the trainee learns the rules and regulations procedures by observing their day-to-day applications. He can, therefore, be easily sized up by the management. Fourthly, this type of training is a suitable alternative for a company in which there are almost as many jobs as there are employees. Finally, it is most appropriate for teaching the knowledge and skills which can be acquired in a relatively short period, say, a few days or weeks.

Demerits: The principal disadvantage of on-the-job training is that instruction is often highly disorganised and haphazard and not properly supervised. This is due to such reasons as the inability of the experienced employee to impart skills to the trainee, the breakdown of the job for the purpose of instructions, and the lack of motivation on the part of the trainee to receive training. Moreover, learners are often subjected to distractions of a noisy shop or office. Further, the other drawback is e low productivity, especially when the employee is unable to fully develop his skills.

However, this training is generally given in a large number of organisations, and is suitable for all levels of operatives, supervisors and executives, for it needs no schools, and the employee's contribution adds to a output of the enterprise.

Job Instruction Training (JIT)

This method is very popular in the States for preparing supervisors to train operatives. The JIT method requires skilled trainers, extensive job analysis, training schedules, and prior assessment of the trainee's job knowledge. This method is also known as "training through step-by-step learning." It involves listing all necessary steps in the job, each in proper sequence. These steps show what is to be done. Alongside each step is also listed a corresponding "Key point," which show how it is to be done and why.

The actual training follows a four-step process, beginning with (i) the preparation of the trainee for instruction. This includes putting him at ease, emphasising the importance of the task and giving a general description of job duties and responsibilities; (ii) presentation of the instructions, giving essential information in a clear manner. This includes positioning the trainee at work site, telling and showing him each step of the job, stressing why and how each step is carried out as it is shown; (iii) having the trainee try out the job to show that he has understood the instructions, if there are any errors they are corrected; and questions and allowing the trainee to work along and the trainer follows up regularly.

The JIT method provides immediate feedback on results quick correction of errors, and provision of extra practice when required.

However, it demands a skilled trainer and can interfere with production and quality.

Vestibule Training (Or Training-centre Training)

This method attempts to duplicate on-the-job situations in a company classroom. It is a classroom training which is often imparted with the help of the equipment and machines which are identical with those in use in the place of work. This technique enables the trainee to concentrate on learning the new skill rather than on performing an actual job. In other words, it is geared to job duties. Theoretical training is given in the classroom, while the practical work is conducted on the production line. It is a very efficient method of training semi-skilled personnel, particularly when many employees have to be trained for the same kind of work at the same time. It is often used to train clerks, bank tellers, inspectors, machine operators, testers, typists etc. It is most useful when philosophic concepts, attitudes, theories and problem-solving abilities have to be learnt.

Training is generally given in the form of lectures, conferences, case studies, role-playing and discussion.

Merits: This method has several merits. First, as training is given in a separate room, distractions are minimised. Second, a trained instructor, who knows how to teach, can be more effectively utilised. Third, the correct method can be taught without interrupting production. Fourth, it permits the trainee to practise without the fear of supervisors/ co-workers' observation and their possible ridicule.

Demerits: First, the splitting of responsibilities leads to organisational problems. Second, an additional investment in equipment is necessary, though the cost may be reduced by getting some productive work done by trainees while in the school. Third, this method is of limited value for the jobs which utilise equipment which can be duplicated. Finally, the training situation is somewhat artificial.

However, when the number of trainees is large, vestibule schools are generally utilised; but when the number is small, on-the-job training is preferred.

Training by Experienced Workmen

By this method, training is imparted by experienced senior fellow-workers. It is particularly adaptable where experienced workmen need helpers. It is useful for departments in which workmen advance through successive jobs to perform a series of operations.

Training by Supervisors

Such training is imparted on the job by the workers' immediate supervisors.

It provides to the trainees opportunities for getting acquainted with their bosses. The bosses, too, have an opportunity to judge the abilities and possibilities of trainees from the point of view of their job performance.

The success of both these methods depends upon the fact that:

(a) The experienced supervisors must be good teachers;

(b) They should have incentives and sufficient time for carrying out the training programmes; and

(c) They should be provided with an accurate account of the training needs of the trainees they are to teach.

Demonstrations and Examples (Or Learning by Seeing)

In the demonstration method, the trainer describes and displays something, as when he teaches an employee how to do something by actually performing the activity himself and by going through a step-by-step explanation of "why" and "what" he is doing.

Demonstrations are very effective in teaching because it is much easier to show a person how to do a job than to tell him or ask him to gather instruction from the reading material. Demonstrations are often used in combination with lectures, pictures, text materials, discussions, etc.

"Teaching by example is effective in mechanical operations or interpersonal relationships, for job duties and responsibilities, for informal group standards, supervisory expectations, and the like."

Demonstrations are particularly effective in the training for the acquisition of skills; but their usefulness is limited when it is a question of training management personnel. In a demonstration, the emphasis is primarily on know-how, the principles and theory of a job must, therefore, be taught by some other method.

Simulation

"Simulation is a technique which duplicates, as nearly as possible, the actual conditions encountered on a job." The vestibule training method or the business-game method are examples of business simulations. Simulation techniques have been most widely used in the aeronautical industry.

Trainee interest and employee motivation are both high in simulation exercise because the actions of a trainee closely duplicate real job conditions. This training is essential in cases in which actual on-the-job practice might result in a serious inquiry, a costly error, or the destruction of valuable materials or resources. It is for this reason that the technique is a very expensive one.

Apprenticeship

For training in crafts, trades and in technical areas, apprenticeship training is the oldest and most commonly used method, especially when proficiency in a job is the result of a relatively long training period of 2 years to 3 years for persons of superior ability and from 4 years to 5 years for others. The field in which apprenticeship training is offered are numerous and range from the job of a draughtsman, a machinist, a printer, a tool-maker, a pattern designer, a mechanic, carpenters, weavers, fitters, jewellers, die-sinkers, engravers, and electricians. A major part of training time is spent on-the-job productive work. Each apprentice is given a programme of assignments according to a pre-determined schedule, which provides for efficient training in trade skills.

The merits of this method are: (i) A skilled workforce is maintained; (ii) Immediate returns can be expected from training; (iii) The workmanship is good; (iv) The hiring cost is lower because of reduced turnover and lower production costs; (v) The loyalty of employees is increased and opportunities for growth are frequent.

Class-room or Off-the-job Methods

"Off-the-job training" simply means that training is not a part of everyday job activity. The actual location may be in the company class-rooms or in places which are owned by the company, or in universities or associations which have no connection with the company.

These methods consist of:

1. Lectures;
2. Conferences;
3. Group Discussions;
4. Case Studies;
5. Role-playing;
6. Programmed Instructions;
7. Laboratory Training.

1. Lectures (or Class-Room Instruction): Lectures are regarded as one of the most simple ways of imparting knowledge to the trainees, especially when facts, concepts, or principles, attitudes, theories and problem-solving abilities are to be taught. Lectures are formal organised talks by the training specialist, the formal superior or other individual specific topics.

In training, the most important uses of lectures include:

(1) Reducing anxiety about upcoming training programmes or organisational changes by explaining their purposes.

(2) Introducing a subject and presenting an overview of its scope.

(3) Presenting basic material that will provide a common background for subsequent activities.

(4) Illustrating the application of rules, principles; reviewing, clarifying and summarising.

2. The Conference Method: In this method, the participating individuals 'confer' to discuss points of common interest to each other. A conference is basic to most participative group-centered methods of development. It is a formal meeting, conducted in accordance with an organised plan, in which the leader seeks to develop knowledge and understanding by obtaining a considerable amount of oral participation of the trainees. It lays emphasis on small group discussions, on organised subject matter, and on the active participation of the members involved. Learning is facilitated by building up on the ideas contributed by the conferees.

3. Seminar or Team Discussion: This is an established method for training. A seminar is conducted in many ways:

(i) It may be based on a paper prepared by one or more trainees on a subject selected in consultation with the person in charge of the seminar. It may be a part of a study or related to theoretical studies or practical problems. The trainees read their papers, and this is followed by a critical discussion. The chairman of the seminar summarises the contents of the papers and the discussions which follow their reading.

(ii) It may be based on the statement made by the person in charge of the seminar or on a document prepared by an expert, who is invited to participate in the discussion.

(iii) The person in charge of the seminar distributes in advance the material to be analysed in the form of required readings. The seminar compares the reactions of trainees, encourages discussion, defines the general trends and guides the participants to certain conclusions.

(iv) Valuable working material may be provided to the trainees by actual files. The trainees may consult the files and bring these to the seminar where they may study in detail the various aspects, ramifications and complexities of a particular job or work or task.

4. Case Studies (or Learning by Doing): This method was first developed in the 1800s by Christopher Langdell at the Harvard Law School "to help students to learn for themselves by independent thinking and by discovering in the ever-tangled skein of human affairs, principles and ideas which have lasting validity and general applicability. A collateral object is to help them develop skills in using their knowledge."

5. Role-playing: This method was developed by Moreno, abenetian psychiatrist, coined the terms role-playing "role-reversal" "socio-drama," "psychodrana," and variety of specialised terms, with emphasis on learning human relation skills through practice and insight into one's own behaviour and its effect upon others. It has been defined as "a method of human interaction which involves realistic behaviour in the imaginary situations." As Norman Major has pointed out, a "role-playing experience soon demonstrates the gap between 'thinking' and 'doing.' The idea of role-playing involves action, doing and practice."

Role-playing, trainees act out a given role as they would in a stage play. Two or more trainees are assigned parts to play before the rest of the class. These parts do not any memorisation of lines or any rehearsals. The players are simply informed of a situation and of the respective roles they have to play. Sometime after the preliminary planning, the situation is acted out by the role-players. Role-playing primarily involves emploplyee-employer relationships — Hiring, discussing a grievance procedure, conducting a post-appraisal interview or disciplining a subordinate or a salesman making a representation to a customer.

6. Programmed Instruction (or Teaching by the Machine Methods): Programmed instruction involves a sequence of steps which are often set up through the desired central panel of an electronic computer as guides in the performance a desired operation or series of operations. It incorporates a pre-arranged, proposed, or desired operation course of proceedings pertaining to the learning or acquisition of some specific skills or general knowledge. A programmed instruction involves breaking information down into meaningful units and then arranging these in a proper way to form a logical and sequential learning programme or package in such a programme, knowledge is imparted with the use of a textbook or problems to teaching machine. The programme involves: presenting question, fact or problem to the trainee to utilise the information given; and the trainee instantly receives feedback (and sometime rewards or penalties) on the basis of the accuracy of his answers.

7. Laboratory Training. (i) Sensitivity Training — Sensitivity training is an experimental approach to training. It provides participants an opportunity to actually experience some concepts of management just as a manager would experience them in his own organisational situation. Sensitivity training is a group training method that uses intensive participation and give immediate feedback for self analysis and change.

Implementation of Training

Once the training programme has been designed, it needs to be implemented. Implementation is beset with certain problems. Firstly, most managers are action-oriented and frequently say no to training efforts. Secondly, there is problem of locating suitable trainers within an organisation. Any training programme implementation involves action on the following lines:

(1) Deciding the location and organising training and other facilities.
(2) Scheduling the training programme.
(3) Conducting the programme.
(4) Monitoring the progress of trainees.

Training Evaluation

Objectives of training evaluation is to determine the ability of the participant in the training programme to perform jobs for which they were trained, the specific nature of training deficiencies, whether the trainees required any additional on the job training, and the extent of training not needed for the participants to meet job requirements.

Principles of Evaluation

Evaluation of the training programme must be based on the following principles:

(1) Evaluation specialist must be clear about the goals and purposes of evaluation.
(2) Evaluation must be continuous.
(3) Evaluation must be specific.
(4) Evaluation must provide the means and focus for trainers to be able to appraise themselves, their practices, and their products.
(5) Evaluation must be based on objective methods and standards.

(6) Realistic target dates must be set for each phase of the evaluation process. A sense of urgency must be developed, but deadlines that are unreasonably high will result in poor evaluation.

There are various approaches to training evaluation. To get a valid measure of training effectiveness, the personnel manager should accurately assess trainee's job performance two to four months after completion of training.

Two writers have suggested that four basic categories of outcomes can be measured.

1. **Reaction:** Evaluate the trainee's reaction to the programme. Did he like the programme? Did he think it worthwhile?
2. **Learning:** Did the trainee learn the principles, skills and fact that the supervisor or the trainer wanted him to learn?
3. **Behaviour:** Whether the trainee's behaviour on the job changed because of the training programme?
4. **Results:** What final results have been achieved? Did he learn how to work on machine? Did scrappage costs decrease? Was turnover reduced? Are production quotas now being met? etc.

Questionnaires or structured interviews with the immediate supervisor of the trainees are acceptable methods for obtaining feedback on training. The supervisor is asked to rate the former trainee on job proficiency directly related to the training objectives.

Another approach is to involve the use of experimental and control groups. Each group is randomly selected, one to receive training (experimental) and the other not to receive training (control). The random selection helps to assure the formation of groups quite similar to each other. Measures are taken of relevant indicators of success (e.g., words typed per minute, units of work produced per hour, reduction in wastage and turnover, etc.), before and after training for both groups. If the results shown by the experimental group are significantly greater than those of the control group, the training can be considered as successful.

Another method involves longitudinal or time series analysis. A series of measurements are taken before the programme begins and continues during and after the programme is completed. The results obtained are plotted on a group to determine whether changes have occurred and remain as a result of the training effort.

Besides, pre-and-post tests be administered to the training groups. Prior to the training, a test related to the training material is applied, and the results of this pre-test are compared with results on the same or similar test administered after the programme has been completed.

Why Training Fails?

The following factors have been regarded as the main reasons for failure of training programmes:

(1) The benefits of training are not clear to the top management.

(2) The top management hardly rewards supervisors for carrying out effective training.

(3) The top management rarely plans and budgets systematically for training.

(4) The middle management, without proper incentives from top management, does not account for training in production scheduling.

(5) Without proper scheduling from above, first line supervisors have difficulty in production norms if employees are attending training programmes.

(6) Behavioural objectives are often imprecise.

(7) Training external to the employing unit sometimes teaches techniques on methods contrary to practices of the participants' organisation.

(8) Timely information about external programmes may be difficult to obtain.

(9) Trainers provide limited counselling and consulting services to the rest of the organisation.

Improving Effectiveness of Training

The training programmes can be made effective and successful if the following hints are considered:

1. Specic training objective should be outlined on the basis of the type of performance required to achieve organisational goals and objectives. An audit of personal needs compared with operational requirements will help to determine the specific training needs of individual employees. This evaluation should form a well-defined set of performance standards towards which each trainee should be directed.

2. Attempt should be made to determine if the trainee has the intelligence, maturity, and motivation to successfully complete the training programmes. If deficiencies are noted in these respects, the training may be postponed or cancelled till improvements are visible.
3. The trainee should be helped to see the need for training by making him aware of the personal benefits he can achieve through better performance. He should be helped to discover the rewards and satisfactions that might be available to him through changes in behaviour.
4. The training programme should be planned so that it is related to the trainee's previous experiences and background. This background should be used as a foundation for new development and new behaviour.
5. Attempts should be made to create organisational conditions that are conducive to a good learning environment. It should be made clear why changes are needed. Any distractions, in the way of training environment, should be removed. The support of the upper levels of management should be obtained before applying training at lower levels.
6. If necessary, a combination of training methods should be selected so that variety is permitted and as many of the senses as possible are utilised.
7. It should be recognised that all the trainees do not progress at the same rate. Therefore, flexibility should be allowed in judging the rates of progress in the training programme.
8. If possible, the personal involvement or active participation of the trainee should be got in the training programme. He should be provided with opportunity to practise the newly needed behaviour norms.
9. As the trainee acquires new knowledge, skills or attitudes and applies them in job situations, he should be significantly rewarded for his efforts.
10. The trainee should be provided with regular, constructive feedback concerning his progress in training and implementation of the newly acquired abilities.
11. The trainee should be provided with personal assistance when he encounters learning obstacles.

Chapter - 12

Performance Appraisal

Once the employee has been selected, trained and motivated, he is then appraised for his performance. Performance appraisal is the step where the management finds out how effective it has been at hiring and placing employees. If any problems are identified, steps are taken to communicate with the employee and to remedy them. A "performance appraisal" is a process of evaluating an employee's performance of a job in terms of its requirements? Heyel observes; "It is the process of evaluating the performance and qualifications of the employees in terms of the requirements of the job for which he employed, for purposes of administration including placement, selection for promotions providing financial rewards and other actions which require differential treatment among the members of a group as distinguished from actions affecting all members equally." Others regard it as a "process of estimating or judging the value, excellence, qualities or status of some object, person or thing". Individually and collectively, it is a part of all the other staffing processes, viz., recruitment, selection, placement and indoctrination.

Terminology Used

Employee appraisal techniques are said to have been used for the first time during the First World War, when, at the instance of Walter Dill Scott, the US Army adopted the "Man-to-man" rating system for evaluating military personnel. During the 1920-30 period, rational wage structures for hourly paid workers were adopted in industrial units. Under this system, the policy of giving grade wage increments on the basis of merit was accepted. These early employee plans were called merit rating programmes, which continued to be so called up to the mid-fifties. By then, most of these plans were of the rating-scale type, where emphasis was given to factors, degrees and points. In the early fifties, however, attention began to be devoted to the performance appraisal of technical, professional and managerial personnel. Since then, as a result of experiments and a great deal of study, the philosophy of performance appraisal has undergone tremendous changes.

Consequently, a change has also taken place in the terminology used. Now, the older phrase merit rating is largely restricted to the rating of hourly paid employees, and is used frequently in developing criteria for salary adjustments, promotions, transfers, etc. The later phrase, personnel appraisal, places emphasis on the development of the individual as and widely used to evaluate technical, professional and managerial personnel.

Importance and Purposes

Performance appraisal has been considered as a most significant and indispensable tool for an organisation, for the information it provides is highly useful in making decisions regarding various personal aspects such as promotions and merit increases. Performance measures also link information gathering and decision-making processes which provide a basis for judging the effectiveness of personnel sub-divisions such as recruiting, selection, training and compensation. Accurate information plays a vital role in the organisation as a whole. They help pinpoint weak areas in the primary systems (e.g., marketing, finance and production). It is easier for managers to see which employees need training or counselling, because jobs are grouped by categories (e.g., production foreman, sales manager, financial analyst). These categories can be broken into smaller and smaller groups, if necessary. If valid performance data are available, timely, accurate, objective, standardised and relevant, management can maintain consistent promotion and compensation policies throughout the total system.

McGregor says: "Formal performance appraisal plans are designed to meet three needs, one of the organisation and the other two of the individual, namely:

(i) They provide systematic judgements to back up salary increases, transfers, demotions or terminations.

(ii) They are means of telling a subordinate how he is doing, and suggesting needed changes in his behaviour attitudes, skills, or job knowledge. They let him know "where he stands" with the boss.

(iii) They are used as a base for coaching and counselling the individual by the superior.

According to Roland Benjamin, a "performance appraisal determines who shall receive merit increases; counsels employees on their improvement;

determines training needs; determines promotability; identifies those who should be transferred. Moreover, it improves employee job performance; encourages employees to express their views or to seek clarication on job duties; broadens their outlook, capacity and potential; promotes a more effective utilisation of manpower and improves placement; facilitates selection reward and promotion of the best qualified employee; prevents grievances and increases the analytical abilities of supervisors."

Levinson has given three functions of performance appraisal: It seeks to provide an adequate feedback to each individual for his or her performance. (it purports to serve as a basis for improving or changing behaviour toward some more effective working habits at providing data to managers with which they may judge future job assignments and compensation. He stresses the fact that the existing systems of performance appraisal do not serve any of these functions effectively but focus on "outcome of behaviour".

According to Cummings, "the overall objective of performance appraisal is to improve the efficiency of an enterprise by attempting to mobilise the best possible efforts from individuals employed in it. Such appraisals achieve four objectives include in the salary reviews, the development and training of individuals, planning job rotation and assistance promotions".

On the basis of merit rating or appraisal procedures of various companies in India, the main objectives of employee performance appraisal are:

(i) To enable an organisation to maintain an inventory of the number and quality of all managers and to identify and meet their training needs and aspirations;

(ii) To determine increments rewards, and provide a reliable index for promotions and transfers to positions of greater responsibility;

(iii) To maintain individual and group development by informing the employee of his performance standard;

(iv) To suggest ways of improving the employee's performance when he is not found to be up to the mark during the review period;

(v) To identify training and development needs and to evaluate effectiveness of training and development programmes; and

(vi) To plan career development, human resources planning based on potentialities.

It will, thus, be seen that performance appraisal is an important tool of personnel management. It is a judgement of the characteristics, traits and performance of employees and has a wide range of utility. For example:

(i) It unifies the appraisal procedure so that all employees are rated in the same manner, utilising the same approach so that the ratings obtained of separate personnel are comparable.

(ii) It provides information which is useful in making and enforcing important decisions about selection, training, promotions, pay increases, transfers, lay-offs, discharges, salary adjustments, etc. The information is supplied well in advance so that spot judgements may be avoided.

(iii) It provides information in the form of records about ratings which may be produced as evidence when decisions on ratings are challenged in a court of law. Even arbitrators accept these in the course of grievance handling procedures as authentic records.

(iv) It serves to stimulate and guide employee development. Appraisal programmes provide information on the weaknesses of employees and enable them to gauge their own value and accomplishments and to know what they are doing. The weaknesses provide the basis for an individual development programme. If used properly, such periodical appraisals will establish an atmosphere in which criticism can be taken without resentment and can be used constructively for self-improvement.

(v) By finding out an employee's qualifications, and his work and comparing it with job requirements, inefficient employees and those whose views are not in harmony with the company's objectives or management philosophy can be weeded out or persuaded to adjust themselves.

(vi) A periodic and accurate appraisal constrains a supervisor to be alert and competent in his work, i.e., it improves the quality of supervision by giving him an incentive to do the things that he should normally be doing anyway.

(vii) It gives supervisors a more effective tool for rating their personnel, enables them to make a careful analysis of their men and gives them a better knowledge and understanding of them.

(viii) It makes for better employer-employee relations through mutual confidence, which comes as a result of frank discussions between a supervisor and his men.

What Should be Rated?

The seven criteria for assessing performance are:

1. **Quality:** The degree to which the process or result of carrying out an activity approaches perfection.
2. **Quantity:** The amount produced, expressed in monetary terms, number of units, or number of completed activity cycles.
3. **Timeliness:** The degree to which an activity or a result produced.
4. **Cost Effectiveness:** The degree to which the use of the organisation's resources (e.g. human, monetary, technological, material) is maximised in the sense of getting the highest gain.
5. **Need for Supervision:** The degree to which a job performer can carry out a job function without supervisory assistance.
6. **Interpersonal Impact:** The degree to which a performer promotes feelings of self-esteem, goodwill and co-operation among co-workers and subordinates.
7. **Training:** Need for training for improving his skills and knowledge . The above criteria relate to past performance and behaviour of an employee. There is also the need for assessing the potential of an employee for future performance, particularly when the employee is tipped for assuming greater responsibilities.

Approaches to Performance Appraisal

Generally speaking three approaches are used in making performance appraisal:

(a) **A causal, unsystematic, and often haphazard appraisal**: This method was commonly used in the past, but now it has given place to a more formal method the main basis being seniority or quantitative measures of quantity and quality of output for the rank-and-file personnel.

(b) **The traditional and highly systematic measurement of** (i) employee characteristics, and (ii) employee contributions, or both. It evaluates all the performances in the same manner, utilising the same approach, so that the ratings obtained of separate personnel are comparable.

(c) **The behavioural approach, emphasising mutual goal-setting:** According to McGregor, in the traditional approach, the supervisor is placed in the position of "Playing Gods." He judges and at times criticizes the personal worth of his men. Therefore, emphasis has been laid upon providing mutual goal-setting and appraisal of progress by both the appraiser and the appraisee. This approach is based on the behavioural value of fundamental trust in the goodness, capability and responsibility of human beings.

The Evaluation Process

Stolz observes that "the process of performance appraisal follows a set pattern, viz., a man's performance is periodically appraised by his superiors. Questions are raised — Is his potential the greatest as a manager or as a staff specialist? What are his strengths and weaknesses? Where can he make his great contribution? Next, sometimes in consultation with the man himself, tentative decisions are made on what might be done to advance his development.

"Usually, the resulting plan is then reviewed at a higher echelon of management, where it may be challenged, changed or added to. But out of the discussion and debate emerges a development plan tailored to the individuals unique needs.

Broadly speaking, 'the process of evaluation begins with the establishment of performance standards.' At the time of designing a job and formulating a job description, performance standards are usually developed for the position. These standards should be clear and not vague, and objective enough to be understood and measure these standards should be discussed with the supervisors to find out which different factors are to be incorporated, weights and points to be given to each factor and these then should be indicated on the Appraisal Form, and later on used for appraising the performance of the employees.

The next step is to communicate these standards to the employees, for the employees left to themselves, would find it difficult to guess what is expected of them. To make communication effective, 'feedback' is necessary from the subordinate to the manager.

Satisfactory feedback ensures that the information communicated by the manager has been received and understood in the way it was intended.

The third step is the 'measurement of performance.' To determine what actual performance is it is necessary to acquire information about it. We should be concerned with how we measure and what we measure. Four sources of information are frequently used to measure actual performance: personal observation, statistical reports, oral reports, and written reports.

The fourth step is the comparison of actual performance with standards. The employee is appraised and judged of his potential for growth and advancement. Attempts are made to note deviations between 'standard performance' and 'actual performance'.

At the next stage, the results of appraisal are discussed periodically with the employees, where good points, weak points, and difficulties are indicated and discussed so that performance is improved. The information that the subordinate receives about his assessment has a great impact on his self-esteem and on his subsequent performance. Conveying good news is considerably less difficult for both the manager and the subordinate than when performance has been below expectations.

The final step is the initiation of corrective action when necessary; immediate corrective action can be of two types. One is immediate and deals predominantly with symptoms. The other is basic and delves into causes. Immediate corrective action is often described as "putting out fires," whereas basic corrective action gets to the source of deviation and seeks to adjust the difference permanently. Coaching and counselling may be done or special assignments and projects may be set: persons may be deputed for formal training courses, and decision-making responsibilities and authority may be delegated to the subordinates. Attempts may also be made to recommend for salary increases or promotions, if these decisions become plausible in the light of appraisals.

The details given above may vary from an organisation to organisation, but these steps usually form the principal steps/ features of a sound evaluation programmes.

ESTABLISHMENT PERFORMANCE STANDARDS
COMMUNICATE PERFORMANCE EXPECTATION TO EMPLOYEES
MEASURES ACTUAL PERORMANCE
COMPARE ACTUAL PERFORMANCE WITH STANDARD
DISCUSS THE APPRAISAL WITH THE EMPLOYEE
IF NECESSARY, INITIATE CORRECTIVE ACTION

Fig. 10.2: The Evaluation Process.

Methods, Techniques or Tools for Appraising Performance

Several methods and techniques of appraisal are available for measurement of the performance of an employee. The methods and scales differ for obvious reasons. First, they differ in the sources of traits or qualities to be appraised. The qualities may differ because of differences in job requirements, statistical requirements and the opinions of the management.

Second, they differ because of the different kinds of workers who are being rated, viz., factory workers, executives or salesmen. Third, the variations may be caused by the degree of precision attempted in an evaluation. Finally, they may differ because of the methods used to obtain weightings for various traits.

There is little agreement on the best method to evaluate managerial, professional or salaried performance. Different authors have suggested different approaches. For example:

Rock and Lewis have classified the methods into two broad categories, viz., the narrow interpretation and broad interpretation of appraisal. The former is considered as "a post-mortem of a subordinate's performance by his superior during a pre-determined period of time, often, the preceding year. It involves assessment of performance vis-a-such as the traits or characteristics' rating scale, the ranking method, the employee comparison method and performance standard method are included under this category."

The latter, "also known as accountability management, management by objectives or management by end-results, involves a broad purview, and aims at improving the entire managing process and the individual managers on a year round basis".

Robbins gives three categories, viz., (i) Single-trait, single subject, in which subjects are not compared with any other person and each trait is measured alone. The check-list, the numerical and graphic scale methods are more popular of such category. (ii) Single-trait, multiple-subject, in which the subjects are compared with other subjects. Group order ranking, individual ranking and pair comparison methods belong to this category. (iii) Multiple-trait, single-subject, in which force choice rating is done by either the subject himself or the evaluation, into traits offered for evaluation.

The widely used categorisation is that given by Strauss and Sayles. "They have classified performance appraisal methods into traditional, and newer or modern methods. The traditional methods lay emphasis on the rating of the individual's personality traits, such as initiative, dependability, drive, responsibility, creativity, integrity, leadership potential, intelligence, judgement, organising ability, etc. On the other hand, newer methods place more emphasis on the evaluation of work results job achievements than on personality traits. Results oriented appraisals tend to be more objective and worthwhile, especially for counselling and development purposes."

Chart 10.1

Methods of performance appraisal	
Traditional methods	***Modern methods***
1. Straight ranking methods 2. Man- to man comparison methods 3. Grading 4. Graphic rating scale 5. Forced choice description methods 6. Forced distribution methods 7. Check list 8. Free from easy methods 9. Critical incident 10. Groups appraisal 11. Fields reviews methods	1. Assement center 2. Appraisal by result or management by objective 3. Human asset accounting methods 4. Behaviourly anchored rating scale

Components of Appraisal Evaluation

As we have seen, performance evaluations can be made for a variety of reasons-counselling, promotion, research, salary, administration or a combination of these. So it is necessary to being by stating very clearly the objectives of the evaluation programme. Having done this, the personnel evaluation system should address the questions who, what, when, where, how? of performance appraisal.

So, the 1st question involved is who? and this issue states "who should be rated, and who should do the rating." The answer to the first issue is that all employees of an organisation should be appraised, from the operator to the top-level management need be appraised for one reason or the other. Regarding the second issue, it may be said that personnel experts assist and advise the top and line management, who should participate in the appraisal programme; and the line management should actually do the evaluation work. The personnel officer obtains the ratings of different raters and analyses and determines the reliability and validity of such ratings. Such validity can be checked against certain objective evidence such as production quantities, quality, absenteeism, and by comparing the results of one system with those of another. The ratings should not be change by the personal expert however he has been obligation to point out inconsistencies to the rater.

"Who" of the Appraisal?

As Ruderman observes, "the appraisal can be accomplished by one or more individuals involving a combination of the immediate supervisor, other managers acquainted with the assesses work a higher lever manager, a personnel manager, the assessee's peers, the assessee himself and the assessee's subordinates.

Usually the immediate supervisor must be entrusted with the task of rating the assessee because he is most familiar with his work; and because he is also responsible for recommending or approving personnel actions based on the performance appraisal; and for providing a feedback of performance appraisal to the subordinate. Because of these reasons supervisors' ratings are regarded as the best possible assessment; and they are often considered as the "heart of the most appraisal systems. This is so because getting supervisor's appraisal is relatively easy and also makes sense. Therefore, most appraisal systems rely heavily on the supervisor evaluation. In such rating hierarchical control is maintained over the appraisal process.

Appraisal is also done, by the staff specialists, i.e., the personnel officers. They may advise the supervisor while evaluating their subordinates stressing the need for evidence. For making specific appraisal judgements and comparing a particular subordinate's evaluation with those of others.

The appraisal of an individual may also be done by his peers. Such appraisal proves effective in predicting future management success. Researchers have veried that ratings made—by peers have been quite accurate in predicting which persons would be promoted and which would not.

Sometimes self-evaluation is also employed for evaluating performance. Self-rating emphasises human relations, which supervisors focus on technical knowledge and initiative. Flippo observes: "The major value lies in the development and motivation areas, it being claimed that this approach: (1) results in a superior upward flow of information, (2) forces the subordinate to become more personally involved and, to some extent constrains him to think about himself and his work, (3) improves communication between superior and subordinate, in that each is given more information by the other when disagreements are discovered, and (4) improves motivation as a result of great participation." "But this approach has its disadvantage that the individual may rate himself excessively high than it would be if he was rated by his superior. Because of this fairly consistent upward bias in self-appraisals, the best thing would be to use these appraisals for counselling and developing subordinates. They are not as useful for making salary and promotion decisions."

Many companies use Rating Committees to evaluate employees. These committees consist of supervisors, peers, and subordinates. Everyone on the Committee is a person who is able to intelligently evaluate some aspect of the employee's performance. Many discrepancies in the ratings may occur - such as "very strict" or "very lenient" ratings — when evaluations are done by individuals. It has, therefore, been felt that "the combined use of several rates" can help "cancel out" problems like 'bias' as 'halo' effect on the part of the individual rates. Second the raters at different levels in the organisation usually observe different facets of an employee's job performance and the appraisal by a group reflect these differences.

Last, in many companies, subordinates and superiors jointly establish goals and periodically evaluate the subordinate's performance with respect to these goals.

"What" of Appraisal

The "what" of the performance appraisal consists in appraising non-supervisory employees for their current performance, and managers for future potential. It also includes evaluation of human traits.

The "Why" of Appraisal

The 'why' of an appraisal is concerned with:

(a) Creating and maintaining a satisfactory level of performance of employees in their present jobs;

(b) Highlighting employee needs and opportunities for personal growth and development;

(c) Aiding in decision-making for promotions, transfers, lay-offs and discharges;

(d) Promoting understanding between the supervisor and his subordinates; and

(e) Providing a useful criterion for determining validity of selection and training methods and techniques and forming concrete measures for attracting individual of higher caliber to the enterprise.

The "When" of Appraisal

The 'when' answers the query about the frequency of appraisal. It has been suggested informal counselling should occur continuously. The manager should discuss an employee's work as soon as possible after he has judged it. He should use good work as an opportunity to provide positive reinforcement and use poor work as a basis for training.

In most organisations employees are formally evaluated once a year, in others twice a year. New employee rated more frequently than the older ones the ideal thing is that employee should be rated three months after being assigned to a job, after six months on the job, and every six months thereafter. The time of rating should not concide with the time of salary review, for if two occur together constructive evaluation and consideration of self-development will probably take second place to pressures of pay.

The "Where" of Appreciation

The 'where' indicates the location where an employee may be evaluated. It is usually done at the place of work or office of the supervisor.

Informal appraisals may take anywhere and everywhere, and everywhere, both on the job in work situations and off the job.

Factors Deterring Objective Evaluation or Problems of Appraisal

The ideal approach to performance evaluation is that in which the evaluator is free from personal biases, prejudices, and idiosyncrasies. This is because when an evaluation is objective, it minimises the potential capracious and dysfunctional behaviour of the evaluator which may be detrimental to the achievement of the organisational goals. However, a single foolproof evaluation method is not available. Inequities in evaluation often destroy the usefulness of the performance system — resulting in inaccurate, invalid appraisals, which are unfair too.

There are many significant factors which deter or impede objective evaluation. These factors are:

1. **The Halo Effect or Error:** The "halo effect" is a "tendency to let the assessment of an individual one trait influence the evaluation of that person on other specific traits. There is this effect in appraisal when the appraiser assigns the same rating to all traits regardless of an employee's actual performance on these traits. The 'halo' effect refers to the tendency to rate an individual consistently high or low or average on the various traits, depending upon whether the rater's over-all impression of the individual is favourable or not. This means that the halo effect allows one characteristic, observation or occurrence (either good or bad) to influence the rating of all-performance factors. The halo effect arises when traits are unfamiliar, ill defined and involve personal relations. This often occurs when an employee tends to be more conscientious and dependable, that the appraiser might become

biased toward that individual to the extent that the appraiser rates him high on many desirable attributes; or when the employee is more friendly or unfriendly toward the appraiser. In such case, a very high rate may be given to a favoured employee, whereas a low rating may be given to an unfriendly employee so that he may be bypassed even though he is a very capable one, when the question of a promotion arises.

Another example may be of the students who tend to rate a faculty member as 'outstanding' on all criteria when they are particularly appreciative of a few things he does in the class room. Similarly, a few bad habits like coming late for lectures, being slow in returning papers, or assigning an extremely demanding reading requirement — might result in student's evaluating the lecturer as "lousy" across-the-board.

The halo effect problem can be alleviated by: (i) providing a five to ten minutes training programme to the evaluators; (ii) restructuring the questions by requiring the evaluator to consider each question independently; and (iii) having the evaluator appraise all rates on each dimension before going to the next dimension.

2. **Leniency or Strictness Tendency or Constant Errors:** Every evaluator has his own value system which acts as a standard against which he makes his appraisals. Relative to the true or actual performance an individual exhibits, some supervisors have a tendency to be liberal in their ratings, i.e., they consistently assign 'high values' to their employees, while at other times they may have a tendency to assign consistently 'low ratings'. The former tendency is known as 'positive leniency error'; while the latter as 'negative leniency error'. When an evaluator is positively lenient in his appraisal, an individual's performance becomes overstated, i.e., rated higher than it actually should. Similarly, under the negative tendency, performance is understated than what it should be. Both these trends usually arise from varying standards of performance observed by supervisors and from different interpretations of what they evaluate in employee performance. The tendency can be avoided by holding meetings or training sessions for raters so that they may understand what is required of them in rating.

3. **The Central Tendency Problem:** It is the most commonly found error. It assigns "average ratings" to all the employees with a view

to avoiding commitment or involvement; or when the rater is in doubt or has inadequate information or lack of knowledge about the behaviour of the employee, or when he does not have much time at his disposal. Such tendency seriously distorts the evaluations, making them most useless for promotion, salary, or counselling purposes. The ranking tools discussed earlier are aimed at avoiding this problem.

4. **Similarity Error:** This type of error occurs when the evaluator rates other people in the same way he perceives himself. For example, the evaluator who perceives himself as aggressive may evaluate others by looking for aggressiveness. Those who show this characteristic may be benefited while others may suffer. This error also washes out if the same evaluator appraises all the people in the organisation.
5. **Miscellaneous Biases:** Bias against employees on ground of sex, race, religion or position is also a common error in rating. For example, a higher rating may be assigned to a senior employee. The rater may also be influenced by organisational influence and give higher ratings to those holding higher positions. Besides these, there may be opportunity bias, group characteristic bias and knowledge-of-predictor bias. Beach observes: "Actual experience with rating has demonstrated that supervisors will rate their people near the middle of the spectrum (average) if their bosses put pressure on them to correct the sub-par performers (or get rid of them) and if they are called upon to really justify an outstanding rating. In other words, they will follow the path of least resistance, because they know that the 'Big Boss' will question them about those rated low or very high."
6. **Social Differentiation:** Rating is sometimes impeded by the evaluator's style of rating behaviour. Pigou has classified raters as: "high differentiators" i.e., using all or most of the scale; or "low differentiators" i.e., using a limited range of the scale. He observes: "Low differentiators tend to ignore or suppress difference, perceiving the universe as more uniform than it really is. High differentiators, on the other hand, tend to utilise all available information to the utmost extent and, thus, are better able to perceptually deny anomalies and contradictions than low differentiators.

Social differentiation makes evaluations using 'trait' criteria unreliable.

Why Appraisal Techniques Prove Failure?

Performance appraisal techniques have often failed to give a correct assessment of the employee. According to Zavala, the causes of such failures are:

(a) The supervisor plays dual and conflicting role of both the judge and the helper.

(b) Too many objectives often cause confusion.

(c) The supervisor feels that subordinate appraisal is not rewarding.

(d) A considerable time gap exists between two appraisal programmes.

(e) The skills required for daily administration and employee development are in conflict.

(f) Poor communication keeps employees in the dark about what is expected of them.

(g) There is a difference of opinion between supervisor and a subordinate in regard to the latter's performance.

(h) Feedback on appraisal is generally unpleasant for both supervisor and subordinate.

(i) Unwillingness on the part of supervisors to tell employees plainly how to improve their performance.

How Appraisals may be Made Successful

The rater must be thoroughly well-versed in the philosophy and nature of the rating system. Factors and factor scales must be thoroughly defined, analysed, and discussed.

The success of an appraisal programme depends upon:

(a) The existence of an atmosphere of confidence and trust so that both supervisor and employee may discuss matters frankly and offer suggestions which may be beneficial for the organisation and for an improvement of the employee.

(b) The supervisor must very thoroughly evaluate the employee's performance so that he is capable of meeting challenges about his ratings of his subordinate.

(c) The results of performance rather than personality traits should be given due weight. Suggestions for improvement should be directed towards the objective facts of the job (such as work schedules, output, reports completed, sales made, losses incurred profits earned, accomplishments, etc.). Plans for the future must be developed jointly after consultation with subordinates. The individual as a person should never be criticised.

(d) The supervisor should try to analyse the strengths and weaknesses of an and advise him on correcting the weaknesses.

(e) The appraisal programme should be less time-consuming and less costly. At the same time, it should bring the maximum benefit.

(f) Which particular technique is to be adopted for appraisal should be governed by such factors as the size, financial resources, philosophy and objectives of an between a supervisor and a subordinate.

(g) The results of the appraisal, particularly when they are negative, should be immediately communicated to the employees, so that they may try to improve their performance.

(h) A post-appraisal interview should be arranged so that employees may be supplied with feedback and the organisation may know the difficulties under which employees work, so that their training needs may be discovered.

Norman Maier suggests three such interviews: (a) Tell-and-Sell Method, to communicate to the employee information about his performance, gain his acceptance of it, and draw up a plan for future improvement, if necessary. (b) The Sell-and-Listen Method, to communicate the evaluation results to the employee and get his reactions to them. (c) Problem-solving Approach, under which the rate and the rater sit together and find out alternative solutions for improving performance.

(i) The standards of performance appraisal can be improved by training of the evaluators. It has been indicated that appraisers who are trained in how to evaluate subordinates tend to be more effective appraisers than those who had not undergone such training.

(j) Lastly, many of the problems or hindrances can be minimised if right appraisal tools are chosen.

Ethics of Appraisal

In any performance appraisal, due consideration must be given to the ethics of appraisal, failing which many organisational problems may crop up and the very purpose of appraisal may be defeated. In this connection, M.S. Kellog has suggested the following:

(i) Don't appraise without knowing why the appraisal is needed;

(ii) Appraise on the basis of representative information;
(iii) Appraise on the basis of sufficient information;
(iv) Appraise on the basis of relevant information;
(v) Be honest on your assessment of all the facts you have obtained;
(vi) Don't write one thing and say another;
(vii) In offering an appraisal, make it plain that this is only your personal opinion of the facts as you see them;
(viii) Pass on appraisal information only to those who have good reason to want it;
(ix) Don't imply the existence of an appraisal that has not been made;
(x) Don't accept another's appraisal without knowing the basis on which it was made.

Kellog maintains that these "ethical standards are most certain to be met if appraisals are accomplished by such qualifiers as:

(i) The fact on which an appraisal is based;
(ii) The time period covered;
(iii) The purpose for which an appraisal is made;
(iv) The situational factors which shed light on the facts presented;
(v) The nature of the appraiser's working relationship with the appraised; and
(vi) An explanation of how and where the facts were obtained.

Edward Deming on Performance Appraisal

Towards the end, it is worthwhile to note Edwar Demeng evaluation. Deming is opposed to employee assessment, because it:

(i) Rewards people for manipulating the system rather than improving it.
(ii) Is often self-defeating.
(iii) Is inconsistent with team-work.
(iv) Acts as a substitute for proper management.
(v) Is inherently unfair.

His alternatives to performance appraisal are:

(i) Meticulous selection of leaders.
(ii) Educating workers about their obligations, and improved training and education after selection.
(iii) Getting leaders to function as colleagues rather than as judges.

(iv) Subordinate performance to be assessed using statistical data.
(v) Annually, three to four hour interviews with subordinates aimed at support and encouragement.
(vi) Accommodation to lone workers.

Index

C

D

E

F

M

Q

R

U

V

W